ON BEING HUMAN

A Systematic View

ON
BEING
HUMAN

A Systematic View

G. MARIAN KINGET

MICHIGAN STATE UNIVERSITY

HARCOURT BRACE JOVANOVICH

NEW YORK   CHICAGO   SAN FRANCISCO   ATLANTA

ISBN: 0-15-567491-9

Library of Congress Catalog Card Number: 75-966

Printed in the United States of America

ACKNOWLEDGMENTS AND COPYRIGHTS

For permission to use the selections reprinted in this book, the author is grateful to
the following publishers and copyright holders:

Mortimer J. Adler. For excerpts from *The Difference of Man and the Difference It
Makes*. Copyright © 1967 by Mortimer J. Adler. Reprinted by permission of the
author.

Atheneum Press. For excerpts from *The Territorial Imperative* by Robert Ardrey.
Copyright © 1966 by Robert Ardrey. Reprinted by permission of the publisher.

John Ciardi. For "The Gift" from *39 Poems* by John Ciardi. Copyright 1959 by
Rutgers University Press. Reprinted by permission of the author.

Columbia University Press. For excerpts from *The Human Imperative* by Alexander
Alland. Copyright © 1972 by Columbia University Press. Reprinted by permission
of the publisher.

E.P. Dutton & Co., Inc. For excerpts from *They Became What They Beheld*, written
by Edmund Carpenter, photographed by Ken Heyman. Copyright © 1970 by
Edmund Carpenter and Ken Heyman. Reprinted by permission of the publishers,
Sunrise Books, a subsidiary of E.P. Dutton and Co., Inc.

The Encyclopaedia Britannica. For excerpts from "Code of Hammurabi" by Cyril
John Gadd, "Jurisprudence" by L. F. Fuller, and "Primitive Law" by E. A. Hoebel
from *The Encyclopaedia Britannica*. © Encyclopaedia Britannica, 1972. Reprinted
by permission of the Encyclopaedia Britannica.

Estate of Frederick S. Perls. For "Gestalt Prayer" by Frederick S. Perls. Copyright
© Real People Press, 1969. All rights reserved.

Faber and Faber Ltd. For "The Hollow Men" from *Collected Poems 1909–1962* by
T. S. Eliot. Reprinted by permission of Faber and Faber Ltd.

(Continued on page 255)

PREFACE

Suddenly, the term *humanistic* has become a favorite on the contemporary scene. Psychology, sociology, medicine, architecture, urbanization, ecology, art, and religion—all are claiming humanistic concern as the growing edge of their endeavors. All this bespeaks a constructive and promising outlook. However, the frequent confusion of the terms *human, humane,* and *humanistic* indicates that many do not clearly understand the meaning of the humanistic stance. To qualify as humanistic, it is not enough to concern human beings. Playing, working, building, traveling, organizing, are all *human* activities. This, however, does not make them humanistic. Similarly, when these activities are performed, for instance, for charitable or philanthropic purposes, they are then raised to a humane or *humanitarian* status, which may be of vital importance but still does not make them humanistic. For an endeavor or a viewpoint to qualify properly as humanistic, it must imply and focus upon a certain concept of man—a concept that recognizes his status as a person, irreducible to more elementary levels, and his unique worth as a being potentially capable of autonomous judgment and action. A pertinent example of the difference between the humane and the humanistic outlook is found in the case of behavior control that relies entirely upon positive reinforcement. Such an approach is humane (or humanitarian), since it implements generous and compassionate attitudes. But it is not humanistic, because the rationale behind systematic behavior modification by purely external forces is incompatible with a concept of man as a self-purposive and proactive, rather than merely reactive, being.

The focus of humanistic psychology is upon the specificity of man, upon that which sets him apart from all other species. It differs from other psychologies because it views man not solely as a biological organism modified by experience and culture but as a person, a symbolic entity capable of pondering his existence, of lending it meaning and direction.

Presently humanistic psychology manifests two markedly different trends. One, sometimes referred to as "the human potential movement," centers around a variety of experiential, affective processes, such as those dealt with in encounter-group work; training groups, or T-groups; and similar forms of social-emotional expression. The other, of which this book is representative, has a more encompassing, more diversified, and more scholarly concern. It is conceptual as well as experiential and widely interdisciplinary. Common to both is an interest in furthering the growth and fulfillment of the person and an opposition to the mechanistic and atomistic philosophies of traditional approaches. However, the ways and means each of them uses to achieve this goal are rather strikingly divergent.

The human potential movement focuses upon action in terms of self-expression, self-disclosure, and candid communication in the here and now of social-emotional contexts. Curiously, considering the academic stature of some of its originators and major proponents (for example, Carl Rogers and Abraham Maslow, both former presidents of the American Psychological Association), the approach is essentially and deliberately noncognitive, nonsystematic, and nonacademic. Its proponents are not, of course, denying the value of conceptualization and orderly thinking (or even of academia) *per se*. Rather their position is a considered reaction against the intellectualistic, abstract, and life-estranged character of most programs of training in psychology.

The scholarly wing of humanistic psychology is also interested in personal and social relevance and opposed to unilateral intellectualism; but it attempts to achieve these goals by the more traditional means of inquiry, reflection, description, and research (not necessarily of the quantitative type) rather than by direct self-expression and social-emotional exchange. Because it focuses on the whole man rather than on isolated data, this psychology deals with both feeling *and* fact, behavior *and* experience, unconscious *and* conscious processes, the tangible *and* the imponderable—the whole of it considered in the perspective of integration, not only of analysis. The ultimate objective, which a growing number of its leading members are pursuing, is the creation of a specifically human science, organized according to a genuinely human model rather than one borrowed from the physical sciences.

While humanistic psychology originated as a protest against established forms of psychology, this strictly antithetical stance is no longer necessary. The wholistic, pluralistic nature of this new psychology, its unifying rather than divisive stance, is so rapidly gaining recognition that its potential as a synthesis now needs to be emphasized more than the value of its difference. Frank Severin aptly characterizes this new approach when he stated that "humanistic psychology is, in effect, all of psychology viewed through a wide-angle lens."

Among the many persons on whose thinking I have drawn in preparing this work and to whom I wish to express my thanks are, in particular, Dr. Carl R. Rogers; Dr. Russell J. Becker; Dr. Walter Smet; Dr. Arthur Schrynemakers; Dr. Vincent Lombardi; Dr. Willard Frick and Mr. Michael Corriveau for their careful reading of the manuscript, their helpful comments and encouragements; Dr. John F. A. Taylor for reading the chapter dealing with The Ethical Animal; Dr. Eleanor Huzar for countless enlightening conversations; Dr. W. A. Saucier and Dr. Hector P. Callewaert for the tireless and scholarly example of their lives; and K. Anne Belleville for her patience and care in typing the manuscript and indexing the book. Grateful acknowledgment is also made to Michigan State University for supporting the preparation of this work by awarding me several All-University Research Grants.

G. MARIAN KINGET

CONTENTS

What Is Human
About
Human Beings?

The Difference of Man

That humans differ from all other animals is one thing about which there is no controversy. Man would not be a separate species if he could be entirely reduced to another. Common sense, moreover, confirms taxonomy: though we see occasionally a fellow human being who looks slightly simian or people who act like trousered apes, we know at a glance they aren't.

What we don't know at a glance is just what the difference consists of. When asked about it, the answer is apt to be on the level of "Man has feelings"—not only a platitude but an inadequate one. For animals have feelings, too. Only they do not know they have. (The latter proposition, however elementary, is already something of a firecracker, capable of sparking the liveliest debate among students as well as among specialists.) Another stock-in-trade answer is "Man has dignity." True enough. However, when asked just what dignity is and what justifies ascribing it to man and man alone, not much of an answer is usually forthcoming.

MAN THE UNKNOWN. When it comes to articulating the *specificity* of humanness, Alexis Carrell's *Man the Unknown* (1935) apparently still characterizes the situation. Essential questions go unanswered, and available essential knowledge is not broadly disseminated in a society that values occupational know-how over liberal education. On the other hand, one must beware of overplaying man's ignorance about his kind. The human animal is endowed with common sense—or at least the potential for it. On a preconceptual level, "deep down," he recognizes what is characteristically human from what is not. Take, for instance, the amazement of the circus-going public at the sight of the human-*like* things that animals can do.

Of course, there is considerable—and considerably more dignified—evidence that people know the difference between the ways of humans and animals. They know, if not always with conceptual sophistication, then at least with practical effectiveness. Thus, in most areas of everyday life, people tend to treat their fellow men, roughly speaking (sometimes quite roughly!), as human beings. People seem particularly able to discriminate between human and inhuman treatment when they are the object of the treatment or when their ego is at stake. Rightly or wrongly, they are then apt to make distinctions so preciously fine they are invisible to anyone but themselves.

In the following chapters I attempt to describe the basic attributes that distinguish man from other animate life, especially from those species closest to him on the phylogenetic scale. Because of this phylogenetic closeness, certain species exhibit instances of behavior that are humanlike at first sight but reveal their distinctly nonhuman nature when examined from the point of view of the critical difference of man. This mapping out of man's specific function and characteristics may not appear to be extremely relevant. It serves, however, only as a paradigm for my actual purpose: to bring about a focused—and potentially joyful—awareness of the prodigiously capable, versatile, and inexhaustingly fascinating being that is man. At the same time, I hope the approach formulates a tentative basis for the answer to the essential question that everyone must work out for himself: *What is man for?*

A Capsule Preview

At the outset it may be useful to offer a certain perspective on the many angles from which the specificity of man may be observed. Following is a sampling of characteristically human dimensions organized in two groups. The criterion for their grouping here, although not in the text, is methodological: the manner, *objective* or *subjective*, in which the characteristics listed are commonly (though not exclusively) studied. The phenomena subsumed under the first category are primarily behavioral; consequently, they are accessible to direct observation. Those in the second category are primarily experiential and require the application of multiple criteria: a judicious and carefully checked blend of intuitive hypothesizing; subjective reports; inferences; and interpretation—the whole of it checked against related observational data (a blend that, incidentally, is part of the methodology of the "hard" sciences as well). All of the characteristics mentioned in each of the two groups are peculiar to man—either because he has the monopoly on these functions or (depending upon the school of thought to which researchers adhere) because he manifests these functions in significantly greater measure than any other species.

Representative of the behavioral group of characteristics are the chapters on:

- Language, in the sense of speech, not merely biosocial communication—which is common to both humans and animals. Animals communicate, also, and very effectively for their purposes. But man's language is propositional, organized in sentences, and governed by rules that are in part specific to the culture and in part universal, that is, inherent.
- Toolmaking, in the most encompassing sense, including not only what we commonly call tools, utensils, and instruments but also fire as a major technological means; tools that make tools; and the manufacture of clothing, food, and shelter (living quarters that vary widely within the species, not just the stereotypical structures produced by birds, beavers, ants, etc.).
- Culture making, a social process pertinent to all human activities and products whose patterns are distinctive in a given society. Such patterns can be discerned in the endless variety of customs, institutions, laws, language, religion, politics, entertainment, ritual, cooking, dress, art, and architecture prevailing within a society during a certain, often extensive, segment of its history. The combined stability and flexibility of these patterns is made possible by the interplay of man's creative urges and his unique capacity to transmit acquired learnings. Culture making refers, then, to those activities determined not by strictly biological needs but by socially determined *modes* of satisfying those and other, nonbiological, needs.

The characteristics that make up the next group are primarily experiential; their existence is known not merely from *observing* humans but from *being* human. Experiential characteristics, however, are not entirely private phenomena. They have behavioral correlates. For instance, thinking or, for that matter, loving, enjoying, or remembering are not directly amenable to assessment by external means but are typically expressed in corresponding activities that can be assessed in this fashion.

- Reflective awareness as the ability not only to know but to know that one knows—hence, the ability to engage in imagination, self-scrutiny, scientific hypothesizing, philosophical speculation, the evolution of a self-concept, and similar internal behaviors without which the existence of countless observable behaviors and products (e.g., literature, biography, ritual, and commemoration) could not be accounted for.
- Ethical concern as a sense of right and wrong, good and bad, transcendent values, and scales of values. This attribute cannot be

reduced to social conditioning even though it is not, of course, independent of it—just as the ability to speak a language is not independent of the social environment but cannot be accounted for *solely* by it.

- Esthetic urges as expressed in activities whose process or outcome serves solely the purpose of sensory or symbolic enjoyment. Thus man, and only man, decorates himself, his dwelling, tools, utensils, and instruments; produces sounds and complex patterns of sounds and motion for the pleasure of his eyes, ears, and total organism; distills intoxicating scents and beverages that transport him, symbolically, to other worlds—all of these devoid of utilitarian concern.
- Historical awareness as a sense of time; the capacity to move with effectiveness and precision along a vast continuum of past, present, and future; the ability to look back and plan ahead and to have foreknowledge of death—capacities of which there is no evidence in any other species.
- Metaphysical concern as the ability to conceive of ultimate questions—that is, questions that transcend the realm of the visible or the sensory, that deal with such "beyonds" as infinity, eternity, and the ultimate origin, nature, and purpose of things. These concerns account for some of the most ancient, durable, and venerable elements of man's cultural heritage.

About the reality of all this in mankind as a whole—not necessarily in every individual member of the species—there is no controversy. Although B. F. Skinner denies the substantive character of experiential phenomena —granting them only the epiphenomenal reality that belongs, for instance, to optical illusions—he admits the existence of experience, feeling, questioning, concern, and the like. But despite basic consensus on the presence of these characteristics in man, debate continues as to their significance. Specialized researchers differ on the question of whether these attributes are exclusively human or whether at least some of them are to some degree shared with certain animals—a question that runs throughout this book.

Though far from being a homogeneous group, humanistic psychologists, on the whole, are committed to the belief that the above-mentioned attributes are specifically and exclusively human. Indeed, the comparative psychologists and related social scientists have so far failed to offer conclusive evidence to the contrary. Substantiation for the humanistic thesis in light of the research of the comparative psychologists is largely the subject matter of the following chapters.

Justification for labeling as *scientific humanism* (Bonner, 1965) the kind of psychology introduced in this book is precisely the dialectical nature of the subject matter—the back and forth process of reference to observational and experiential data and to pro and con positions. Because of the interdisciplinary and unusually diversified material encompassed by humanistic psychology, frequent references will be made to the testimony of leading authorities in each of the many fields touched upon. The psychological outlook that this introduction attempts to reflect is not, indeed, ideological but essentially empirical—in the original sense of that word, not necessarily referring to experimental data, which are often barely empirical (Bakan, 1967), but to the data of experience, both sensory and conceptual.

I Homo Symbolicus

Characterizing man, the most complex of beings, with a single stroke that sets him apart from all else can hardly be a simple task. Taxonomists over the generations nevertheless have endeavored to pinpoint the specificity of man. The latest and most fundamental outcome of such attempts is the designation *homo symbolicus:* the animal capable of evolving and handling symbols and complex systems of symbols.

It is claimed by some, however, that the capacity for symbolic activity is not unique to man. The question is whether the claim is justified. We know that anything—in this case, symbolic activity—can be defined so as to suit the purpose of him who does the defining. This results, of course, in confusion and error.

As far as can be seen at the present time, symbolic capacity is the key to man's uniqueness. All the specifically and exclusively human capacities described in the following chapters can be traced back to this fundamental capacity. Symbolic ability allows man not only to know, as all animals do in variable measure, but to know that he knows, to reflect and to conclude. It manifests itself excitingly, though not most conspicuously, in the time dimension of his existence—one of the latest foci of psychological inquiry. Man is the animal who not only measures time, or what he thinks is time, but creates it in any existentially meaningful sense. His symbolic capacity accounts also for his capacity to free himself conceptually from the here and now of the stimulus situation, allowing him to conceive of new modes and models, to conjure new dimensions, new worlds.

1 The Symbolic Animal

Ever since grade school we have been taught that man stands apart from other animals by virtue of his reason: in the zoological table, he is proudly billed as *the rational animal*. The designation is perfectly valid insofar as man is endowed with the potential for abstraction, generalization, and logical exercise. For several reasons, however, it is less and less favored for characterizing the particular primate that is man. What accounts for the decline of the classical designation is, in part, its exalted flavor. There is something of an aura about the term *rational*, something that tends to evoke the glorified image of man depicted by Shakespeare in these lines:

> What a piece of work is a man!
> How noble in reason, how infinite in faculty!
> in form, in moving, how express and admirable!
> in action how like an angel!
> in apprehension how like a god!

> (*Hamlet*, II, ii.)

However, rhetorical flights such as these ring false in the ear of modern man, keenly aware of the dark side of human history and too disenchanted by the events of the twentieth century to appreciate sublime characterizations of this sort. Significantly, perhaps, the contemporary mood tends rather to be attuned to T. S. Eliot's dismal lines:

> We are the hollow men
> We are the stuffed men
> Leaning together
> Headpiece filled with straw. Alas!*

* T. S. Eliot, "The Hollow Men," *Collected Poems 1909–1962* (New York: Harcourt Brace Jovanovich, 1963).

Actually, these two images of man—one euphoric and the other depressing—are but extreme samples of a vast spectrum of attributes that can be stated in far more sober, neutral, and even operational terms, such as those evolved by the combined efforts of scientists and scholars and presented in the following pages.

The "Unreasonable-Rational" Animal

One reason, then, for the decline of the traditional designation *rational* is its value-laden character, which tends to exclude it from scientific use. Not, incidentally, that values are incompatible with science: the theory of a value-free science (Weber, 1949) has long been discredited. Instead, it is now recognized that the *practice* of science—as distinct from its *product(s)* or findings—is pervaded with judgments pertinent to value (Bronowski, 1959). What is improper in scientific discourse is the arbitrary or impertinent use of value judgments and/or terms. And *rational* is gradually being regarded as belonging to this category, sounding like a title rather than an attribute—as if man were classified as the "lordly" animal.

The statement that man stands out above all other creatures by virtue of his reason tends to suggest, though it does not actually claim, that he acts and lives reasonably—obviously a most unreasonable position in the face of his behavioral record. Man may be the *rational* animal, but he is unquestionably the most *unreasonable* of animals (A. Huxley, 1946). In fact, since the potential for reason is a prerequisite for unreasonableness, he is the only unreasonable animal.

RATIONAL VERSUS REASONABLE. The paradoxical notion of unreasonable-rational man is rooted in an awkward combination of etymology and usage. Although both words share the same root, each has acquired a different function. *Rationality,* whether in thought or in action, refers to a logical, internally consistent organization or sequence of elements. The term belongs, therefore, in the context of more or less rigorous or learned discourse—even though the spread of literacy caused its use to spill over into the vernacular. *Reasonable,* on the other hand, points to the realm of common sense and refers to practical rather than conceptual matters. It is a broad, life-related term that may encompass even irrational (or nonrational) phenomena—as emotions are commonly classified. Thus, we can say that it is reasonable or "stands to reason" if a person gets angry or anxious or fearful in certain situations. Similarly, we speak of maturity as a certain state of reasonableness, by which we mean a certain balance between intellect and emotion. Consequently, not all that is rational is, strictly speaking, reasonable, and vice versa.

Homo Symbolicus Dethrones Homo Sapiens

Another, more substantial factor that accounts for the declining use of *rational* as a designation for the human animal is its lack of precision and empirical value, which affects its worth as a criterion for the experimental identification of species differences. Better suited for such purposes is an operational criterion stated in terms of directly observable performance. For instance, certain animals can acquire certain noninstinctive behaviors in response to stimuli toward which they are not naturally or inherently sensitive. These learned behaviors are elicited by rewards—either the satisfaction of need or the avoidance of pain. Consequently, they are goal directed—however mechanically—and can be extraordinarily useful to humans; for example, the skills that the bottlenosed dolphin can be taught.

Should one conclude that these behaviors or their agents are rational? Some might say yes, others no, depending on how broadly or narrowly they define the complex notion of rationality. However, if we can find an operation that is typically performed by one species and that no other species proves able to perform, we have an operational criterion: a means by which interspecies differences can be assessed experimentally, at least *in principle*. Such a means allows one—again, in principle—to resolve some of the controversies that may arise in connection with identification of critical differences among species.

In recent decades scientists from a variety of disciplines have come to recognize one such variable within the infinitely diverse behavioral reper- toire of humans: symbolic capacity. Authorities on the subject unani- mously agree that humans manifest an extraordinary capacity, *unmatched by any other species,* for dealing with symbols. Note, however, the italicized phrase. For, again, there remains an important core of con- troversy within this unanimity.

Indeed, operational criteria are not absolute. They are valuable in that they come closer to what is called the "facts"; that is, the publicly observable and recordable aspects of a problem. Unfortunately, there are no facts without some measure of interpretation, and this is where the human factor again creeps in. Imagine, for example, the facts derived from any systematic but simple observation made at ages eight, twenty, or fifty. Would not the observed facts vary according to the experiential context of the observer? As Bridgman, the father of operationism, con- cluded, "We never get away from ourselves" (1959, p. 6).

Bridgman's conclusion is well taken: the perceiving subject, with his intellectual orientation, his beliefs and presuppositions, and so forth, influences what is actually perceived from among the myriad factors present within a situation. A ten-year-old reading a history book per- ceives the reported facts in terms of his limited experience; he sees con- siderably less than an eighteen-year-old, and the latter may quite likely see less than a thirty-year-old individual reading the same historical analysis.

A QUALITATIVE OR A QUANTITATIVE DIFFERENCE? Where the experts' unanimity about man's symbolic capacity breaks down is over the question of *the nature of the difference:* Is it merely quantitative (a difference in degree), or is it qualitative (a difference in kind)? Is man simply excelling along the symbolic dimension, or is he the only organism to have specifically symbolic capacity?

The cleavage between authorities in regard to this question is not ideological—that is, not involved with world views or religious positions— as was the case with the controversy surrounding the theory of evolution. More precisely, it is not *obviously* so rooted, but ideological positions can be disguised as scientific truth. Paradoxically, neither is the controversy centered strictly around the facts! By their very nature, facts or data of observation are "out there" for all to assess: bottlenosed dolphins do show an extraordinary capacity to learn; apes do exhibit rule-following behavior; dancing honey bees do give precise information to the group as to the location of remote food sources; and so on. Controversies of this sort hinge either upon the interpretation or, as is the case here, around the often insufficiently examined epistemologies or linguistics involved. Indeed, it is now clearly recognized that "scientific observations are not 'theory-neutral,' as scientists once claimed, but can be heavily 'theory-laden'."*

To understand how easily a controversy can develop around otherwise crystal-clear facts, one must remember that the study of complex matters usually involves a spontaneous division of labor: some workers gather the data and conduct the experiments; others examine the work from the point of view of design, statistics, logic, linguistics, semantics, and other critical angles. In the case at hand, the comparative psychologists and the ethologists are the authorities in animal behavior and learning. However, the very fact that they are specialized in one area usually precludes their being the final authority in other areas. Thus, a researcher's methodology may have been perfectly watertight, but he may err in the verbalization of either the process or the outcome of his work. Here, then, is where "theory" may creep subliminally into the reporting. When such is the case, conclusions are apt to be faulty—or at least faultily conceptualized—regardless of the excellence of the design and execution of the project. A semantic slip or theoretical bias rooted in the limitations of a specialized background apparently accounts for the comparative psychologist's choice of the term *symbol* to designate something that more properly belongs in the category of *signs.*

* The terms "theory-neutral" and "theory-laden" are attributed to Harvard's Everett Mendelsohn.

To give an idea of the magnitude of the error involved in this mis-labeling, let us compare the case under discussion with one more familiar. The use of *symbol* to designate what is actually a *sign* is comparable to saying that coffee is an amphetamine because amphetamines are stimulants and coffee is a stimulant. Both products have, undeniably, a common dimension in their effect. But the fact that both can be situated legitimately along *one* common parameter does not justify the reduction of amphetamines to coffee, for coffee is not in any way a simpler or milder form of amphetamine.

Now, to gain an insight in terms of the case itself, let us proceed to a brief but thorough analysis of the concept of *symbol*, for it is the key concept in the behavioral identification of the specificity of man. It is also the pivot around which several chapters in the following presentation turn. It will become clear from this analysis that the source of the difficulty lies in a semantic error—incidentally, only one of several semantic errors into which reductionist social scientists have repeatedly fallen in their failure to distinguish between *conceptual* and *perceptual* thinking, between *methodological* and *ontological* determinism (Adler, 1967), and between *empirical* and *experimental* approaches (Bakan, 1967).

The Key Issue: Symbols Versus Signs

Since the problem centers around the ambiguity of two terms, let us begin this comparison by stating what signs and symbols have in common. In the first place, *each stands for something other than itself.* Reichenbach (1947) chooses to use *sign* as the more fundamental, hence the larger, concept. Signs are physical things that represent things other than themselves with regard to the sign user—e.g., chalk marks on a blackboard, ink marks on paper, sound waves produced in the throat. According to Reichenbach, then, *all symbols are signs, but not all signs are symbols.*

Adler (1967), realizing the confusion that Reichenbach's use of *sign* is apt to generate—because it represents both a category and a subcategory of phenomena—proposes instead the term *signifier* as the common denominator of signs and symbols. Beyond the fact that each signifies something other than itself, signs and symbols differ along every one of their semantic dimensions.

THEIR DIFFERENTIAL MEANING. Different authors characterize the difference between sign and symbol in different terms—fortunately, all their characterizations are compatible and complementary. Most widely used, perhaps, is Reichenbach's analysis (1947). Using the concept of *sign* as the generic term, he distinguishes three classes: the first comprises the *indexical signs,* which acquire their sign function through a causal connection between sign and object signified. Smoke, then, is a sign of fire, fever a sign of infection. In both examples, there is a causal relationship between sign and object. In the second class are the *iconic signs,* whose sign function rests on a relationship of similarity to the objects they designate: for example, a photograph of a person or a representation of a spoon and fork on a sign advertising food. The third class comprises purely arbitrary or *conventional signs,* whose relation to the object is established by common accord, as is the case with the vast range of intellectual and technological symbols (letters, words, digits). Within this classification, *only the latter category,* comprising the conventional signs, *corresponds to the notion of symbol.*

Very useful also is Cassirer's distinction between symbols that function as *designators* in human behavior and signals that function as *operators* in both human and animal behavior. The meaning of designators is inferential: they tell *what* or *how* a thing *is;* for example, "the word 'danger' on a roadway sign *can* operate as a warning eliciting alertness; but the word 'danger' as such, by itself refers to a whole class of phenomena" (Adler, 1967, p. 136). As the commonplace saying goes, words mean different things to different people because words are symbols. Signs and signals, on the other hand, do not mean different things to different people. The amazingly unequivocal meaning of signs is demonstrated visually in Henry Dreyfuss's *Symbol Sourcebook* (1972), a fascinating collection of several thousand internationally used signs and signals.

Operators, however, are functional: they "tell" the subject to *do* or *not to do* something and, in certain cases, where to do it. "The cry of an animal in danger operates as a warning, eliciting awareness on the part of animals of the same species" (Adler, 1967, p. 136). Symbols, then, in the proper sense of the term "cannot be reduced to mere signals, for they belong to different universes of discourse. [Signals are] part of the physical world of being, [symbols, part of] the human world of meaning" (Cassirer, 1944, p. 32).

To all this Royce (1964) adds another important feature, pointing out that signs stand in a *one-to-one relation* to the object signified while symbols stand in a *one-to-many relation* to the objects they designate. A road sign signifies only one idea; it is unambiguous. On the other hand, the word *America* can refer to a geographic unit, a shape on a map, democracy, affluence, the flag, world power, the national anthem, baseball, cowboys, westerns, the dollar sign, stars and stripes, Uncle Sam, and so on.

Finally, in an effort to unify and simplify these various classifications, Adler proposes to use *signifier* as the generic term, distinguishing two classes—one for the symbols proper, the other for both signs and signals (since these two share the same characteristics). The relations among these concepts and their classifications are presented in Tables 1–1 and 1–2.

TABLE 1–1 SIGNS AND SIGNALS DRAWING UPON REICHENBACH, CASSIRER, AND ADLER

Adler	Cassirer	Reichenbach
Signifiers	↱ Operators	↱ Indexical signs
		↳ Iconic signs
	↳ Designators	Conventional signs or symbols

TABLE 1–2 THE REALM OF SIGNIFIERS

(combining the views of Cassirer, Reichenbach, and Royce)

SIGNS and SIGNALS (*operator* symbols)	SYMBOLS (*designator* symbols)
are part of the physical world of *being*	are part of the human world of *meaning*
belong to the universe of *practical affairs*	belong to the universe of *description* (or designation)
are *operators:* their significance is *functional;* they "tell" the subject to do or not to do something	are *designators:* their significance is *referential;* they tell *what* or *how* a thing is
are *associated* either by instinct or by learning with the action signified	are typically *instituted* and sanctioned by convention, common consent of the parties; they are socially shared
stand in a one-to-one relationship to the object represented	stand in a one-to-many relationship to the object referred to; can stand for a wide variety of things at different times and places
"stand for" or "point to" *definite* and *specific objects* only—usually concrete objects	can have *definite* or *indefinite,* specific or nonspecific, concrete or abstract, referents
are *stimulus-bound;* that is, tied to perception by the senses	are *independent* of the presence of *sensory stimulation*
are *time*-bound, confined within the present	transcend time, are conceptual in nature
are subject-oriented	can be object-oriented; that is, can be independent of subjective need or reference

Each of the preceding two categories belongs to a different universe of discourse. Consequently, symbols proper (*designators*) cannot be reduced to signs and signals (*operators*). Note: Their verbal or nonverbal character does not constitute a critical difference.

"MINIMAL MAN" VERSUS NONMAN. In the preceding analysis the concept of symbol is described in the strictest of terms; that is, in terms of the meaning it has in the context of symbolic logic. One may wonder why it should be necessary to describe it in quite so abstract and unexistential a fashion in an introductory text on humanistic psychology. The reason for doing so is of crucial importance: a clear understanding of the concept of symbol and, especially, of the difference between sign and symbol is, at the present time, the only empirically valid way to distinguish between specifically human behavior and certain forms of animal behavior that appear similar. But, one may further ask, why is it necessary to proceed in an empirical way? Would not the existential, the phenomenological, the ethical, or the literary way be more suitable to, more commensurate with the richness of the subject matter and much more capable of rendering the fullness of the specificity of man? Why argue the case of man in minimal terms?

The reason for focusing upon what Krutch (1954) calls "minimal man" is the following. Each historical period has its own language. At the time of romanticism, things were argued in lofty, exalted terms; at the turn of the century, discussion took on either a materialistic or a moralistic, Victorian perspective. At the present time it is the language of research that has our ear. Whether or not research is the most appropriate method of inquiry for a given subject matter, it is important to state one's case in the language of one's time. More significantly, priority should be given to empirical evidence over rational inference, intuitive insight, or arguments of authority wherever the subject matter permits. Such is a requisite of scientific and sound procedure. True, the *significance* of empirical evidence stands in inverse relation to its *certitude,* but established psychology attaches considerably greater weight to certitude than to significance. Since humanistic psychology assumes as one of its tasks the refutation of established psychology, it must be able and willing to argue in terms of its opponent. Such an approach does not exclude drawing upon other, more meaningful approaches as well, but it avoids arguing the case solely in what Skinner calls rhetorical terms.

This, then, is the reason for which the chapters dealing with directly observable phenomena (toolmaking, language, lawmaking, esthetic activity) make reference to pertinent findings of comparative psychology (animal psychology) and/or ecology. In each case, these findings are examined according to a criterion—the distinction between sign and symbol —in an effort to test the validity of the distinction between specifically and nonspecifically human behavior.

The Power of Symbols

The invention of the wheel is often cited as the single most important event in the process of civilization. Its role in the diffusion of culture and in the advancement of technology is indeed beyond question. But the invention of abstract symbols is incomparably more significant and more basic to the cultural process. Among man's innumerable inventions, none is more indicative of his creative potential and none, it seems, has served the actualization of that potential as the alphabet has. Indeed, none of the symbolic universes originated by man has proved more fruitful nor more instrumental in generating communication, enlightenment, power, and intelligent enjoyment than the system of twenty-six (more or less in different languages) characters called the alphabet.

It is a fascinating and little-known fact that, despite its numerous phenotypical versions, ancient and contemporary, the alphabet seems to have been invented only once. On the question of its uniqueness there is little or no controversy, and Diringer, an outstanding authority on the subject, colorfully outlines his view:

> A learned professor said to me once: "I have been told that you are dealing with the history of *the alphabet*. Can you tell me which alphabet you mean—the Egyptian, the Hebrew, the Latin, the Arabic, the Chinese?" I explained to him . . . why the Egyptian, the Chinese, and other similar systems of writing should not be termed alphabets. And I added that in dealing with the history of *the alphabet*, I include all the alphabets, because all of them probably derived from one original alphabet" (1948, p. 195; Diringer's emphasis).

On the question of the precise who, where, and when of this momentous invention, Diringer finds a large core of agreement though something less than unanimity. Mercer (1959) is apparently not far off when he averages expert opinion and places the emergence of the alphabet at about 1500 B.C. among Semitic tribes working in the copper and turquoise mines of the Sinai desert (1959).

Needing a system for keeping records of their production and delivery and the strict ritualistic practices imposed on them by their Egyptian masters for the propitiation of the goddess of turquoise, the tribe invented this extraordinarily flexible system of non-iconic signs. The merits of this remarkably ingenious system were easily recognized by the Egyptians, who adopted it promptly (that is, as promptly as history moved before the era of future shock) and passed it on to the Phoenicians, the Greeks, and the Romans, who diffused it widely. At the present time, its use is the hallmark of civilization—in the sense of literacy—all over the globe.

Relating this historical fragment to what was noted earlier about the differences between symbols and signs, it should be clear that the crucial value and power of the alphabetical system lies in its *non-iconic* character—that is, its use of conventional instead of representational signs. Iconic systems of writing—ideograms or phonograms—appeared, of course, much earlier in the writings of ancient Persia, in Egyptian hieroglyphics, and, for that matter, in the rudimentary graphics of any known civilization before it became acquainted with the alphabetic system. Until such time, the semantic and communicative value of iconic writing was severely limited by the above-mentioned *one-to-one* relation of sign to object and was, of course, hazardously ambiguous. These limitations were overcome by the *one-to-many* relation of symbol to object and opened the way to a rich and relatively unambiguous form of communication.

A SYMBOL FOR NOTHING.   In the realm of mathematics, it was the paradoxical invention of a symbol for nothing, the zero, that proved especially prodigious. With its help, as Langer (1967) remarks, fourth graders can perform mathematical operations for which the ancients, at the peak of their civilization, would have had to use the abacus, the forerunner of the computer. The extraordinary versatility of the zero—which may represent either nothing or infinite tenfolds—again illustrates the power of the one-to-many referential capacity of the symbol.

More effectively than any other symbolic medium, mathematical symbols enable man to transcend the realm of the tangible, to engage in intellectual adventures independent of the factual data of sensory evidence. As Langer points out:

> Behind these symbols lie the boldest, purest, coolest abstraction mankind has ever made. No schoolman* speculating on essences and attributes ever approached anything like the abstractness of algebra. Yet those same scientists who prided themselves on their concrete factual knowledge, who claimed to reject every proof except empirical evidence, never hesitated to accept the demonstrations and calculations, the bodiless, sometimes avowedly "fictitious" entities of the mathematicians. Zero and infinity, square roots of negative numbers, incommensurable lengths and fourth dimensions, all found unquestioned welcome in the laboratory (1963, p. 18).

It is a source of lasting wonderment to observe how the hardnosed scientist who swears only by factual, sensory data readily submits to the mathematician's juggling of the immaterial and sometimes admittedly "fictitious" entities conveyed by mathematical symbols, the use of which now undergirds man's ventures into limitless space. "The faith of scientists in the power and truth of mathematics is so implicit that their work has gradually become less and less observation and more and more calculation" (Langer, 1963, p. 19). This is precisely Bakan's point in "Psychology's Research Crisis" (1967): the substitution, under the name of experimental

---

* The term *schoolman* refers to a medieval scholar who applied the speculative methods of scholasticism.

research, of mathematical (symbolic) data for empirical data; that is, for sense observation.

Nonconventional Symbolic Universes

Man's symbolic capacity can be described, of course, in far more exciting and existentially meaningful terms than the preceding. In fact, symbol, as it is commonly understood, refers to some visible object or sign used to represent something invisible or immaterial, usually a meaning that cannot be fully expressed in words. Popular instances of such symbols are, in Western culture, a heart for love, a cross for suffering, a cogwheel for industrialization; in other cultures, a circle to represent perfection, the yin/yang figure for the meaning of the universe, the ankh to symbolize generation or enduring life, and the Buddhist knot for happiness. From the point of view of their form or externality, such symbols are still conventional, even though their meaning is acquired through cultural contagion rather than formal learning. However, the power and quality of their meaning is a function of the subject, of his capacity to realize and participate in a particular universe of meaning, be it love, faith, suffering, the striving for perfection, or any other sphere of experience or aspiration.* In other words, the value of the symbol is a function of the subject: like teaching, it can impart only what the subject is ready to receive.

METAPHOR AND ALLEGORY.   There is a world of symbolism spontaneously created and likewise understood, especially by members of related cultures. Among these nonconventional symbolic universes, metaphor and allegory are outstanding for their originality, kaleidoscopic variety, and pervasive power to communicate significant content. Nowhere is the stimulus-unboundness (that is, the spontaneity and creativity of the human mind) revealed as luminously as in these forms of symbolism.

Metaphor and allegory are verbal or pictorial manifestations of man's tendency to transcend limitation, denseness, obscurity, and dullness and his capacity to lend a bright edge to ordinary experience. Both these forms of figurative expression are special, superior cases of the use of analogy. In them the likeness between symbol and content goes far beyond perceptual associations of similarity and extends into the realm of essential meaning. They liberate insight from the limitations inherent in concreteness and allow it to emerge, clear and sharp, from amorphous experience.

It was aptly put that "for gaining an insight into life, a metaphor is a

---

* This idea of participation between subject and symbol was brought to my attention by my colleague in the social sciences, Dr. V. Lombardi.

sharper and brighter instrument than a syllogism" (Litt.D. citation awarded Robert Frost at Amherst) because it is capable of crystallizing the diffuse and implicit nature of existential truths. Even a one-word metaphor is apt to capture and enliven an idea; thus the word *arrow* in combination with *thought* conveys in one stroke the sharp, swift, focused, and penetrating character of thinking at its best. Note the loss in evocative power of the same metaphor applied to *imagination*. Imagination being playful, leisurely, capricious, gliding, fluttering, its essence is more aptly conveyed by the image of *wings* than by the sharpness of the arrow and the straightness of its path.

Because of the subtle requirements that govern its use, the metaphor, according to Aristotle, who regarded it as the mark of genius, is "the one thing that cannot be learned from others." And Kenneth Burke eulogizes its power in terms to which modern man is particularly responsive: "As the documents of science pile up, are we not coming to see that whole works of scientific research, even entire schools, are hardly more than the patient repetition, in all its ramifications, of a fertile metaphor" (Shibles, 1971, p. vii).

MYTH AND LEGEND. When metaphors are woven into encompassing, interlocking patterns relevant to significant areas of human experience and aspiration, they become myth and legend. They are then, at the summit of their power, able to lend insight into unyielding questions that pose themselves, clearly or dimly, to the human mind. Myth and legend do not have the spotlight quality of the single, dazzling metaphor. More like a floodlight, they are capable of illuminating the nature of enduring questions: the mystery of life and love, of suffering and evil, of birth and death. Myth and legend at their best are endowed with an existential validity. They may not be able to withstand scrutiny in terms of the principles of identity and contradiction, and so forth, but they may sustain man's quest for ultimate answers regarding the nature, conduct, and purpose of his life. Appearances notwithstanding, myths are not so much irrational as transrational. When they lose their power, it is because they have been disowned—but not disproven—by the subject.

RIDDLES, PUNS, AND PUZZLES. Sharing something of the playfulness and charm of the metaphor is the particular symbolism of the wide domain of thought-tickling and mind-stretching riddles and puzzles, the witty realm of puns. Puns may be, as is often claimed, "the lowest form of humor," but they are a clever illustration of the versatility and multidimensionality of man's visual, auditory, imaginative, and intellectual symbolic capacities. As for puzzles and riddles, they are among the most ancient forms of "testing" (remember the riddle that the sphinx posed to Oedipus or Samson's riddle to his in-laws) and reveal man's delight in challenge for challenge's sake and his unmatched skill in devising games out of nothing but his own symbolic genius.

Universal Symbolism

Man's symbolic nature reveals itself not only in theoretical systems, practical inventions, solutions to problems, and esthetic or playful pursuits, but also in his very perception of the world and of himself. That all his perceptions are interpretations is both man's glory and his predicament, the source of much of his delight and distress. For what he perceives is seldom if ever an exact replication of what is presented to his sense organs. It is usually something phenomenologically far more original and richer than its physical counterpart (Michotte, 1963). For perception is intertwined with elements drawn from the vast associational field of the perceiver and stamped with the mark of his personality, maturity, and capability—a creative phenomenon that justifies the apt (if perhaps overstated) observation that we know things not as *they* are but as *we* are.

The symbolic tendency of perception—its capacity to reveal the subject's inner make-up and orientation—has been widely tapped by clinical psychology in the use of projective tests for the diagnosis of personality. A well-known example is the Thematic Apperception Test (TAT), which features pictures of people either alone or in interaction with others and which the subject is asked to interpret. The stories thus produced are believed by clinical psychologists to provide a sampling of the predominantly unconscious dimension of the subject's mental-emotional make-up.

More fascinating yet, man's prodigious symbolic capacity is not limited to the perception of objects or images, verbally or nonverbally presented. It manifests itself also and even more strikingly in nonrepresentational material, as was documented in the fascinating experiments of Krauss (1930). Krauss asked his subjects to use nonrepresentational lines to illustrate emotions (anger, joy, serenity), materials (gold, silver), and ideas (progress, peace) and found that his subjects could significantly categorize these free line structures. The same capacity is demonstrated in an original experiment reported by Köhler (1947) in which subjects were asked to match nonsense words with nonrepresentational line structures.

Recognition of the potential for clinical application of nonrepresentational materials resulted in the construction of numerous projective tests. Actually, as is so often the case, practice preceded theory—to wit, the well-known Rorschach Inkblot Test, which was invented prior to any theoretical investigation of the projective qualities of nonrepresentational material. Less well known but remarkably productive is the Wartegg Drawing Completion Test (Kinget, 1952).

METASYMBOLISM. This section on universal symbolism would be grossly inadequate without mention of Jung's work on the depth-psychological meaning of the symbolic in human experience. Jung labored a lifetime trying to discover and interpret the many analogies existing between the psychic contents of modern man and certain manifestations of the psychology of preliterate peoples and of their myths and cults. His theory of archetypes—primeval and pervasive representations, ideas, and themes that appear in the literary and religious legacies of cultures originally totally removed from one another in time and space—is well known. Everywhere Jung sought parallels and illuminating insights that might provide a deeper understanding of the creative products of the human psyche and its ever-recurring basic manifestations.

Because Jung's work is itself a symbolic system about symbolic systems, it may be labeled a work of metasymbolism (just as metalanguage refers to that part of a language system that deals with the rules of language use). And because all interpretations are to a variable degree subjective and, therefore, projective, his work can be regarded as a high-order combination of symbolism and projection that is largely subjective and tentative but nonetheless fascinating and thought-provoking.

2 Reflective Consciousness

Self-reference is something man cannot escape. Whether he speaks about the future of marriage, the trend in politics, a recent discovery, tall buildings, or small gains, his comments issue from a point in time and space that is unique to that symbolic locus of reference, the "I." Near, far, right, left, high, low—all draw their significance from the shifting position of the individual organism and attending self. "To make a statement about a distant galaxy is to make a statement about oneself" as Bugental (1967) puts it, a bit startlingly but aptly, for distance presupposes a referent. Man's every utterance, then, is of necessity self-anchored.

Man owes his superior cognitive ability to two species-specific attributes: reflective awareness and conceptual thought. Reflection—the capacity of human consciousness for turning in upon itself—allows him not only to know but to know that he knows; to emit and receive the same symbolic content; to re-flect it. As Teilhard de Chardin observes in *The Phenomenon of Man:* "If we wish to settle this question of the 'superiority' of man over the animals . . . I can see only one way of doing so . . . making straight for the central phenomenon, reflection" (1959, pp. 164–65). And he comments further: "The being who is the object of his own reflection, in consequence of that very doubling back upon himself, becomes in a flash able to raise himself into a new sphere. In reality, another world is born. Abstraction, logic, reasoned choice and inventions, mathematics, art, calculation of space and time, anxieties and dreams of love—all these activities of *inner life* are nothing else than the effervescence of the newly-formed centre as it explodes onto itself" (p. 165).

The purest and most complex manifestation of man's symbolic nature is his capacity for conceptual thought; that is, for thought involving sustained and high order abstraction and generalization. Conceptual thought enables man to make himself independent of the stimulus-boundness that characterizes animal thinking. Animals, especially primates, give undeniable evidence of something analogous to human thought—analogous yet radically different in that their thought is bound to the immediate stimulus situation and to the felt impulse of the organism. Animal thinking, too, is riveted to the realm of survival (broadly taken) and therefore encompasses a variety of needs pertinent to the species as well as to the individual. These differences account for the distinction between *conceptual* thought, which is the exclusive prerogative of man, and *perceptual* thought, a cognitive function based directly upon sense perception, which man shares with other animals.

Reflective Awareness

Man, then, is not only the agent of the experiential process going on within him he is also its witness—one not always fully awake and not immune to closing an eye to events about which he would rather not know. But nevertheless a witness who can be called to the stand whenever the situation demands it—and when the necessary safety for the ego is provided. This does not mean that any individual, no matter how articulate, is capable of expressing the linguistic equivalent of what Langer terms "the what and how of the inner show." Language is one-dimensionally linear and discursive; its expression occurs over time. Consciousness, on the other hand, is so rich in dimensions, directions, and overtones that it is truly implosive, occurring along several interlocking, looplike, and centripetal lines.

This peculiar circularity of human awareness is obviously at the root of that primary—if usually implicit—datum of human experience that is the self: a symbolic structure of attributes, capacities, values, purposes, assumptions, illusions, and so on, pertinent to the "I" or "me." According to self-theory, the self-structure plays a major role in the economy of human existence in that it guides and regulates behavior by constant cybernetic reference (feedback) to this organized internal locus of awareness. This guiding self-image is also the basis of individuation and the necessary requisite for conscience, self-scrutiny, guilt, pride, and a host of characteristics that constitute identity or personality. Because he is a reflective center, man is a person, a self.

The human being, then, is of necessity centered in the self or self-centered—a condition not to be equated with egotism or selfishness. His ultimate center of reference is the self—unless he is in love, in which case he is fence-riding two selves, for in that instance, "the existential I is transformed into the co-existential we" (Bonner, 1965, p. 149), as we will see in a later chapter.

Know thyself. Consider these two words, perhaps the most celebrated injunction ever addressed to mankind. Socrates apparently was an early self-theorist. He realized long before what we now call "psychology" that the agency responsible for guiding and regulating human behavior is the self and hence, that it is crucial to endeavor to know just what that agency consists of and what it is up to. Interestingly, none among those who train, regulate, or study the behavior of animals ever aims to convey to his charges even a watered-down version of this principle. Pigeons have been taught to play ping pong—a feat that may hold diplomatic promise—and dolphins to work for the Department of Defense. But no researcher, whether working with rats, dogs, pigeons, or primates, ever tried to tap the animal's potential for engaging in the beneficial exercise of self-scrutiny and self-consultation.

FIRST-PERSON STATEMENTS. Reflective thought and the resulting self-concept enable man, and only man, to make first-person statements—a typical form of human expression. The animal's inability to produce the equivalent of the first-person statement is not due to a lack of the requisite vocal apparatus. Certain birds are able to form sounds and sound-structures, and primates can be taught to use signs for words (Gardner and Gardner, 1969). Their inability to make first-person statements is due to the absence of that symbolic structure, the "I," that is, the product of the reflective function.

Actually, human beings are not only capable of expressing themselves in this mode, they are apt to do so with immoderate fondness. Man's tendency to see and understand in terms of the "I" is often ingenious, sometimes a bit overbearing, and sometimes colorful, as in the following anecdote, a charming instance of this strong and natural bent. It concerns an alert little girl whose parents were typically fond of teaching the child such things as giving her name and address, counting to ten, and reciting the alphabet, all of which the child learned readily and with remarkable accuracy. In the case of the alphabet, however, the parents were surprised to find that she always jumbled the tail end of the series without, however, showing any sign of confusion or hesitation around that area. After listening carefully, they discovered that the child wasn't garbling the sounds, but that she was automatically converting the "u" (you) sounds into the first-person form, making "s, t, *u*, v, *w*, x, y, z" into "s, t, *me*, v, *double-me. . . .*"

Contrast the spontaneously executed little stunt of the three-year-old with the animal's inability to effectively use the pronoun form, as appears from the Gardners' work with the chimp Washoe which they taught intensively in the use of sign language. After twenty-two months, Washoe still proved unable to differentiate basic grammatical relations: "The signs for *me, you,* and *tickle,* for example, have occurred in all possible orders in Washoe's signed sequences. These different orders do not seem to refer to different situations in any systematic way. For the same situation (requesting someone to tickle her), Washoe signed *you tickle* and *tickle you.*

Washoe signed *me tickle* for someone tickling her and again *me tickle* to indicate that she would tickle someone" (Bronowski and Bellugi, 1970, p. 672).

HOW DO WE KNOW THAT ANIMALS DON'T? We have no evidence nor any reason to assume that other forms of life have something comparable or equivalent to reflective awareness as we know it. Nor do we have, in the present state of our methodology, any way to decipher the mode of expression that this form of awareness would take if it existed. Nevertheless, is this sufficient reason to conclude the absence of self-awareness in the animal?

Granted, reflective awareness is clearly not a datum of external observation; it is part of the private world of the subject. What it is that he is reflecting upon at any particular moment cannot, of course, be known directly by another. However, this does not mean he is not reflecting. Similarly, how can we be sure that animals don't reflect? Why cannot the same private world be assumed to exist for them? On the surface, the question seems to call for the simple admission that we cannot know. However, upon reflection we find that the answer is not so simple. Granted, it is impossible for anyone but myself to know *what* I am thinking about or reflecting on *at any particular moment*. But over a span of time (anywhere from a few hours to a few days), it is impossible not to know that I *do* engage in this function—which is the issue here.

How do I substantiate this? By the same means science uses in regard to any other problem—namely, observation and inference in combination with other methods. Thus it is not only permissible to infer the operation of reflective and conceptual thought in man but, as William James, Henri Bergson, Mortimer Adler, and others have made amply clear, it is *necessary* to do so in order to account for the kind of behavior man exhibits over a span of time. The existence of an internal process *must* be inferred for most of man's initiatives to make sense—for example, planning a trip, a meal, an experiment, a lecture, a will—and for reports about such states as doubt, uneasiness, striving—held to be analyzable into sensory elements—to be understandable. Conversely, in the case of subhuman animals, one *need not* infer reflective and conceptual thought because their behavior—which does not transcend the level of elementary associations elicited by an immediate stimulus—does not call for nonobservable explanatory mechanisms.

We may, of course, fantasize about the animal's repertory of capacities. Those of us with a poetic bent may impute reflective thought and planful action to animals because poets have a license to anthropomorphize. Such is also a favorite exercise on the part of authors and scriptwriters, and the results are usually witty and entertaining. But scientists qua scientists do not have this option; the principle of parsimony prohibits them from calling on unnecessary explanatory structures.

SELF-AWARENESS AND THE HUMAN DILEMMA. Self-awareness is at the heart of the human dilemma. The capacity for experiencing the self as both subject and object constantly causes one to oscillate between two opposite—and often contrary—stances.

> We are not simply describing two alternate ways of behaving. Nor is it quite accurate to speak of our being subject and object *simultaneously*. The important point is that our consciousness is a process of oscillation between the two. Indeed, is not this dialectical relationship between experiencing myself as subject and object just what consciousness consists of? The process of oscillation gives me potentiality—I can choose between them, can throw my weight on one side or the other . . . it is the gap between the two ways of responding that is important. My freedom, in any genuine sense, lies not in my capacity to live as "pure subject," but rather in my capacity to experience both modes, to live in the dialectical relationship (May, 1967, p. 9).

Self-awareness also makes for loneliness, for being conscious of separateness, of being torn away from the primary unity with nature. From generation to generation this self-awareness has inevitably led man to ask a profound and unyielding question: What is the meaning of man and the universe? Man realizes the accidental character of birth and death. He is, directly or indirectly, aware of his need for meaning and of the possibility (or actuality) of its loss. He is, therefore, subject to anxiety and even anguish. "To the day of our deaths we exist in an inner solitude that is linked to the nature of life itself. Even as we project love and affection upon others we endure a loneliness which is the price of all individual consciousness—the price of living" (Eiseley, 1970, p. 48).

THE ENDURING RIDDLE. Before moving further into the subject, reference should be made to the process that underlies both perceptual and conceptual thought—consciousness. It is sometimes said that consciousness is an attribute of the cosmos. When properly qualified, there is validity to such a statement. Indeed, consciousness in its most elementary manifestations can be defined as the capacity for sensory discrimination (Royce, 1964). In this elementary sense, all that is alive—even such obscure vegetable phenomena as tree roots "searching" for moisture, heliotropic flowers "following" the sun, and phototropic amoeba "choosing" light over dark— is to some degree endowed with consciousness. At the other extreme is the sort of consciousness with which we are familiar, the kind that flows by "the mind's eye" like an uninterrupted, multiple-track videotape, simultaneously made and viewed, reversed, spliced, or fast-forwarded by simple "eye control" on the part of the subject agent.

Interestingly, the immensity of the difference between these two forms of cognition is not only phenomenological. It is equally vast on the explanatory level. Indeed, the type of "consciousness" that consists in the capacity to discriminate within a narrow range of phenomena has long been explained in physicochemical terms. Conversely, we are as ignorant as ever about the manner in which consciousness "inserts itself into" or "links up with" the tissues (to phrase it, for lack of a better way, in awkwardly mechanistic terms).

We know, of course, about the relationship between consciousness and the brain, but we do not know the nature of that relationship. It is certain, however, that the brain is the necessary condition for consciousness: no (human) brain, no (human) consciousness. But necessary condition does not mean cause. Water is the necessary condition for swimming but not the cause of it; water is also the necessary condition for drowning. The *cause* of thinking is unknown. As Adler (1967) puts it, the brain does not secrete thought the way the liver secretes bile. Therefore, the brain, although an organ, cannot be designated (strictly speaking) as the organ of consciousness in the fully human sense. We have it from neurosurgeon Wilder Penfield that "Time was, when the brain was considered to be the 'organ of the mind' . . . [but] such a point of view is no longer tenable" (1961, p. 13). True, a great deal is known about the physiology and chemistry of the brain and the manner in which these functions affect thought and consciousness. But despite the vastness of the neurological data accumulated in recent decades, we are, in Penfield's words, still in the dark "as much as Aristotle was" (1961, p. 16).

Extending the concept of consciousness to the ability to discriminate, as Royce (1964) proposes, clarifies the qualitative nature of the difference between the reduced form of "consciousness" (discrimination) and consciousness proper, or human consciousness. The ability to discriminate remains operative, to a degree, even in deep sleep when distinctly adaptive motions are made in response to cold, heat, pressure, and the like. Under certain conditions, even a dead and quartered organism maintains a threshold measure of discriminating capacity—proven by "the frog whose croak was heard around the world," as Carpenter (1970) colorfully refers to the frog observed by Galvani, the discoverer of electricity.

One evening in the late eighteenth century an Italian woman was preparing a delicacy—roasted frog legs—for supper. "Look at those muscles move," she said to her husband. "They always seem to come alive when I hang them on copper wire." Indeed, because the cut end of a nerve was in contact with the copper wire, the legs jumped and twitched. The husband, who happened to be Luigi Galvani, looked (Penfield, 1961, pp. 3–4). We know the rest.

There is no common border between such mechanical reactions and the "inner show" of ordinary human consciousness. This extension of the concept of consciousness to mechanical devices—especially computers, which are eminently capable of "discriminating"—has great appeal to the reductionist social scientist committed to the belief that the difference of man is purely quantitative.

THE UNIVERSE BECOMING CONSCIOUS OF ITSELF. The difference between minimal consciousness, or the capacity to discriminate, and the unique self-awareness characteristic of man is masterfully placed in evolutionary perspective by Julian Huxley:

> As a result of a thousand million years of evolution, the universe is becoming conscious of itself, able to understand something of its past history and its possible future. This cosmic self-awareness is being realized in one tiny fragment of the universe—in a few of us human beings. . . . Evolution on this planet is a history of the realization of ever new possibilities by the stuff of which earth (and the rest of the universe) is made—life; strength, speed, and awareness; the flight of birds and the social politics of bees and ants; the emergence of mind, long before man was ever dreamt of, with the production of colour, beauty, communication, maternal care, and the beginnings of intelligence and insight. And finally, during the last few ticks of the cosmic clock, something wholly new and revolutionary: human beings with their capacity for conceptual thought and language, for self-conscious awareness and purpose, for accumulating and pooling conscious experience. For do not let us forget that the human species is as radically different from any of the microscopic single-celled animals that lived a thousand million years ago as they were from a fragment of stone or metal (1968, p. 73).

Conceptual Thought

Because we do not know the nature of consciousness, we do not know of just what the process of thought inherently consists. So far, knowledge about the workings of thought has been obtainable solely via its very use —a striking instance of the self-anchored nature of all knowledge, including, in the last analysis, all scientific knowledge (Bonner, 1965; Polanyi, 1964; Rogers, 1961).

While we cannot observe thought in the making, we can study some of its characteristics from its visible effects. Thus, we may infer that the process involves networks of interconnected memory traces whose activation occurs according to the laws of association. We also know that the content of human thought can be independent of *immediate* sensory stimulation. This independence is evidenced in such cases as congenital blindness or deafness: even total deprivation of one sensory dimension of experience does not constitute an obstacle to the unfolding of conceptual intelligence. Sensory handicaps are only practical, not conceptual. They restrict the range of the perceptual spectrum in that they exclude the symbolization of those elements of the lacking sensory modality. However, wonderfully evident of the organism's compensatory power, we observe that (barring other, structural damage) the absence of one sensory modality usually leads to the development of unusual acuity of another sensory dimension, for example, touch for the blind, visual cues and motion for the deaf.

While the individual's conceptual powers are not basically affected by the absence of one or two sense modalities, it is doubtful that a human being—in the minimal sense of a being issued from human parents—congenitally deprived of all sensory modalities could possibly actualize his conceptual potential. Some avenue of sensory contact with the outside world seems to be an indispensable requisite. But where such contact exists, as is the case with all functioning human beings, thinking does not necessarily require immediate sensory stimulation or support for either its origination or its formulation; for example, mathematical operations are remarkably independent of the stimulus situation.

The capacity for conceptual thought, then, makes the individual independent of the immediate stimulus situation. An important consequence of the liberation from stimulus-boundness is that it enables man to think in terms of not merely what is actually present but also what is possible—the future, the not yet given. This allows him to conceive of alternate courses of action and to compare them in terms of logical, practical, or moral principles. Thus, conceptual thought provides the basic, systemic condition for human freedom.

DO ANIMALS THINK? As I have mentioned previously, animals do engage in communication. Since thought and language are intimately related, one can legitimately ask whether there is also a kind of thought that undergirds or parallels their language. Animals can think in several ways. They are capable of discrimination (in the sense of recognizing differences among objects belonging to the same category), of matching objects with symbols, of learning from experience, of solving problems by trial and error, and even of a measure of insight. Certain experiments have demonstrated that animals are capable even of abstraction and generalization—though only on the perceptual, not on the conceptual, level.

More precisely, the objects from which the animal abstracts and subsequently generalizes must be within the limits of his perceptual field; that is, their size may not extend beyond those limits. For instance, certain animals are able to discriminate between geometric forms of varied sizes, provided that the size of these objects (or representations) can be encompassed by the subject's visual span. Where this is not the case—as where an animal is to match, say, a triangular field with a triangular object by being led around the field—he is incapable of the task. He is apparently unable to conceptualize or, for that matter, to conceive of the problem. By contrast, humans, even blindfolded, prove capable of recognizing a triangular from a rectangular or from a circular field because conceptual thinking—translating percepts into concepts—comes naturally to them.

The key difference here is one between conceptual and perceptual thinking. The latter, which is typical of animal thinking, requires the actual or nearly immediate presence of the pertinent objects. Man's thinking, on the other hand, is independent of the presence of pertinent objects. It is, in fact, independent of objects altogether, as is the case with logical or mathematical exercises. Secondly, the difference between human and animal thinking resides in the fact that, whether or not the object of the mental operation is present, animals cannot make judgments or engage in reasoning. For example, animals are unable to conclude that such and such *is* or *is not* the case in a given situation or that *if* such and such is the case, *then* so and so is not.

In conclusion, the issue here again is not whether animals can think, but whether they can think *in the way that people do*. The answer is clearly no. To conclude otherwise, as behaviorists do, is to violate the principle of parsimony—the precise principle on which these psychologists are so insistent.

Thinking Machines

Future shock, says Alvin Toffler (1970), has to do with the dizzying rate at which things first experienced as outrageous come to be taken for granted. Thinking machines are a case in point. Before we have had the time to recover from the impact of the notion that a machine may be able to think, we have settled for the assumption that it is indeed capable of such and in the very ways of man.

To deal with this question at its growing edge, we can consider the relatively recent concept of Turing's game. This game, which British mathematician A. M. Turing recognizes as a suitable means for testing a machine's ability to think with the flexibility, versatility, and creativity of human thought, involves three players who use an ordinary language such as English—not the fabricated code system of a computer language. Two of the players are behind a screen; one of them is male, one female. The third participant is the interrogator, who asks questions aimed at finding out which of the two is male, which female. Questions and answers are exchanged on typewritten slips of paper so as to eliminate voice cues. The hidden players are not required to answer with the truth; on the contrary, the idea is that they try to escape recognition. In Turing's version of this game, one of the hidden players is a robot. If the robot proves capable of successfully playing this game, this, according to Turing, constitutes the crucial test of its ability to *think in the same manner as man*. Note the italicized phrase. Even if Turing's game ever materializes, it will not prove that man is not qualitatively different from other species. There remains the unyielding question of man's ethical sense, which is not a "manner" of thinking but an orientation, a peculiar bent of his sensibility.

THE ROBOT PROLETARIAT. In connection with this (as yet hypothetical) type of robot, Scriven states: "With respect to all other performances and skills of which the human being is capable, it seems to me clear already that robots can be designed to do as well or better" (1963, p. 254). As for the particular activity that would be the crucial test of the robot's consciousness, he states that he feels "confident that robots can in principle be built that will pass this test too because *they are in fact conscious*" (p. 254; italics added). On the outcome of this prediction depends, in his estimation, "the crucial ontological question of the status of a robot as person and then the proprietary saying that it knows or believes or remembers"; and he concludes, "If it is a person, of course it will have moral rights and hence political rights" (p. 254).

One may wonder, with all due respect, whether Scriven is speaking with tongue in cheek when he says "If *it* is a person." Being a person involves a good deal more than proficient intellectual exercise. Incidentally, should such robots someday be constructed, one may also wonder whether our pragmatic society might not find it more expedient to reduce the status of persons to that of the robot, thus establishing the proletariat of the machine.

While Turing claims that his machine is mathematically conceivable, it is apparently not about to be marketed. Bronowski claims that the possibility of equating man's type of thinking by artificial means is not entirely valid: "I am asserting that there is a mode of knowledge which cannot be spelled out formally to direct a machine. It may be asked, Any machine? If this is a question in the present, then the answer is Yes. For example, we know (from the work of Kurt Gödel and A. M. Turing) that no machine that uses strict logic can examine its own instructions and prove them consistent" (Bronowski, 1968). And in relation to the identity of man, to man as person or self he states: "The knowledge of self cannot be formalized because it cannot be closed, even provisionally; it is perpetually open" (p. 45).

In conclusion, here again, as in the case of the animal's capacity to think, the question is not whether machines *can think* but *in what ways they can*. And again, the answer is that, as of now, there is no existing machine that can do so in the same manner as humans.

3 Existence in Time

Man inhabits not only the three-dimensional world of space but also a continuously flowing stream of what he calls time. From his ever-fleeting "now" he enjoys a double perspective into past and future. Within this infinite before and after, the symbolic animal moves, recalling past experience into present focus and projecting new combinations of it into the future.

The English language reveals a peculiar fondness for the word *time:* good times; hard times; time is money; from time to time; how many times; time and again; in his own good time; against time; behind time; between time; time off; ragtime; time flies; time on one's hands; making time; keeping time; saving time; killing time; serving time. In all these cases we know what is meant; what we do not know is what time *is*—a state of affairs that supports the well-established phenomenological tenet that experience is an interpretation, rather than a representation, of reality. Man's grasp of things is a function of himself as a peculiar organism whose mode of cognition is, in large part, intuitive. More than any other dimension of his experience, his perception of time—as a lived rather than a measured dimension—seems based on radically subjective data.

The Enigma of Time

"Nothing puzzles me more than time and space; yet nothing troubles me less, as I never think about them." Thus wrote Charles Lamb in a New Year's letter to Thomas Manning. Modern man, in contrast with Lamb, seems obsessed by time but, unless he is an existentialist, hardly ever puzzled about it.

The "psychology of time," that is, an interest in time as a primarily psychological rather than physical datum, began well before psychology was founded as an independent discipline. Prior to Kant, the reality of time had not been regarded as a problem, though its nature had long been the object of philosophical dispute. Kant, contrary to Newton, who accounted for time strictly in terms of external motion, proposed that time is not a noumenal reality—that is, something that exists in itself, independent of the subject. Instead, he proposed, time proceeds from the activity of the mind itself and is part of the very structure of the mind. (I do not mean to imply, of course, that the mind is somehow tangible or has an independent existence.)

Curiously, while we "create" time, exist within it, are (physically) bound by it, and organize our life in terms of it, we do not know what it is we are constantly referring to. Both time and space seem to be experienced, subliminally, as vacuums in which we arrange the events and objects that form our life and world. Obviously, however, neither time nor space is merely a vacuum. Again, we find it is the subject who creates his world.

Time and Duration

Not knowing what time is does not deter technological man from measuring it with uncanny precision. There is no agreement, however, among the various disciplines interested in the concept (physics, philosophy, psychology, and biology) on whether what he measures is real and whether it is time. Nevertheless, two concepts of time are currently agreed upon: measurable time, objectively determined and constant regardless of circumstances; and human time, or duration, subjectively experienced and varying according to the situation. "The first is common to animals and man; through learning, activities become synchronous with series of changes. The second is peculiar to man, who is able to make symbols correspond to the various aspects of the changes. Society teaches these symbols to man, who uses them to represent the changes to himself, to orient himself within them, and also to control them" (Fraisse, 1968, p. 26).

IS IT TIME OR IS IT SPACE? Man measures daily time with clocks, historical time with calendars, geological time with carbon dating, and infinitesimal time by micromillimetric screws. In none of these cases, however, is it time that is measured, but motion. Clocks measure mechanical motion—the distance covered by a hand moving over a graduated circular surface at the set rate of a cogwheel of a certain size, the entire mechanism made to correspond to a universe of natural motion.

As far as technological purposes are concerned, motion is indeed an effective device for the measurement of time. For human purposes, on the other hand, the affirmation that every hour is identical in length is of course preposterous. Ask any expectant young father waiting outside the delivery room or any person in pain and waiting for help: an hour can be intolerably long. Conversely, for people who enjoy each other's company but seldom get together, an hour's visit appears fraudulently short. Thus, while time flows continuously, it seldom appears to elapse evenly.

Beginning in the nineteenth century, in a departure from Kant's essentially rationalistic approach to the *nature* of time, men began to study the *perception* of time and developed a psychophysics of time by comparing estimates of duration with the measurements of chronometers. The French psychologist, Henri Pieron, in 1923, was the first to define the psychology of time in a behaviorist framework. This point of view was further developed by his colleague, Pierre Janet (1928), who investigated our adaptation to time. In his widely known work, Jean Piaget (1946) studied the development of the notion of time in the infant, and Paul Fraisse (1963) provided a general analysis of temporal behavior.

While the reality or unreality of time remains a puzzle to philosophers and while everyone is subject to temporal misperceptions and illusions, people easily recognize what time *is not*. Kafka, in "A Common Confusion," describes the plight of a businessman tricked by the enigma of time. He leaves early in the morning for an important appointment with an associate in a town normally just ten minutes away. Although he goes directly there, he arrives at the end of the day and finds his associate has left in anger for the businessman's own home. Bewildered, he returns to his home, arrives there in one second, and collapses in defeat as the associate, who spent the entire day waiting there for him, storms off. Commenting on this tale, Doss (1970) appropriately remarks that one senses some deeper, allegorical meaning in the tale. A story of that sort "cannot be just a story, and least of all a matter of journalism" (p. 193). Nothing of the sort could ever happen. Whatever time is, it is not like that.

We know that we can make major errors in estimating duration. Two sets of variables have been studied in particular. Fraisse (1968) reports that "convergent results show that the more complex an activity and the more attention it requires, the shorter time it seems to involve. Thus, it was found that copying a text or taking it down from dictation seems shorter than reading or listening (for equal objective durations of the activities)" (p. 27).

Because we note fewer changes, a complex activity appears of shorter duration than a simple activity. Furthermore, a complex activity is generally interesting, and that which captivates our interest appears of short duration while that which bores us seems interminable. Everyone has observed this relation in daily life, and many experiments confirm the observation. The notion of time per se emerges with Bergson.

The Temporal Horizon

An individual's temporal horizon is the range or limit of his perception of time. When the child's temporal horizon first develops, it is situated between a recent past and a very close future. One may well wonder how the child acquires the capacity to effectively use such complex and intangible notions as time. Acquisition is apparently related to the periodic recurrence of certain events and cycles of activity. As a result of these conditioning events, "present" signals are perceived as referring to future action. The "present" stimulus, with its previously acquired significance, triggers an activity that anticipates some aspects of the future. These cycles are present in animals as well as in man, but man, in addition to living these dimensions, is able to distinguish the present from what has been and what will be. This ability is manifest from the time the child is able to make adequate use of the adverbs of time (*yesterday, tomorrow,* and so forth) and the verb forms that refer to past and future.

Little by little this horizon expands; use of the adverbs of time becomes more sophisticated. Past memories and future projects are localized with increasing accuracy and range. From the age of seven or eight, this horizon expands beyond personal experiences. The child becomes interested in his country's history and proves able to imagine future events that have not formed a part of previous cycles of his activity (his own marriage, for example). This development is, to a very great extent, a function of intelligence, which allows for better organization of the past and better anticipation of the future (Kastenbaum, 1961).

Past and future are made more precise by learning a society's language, which is the medium for transmission of its representations of past and future. Some of these representations, linked to the great philosophies, have wide currency. Among the Greeks, for example, a *circular* representation of time predominated. The *continuous* representation of time, typical of the Christian world view, started with creation and continued to the end of time. A cyclical conception of years, generations, civilizations, or economic plans, however, is used to some degree by all societies.

More specifically, each social framework (family, profession, church, nation, and so forth) has its own way of conceptualizing time, and in any society the temporal horizon appears to be closely related to the cycle of experienced expectations and satisfactions. Every man has the capacity to evoke very distant pasts or futures, but in practice the horizon that is most substantial and real to him is intimately linked with his own way of life. The time of the farmer is one time, and the time of the city dweller another. And anyone belonging to several social groups has multiple temporal perspectives—family time, office time, leisure time.

Thus, every man, depending on his temperament, his intelligence, and the forms of socialization that shape him, achieves his own temporal horizon, defines its scope and its polarity, assigns different values to the past or the future and sometimes only to the present (Fraisse, 1957).

Time and Being

Around the time that Bergson developed his thesis about time as duration, a significant philosophical development took place with the advent of phenomenology and existentialism. These new viewpoints on the nature of man, particularly on the nature of his cognition, stressed the notion that the soil of and criterion for all knowledge is *living experience* —not primarily reason, as was traditionally held. Only experience in its various and intertwining dimensions—empirical, affective, intuitive, unconscious, preconscious as well as conscious and rational—mediates valid cognition or, in the language of existentialism, truth.

Experimental psychology implicitly confirms this view by demonstrating that even the simplest sensory perceptions are not replicas of the stimuli. Every supposedly elementary perception inserts itself in an experiential context in which it undergoes modification and acquires meaning. Because of its focus upon the personal world of experience rather than the impersonal, logical-abstract dimensions of cognition, the phenomenological viewpoint necessarily evolved into a phenomenological-existential psychology now incorporated into the humanistic trend.

Bergson's notion that time is the very ground of existence (1959) was readily absorbed by the phenomenological and existential approaches, especially by Heidegger in his *Being and Time* (1962). The central theme of this work is the question: What is *being;* what does it mean to *be?* Attempting to answer this question, Heidegger analyzes the presuppositions of the specifically human mode of Being.* With regard to time, Heidegger proposes that man's existence is a temporal rather than a spatial mode of Being. Past, present, and future are connected by our personal existence. We have our Being in time, but we do not exist in time; *time exists in us.* That is, time is not the condition of our existence; *we are the condition for the existence of time.* (This summary of Heidegger's thoughts is based upon Feibleman, 1962, p. 29.)

In his analysis of the predominantly temporal mode of Being, Heidegger also deals at length with the finiteness of human existence and, hence, of time. In other words, he deals with death: Being can be understood only in contrast to non-Being, and death provides the ultimate and inescapable horizon of man's existence.

Unfortunately, the merit of Heidegger's pioneering work is affected by

* The word *Being* is capitalized in translations of Heidegger's work to convey his peculiar use of this term to symbolize Being independently of particular, existing beings.

the obscurity of its language. A keen awareness of the multidimensionality of Being and the ineffability of experienced time led Heidegger to create a vocabulary of nearly untranslatable descriptive terms. As a result, his writings are inaccessible to all but the few who choose to make his *oeuvre* their life-long career. Yet, reference to his seminal insights cannot be omitted in any discussion of time. Realizing the gap likely to separate the formulation of his insights from the reader's understanding, Heidegger asks: "But how can we become properly involved with . . . Being and time? . . . By cautiously thinking over the matters named here . . . not hastily invading (them) with unexamined notions, but rather reflecting on them carefully" (1972, p. 4).

Time and Sanity

Perhaps the first to follow Heidegger's advice and certainly the first to extract practical meaning from his abstruse thinking were three existential psychiatrists and analysts—Binswanger, Boss, and Minkowski who, more than anyone, were responsible for awakening psychology to the significance of the notion of time. (Their main interpreter in this country is Rollo May, especially in this chapter in *Existence* (May, and others, 1958).)

These early psychiatrists discovered that many of their patients manifested a disturbed sense of time. For example, the ability of some patients to think in terms of past or future or to bring the data of either period into present focus was markedly impaired. The inability to deal adequately with time, common to several forms of psychological incapacitation and perhaps most obvious in schizophrenia, is usually interpreted today as a result of the patient's condition. Minkowski, however, proposed that the reverse is more likely the case: a disturbed sense of time is apt to be the cause of the psychological problem. Although this radical interpretation was received with scepticism, Minkowski and other existential analysts succeeded in focusing attention on the significance of the individual's experiencing of time. Increasingly, many psychologists recognize the future as the dominant experiential dimension of the fully functioning person. The intellectually and emotionally flexible individual has the capacity to think in terms of possibilities, of alternatives for action and outlook, and a desire for growth that necessitate future-oriented thought and action.

An insight into the significant relation between time and sanity was glimpsed by Bergson nearly a century ago:

> It could easily be shown that the different degrees of sorrow . . . correspond to qualitative changes. *Sorrow begins by being nothing more*

than a facing toward the past, an impoverishment of our sensations and ideas, as if each of them were now contained entirely in the little which it gives out,* *as if the future were in some way stopped up.* And it ends with an impression of crushing failure, the effect of which is that we aspire to nothingness, while every new misfortune, by making us understand better the uselessness of the struggle, causes us a bitter pleasure" (Bergson, 1959, p. 11; italics added).

Insights of this kind are now commonly being confirmed (in less poetical language than Bergson's) both by clinicians and experimentalists.

Time and the Meaning of Life

Closely related to psychological functioning is our perception of the meaning of life. The relation between an individual's ability to achieve and maintain a sense of meaning, and his outlook upon both his past and his future is hardly farfetched. We all realize that our expectations for the future are determined very largely by the perception of our past. Furthermore, the amount of futurity that one knows or assumes to be his share tends to determine the value he places upon certain other people, objects, events, goals, and ideals.

Man's perspective on his future is particularly significant with respect to his ethical behavior. Confidence in the probability of a future fosters foresight, self-discipline, responsibility, and planning (or acquisitiveness, possessiveness, and power). Doubt or knowledge of its improbability invites a wasteful and perhaps destructive style of life focused upon immediate gratification and disregard of resources, both material and human. In catastrophic situations—wartime, severe illness, or other severe threats to one's future—a radical reversal of values may occur. Persons usually taken for granted may suddenly acquire significance, while formerly all-absorbing objects and pursuits may lose their appeal. Habitual standards and values tend to break down when future falls away.

The individual's tacit relation to time, in particular his awareness or ignorance of its ultimate limit, is a major determinant of behavior, attitudes, values, and mood. This relationship accounts for the insouciance of childhood, the recklessness of youth, the drive of early manhood, and the resignation or despair of those who recognize that their future is rapidly shrinking.

The pervasive effect of the temporal aspect of life, the fact that, for instance, pleasure and pain are not determined solely by the present but

---

* The translator's choice of words: "In the little which it gives out" would come closer to Bergson's meaning and perhaps be better understood if phrased as "in the paucity of its output."

are suffused with an awareness of past and future was long ago recognized and described, again, by Bergson:

> What makes hope such an intense pleasure is the fact that the future, which we dispose of to our liking, appears to us at the same time under a multitude of forms, equally attractive and equally possible. Even if the most coveted of these becomes realized, it will be necessary to give up the others, and we shall have lost a great deal. *The idea of the future,* pregnant with an infinity of possibilities, *is thus more fruitful than the future itself,* and this is why we find more charm in hope than in possession, in dreams than in reality (1959, pp. 9–10; italics added).

Time and Freedom

What most accounts, perhaps, for the existentialist's interest in time is its relation to freedom—the affirmation of which is the central tenet of existential philosophy. Man is the animal who continuously projects himself into the future; he is, therefore, "a being who is always in advance of himself . . . who, though he is always in a particular situation, nevertheless transcends that situation. Existence, then, testifies to human freedom" (Bossart, 1968, p. 66), to the capacity to transcend contingencies. And freedom, like time, "is a spontaneity which has no further ground" (p. 63).

While Heidegger, Husserl, Sartre, Merleau-Ponty, and other existential-phenomenological authors are the major exponents of these theses, their point of departure can be recognized in Bergson's notion of time as a purely qualitative, subjectively apprehended state of being. Although it is impossible here even to summarize existential thinking on the relation of time and freedom, it is, however, so important that an illustration, at least, must be attempted.

Let us take the person whose situation leads to the realistic and unemotional conclusion that, in regard to some prospect, he has nothing to lose. (This attitude differs significantly from the negative evaluation of the future made by one who contemplates suicide.) Though this person may hardly feel exhilarated about such a prospect, he finds himself experiencing an unusual state of freedom that allows him to appraise his situation in a new light, relatively independent of the circumstances of place, status, possessions, and commitments that formerly governed his decisions. He feels liberated, able to recognize what he prizes most and to choose what he wants—within the bounds of the obtainable—largely regardless of antecedents, contingencies, and consequences.

For the symbolic animal, this experience of relative independence from contingencies is the essence of the relation of time to freedom. It endows him with the capacity to restructure his world endlessly and engage in an ongoing internal dialogue that is the privilege of the reflectively conscious human animal.

Time Binding, Space Binding, Energy Binding

Just as space is not a "thing" of a certain size or capacity, neither is time a "thing" of a certain length. It is, rather, a dimension of specifically human existence. Time, therefore, must be characterized in terms of man, rather than the other way around.

In his *Time-Binding: The General Theory,* Korzybski (1924) character-izes the human, the animal, and the vegetable in terms of *the syntheses that each is typically capable of forming with the givens of its respective realm;* that is, in terms of constructive use, the transformation or tran-scendence of those givens. In this respect man is unique in his capacity for time binding; he is able to transcend the present by recalling the past, projecting the future, and connecting both in a beneficial and ongoing conceptual process. The subhuman animal is typified by his capacity for space binding—for connecting the here with the there and the yonder to serve his biological and psychological purposes. Typical of the vegetable realm is its energy binding capacity; that is, its capacity for productive transformation of chemical and biochemical elements. The entire psycho-biological structure appears, then, rather like a reverse pyramid of func-tional complexity in which the higher strata possess the capacities of the lower biological layer(s), plus their own specific binding function.

Restated, and in reverse order, the characteristic function of the vege-table order is to synthesize energy-releasing chemicals. Energy binding is also one of the attributes of the animal realm. But the animal's character-istic attribute is movement—not only the built-in movement of growth, which the animal shares with all life, but the independent movement that allows him to roam through space, to migrate, disperse, and populate. As for man, while he is capable of synthesizing energy as plants do and of binding space as animals do, he represents the only form of life capable of binding time—of conceiving such notions as past and future, bringing these notions into productive focus, and aligning their events, actual or projected, along a continuum between whose poles he "moves" in an in-comparably meaningful manner.

It is, of course, this time-binding capacity that underlies man's ability for cumulative transmission of culture. In turn, this capacity for social transmission of experience through successive generations becomes one of the most visible characteristics of man's uniqueness, for what happens in one generation is made available, to a significant extent, to later generations.

LOCKED IN THE PRESENT. Animals exist physically, but not experientially, in that mysterious time-space we call the world. They have no sense of time except for some awareness of the immediate before and after. The animal's world is bound by the senses, and time is not a sensory datum. This places the nonhuman animal outside the universe of symbols (though not of signs) and consequently outside the universe of time. Several studies have demonstrated that animals are capable of maintaining rudimentary associative ties with specific events of the immediate past. But those events must be so recent that their "recall" is more like a psychological reverberation of recent stimuli than a reinstatement into consciousness of events removed from current sensory impact.

Certainly animals are capable of "remembering"—especially survival-related events such as good or bad treatment. But this recall is associative, triggered by the appearance of a particular sight, sound, or smell; for the animal's memory is stimulus bound. Conversely, while human memory, like animal memory, obeys the laws of association, it does not *need* to be triggered by sensory events. Man can guide the associative process in the direction he chooses—independent of the concrete presence or sensory perception of an object—in order to bring another one into focus.

TO HAVE OR TO BE ONE'S PAST. Animal behavior, like human behavior, is determined not only by species-specific factors but also by learning. In both cases some learning may have been acquired in the distant past, but enacting such past learning does not necessarily mean remembering it in any representational manner. Thus, a dog may behave exactly as he was taught in obedience school without having any memory images, visual or otherwise, of the school, his fellow canine companions, and so on. Similarly, the psychological organization of both man and beast at any particular point in time represents their telescoped past experiences—with, however, one crucial difference. The animal not only *has* a past, he *is* his past and, experientially, nothing more. He is only the bundle of tendencies to perceive and to react that represents his particular organism modified by his past learnings. His learning is both random (happenings) and systematic (training).

Man, on the other hand, is not this passive sum of events. Because he can control his impulses to a variable degree and can symbolize many of the events of his past in conscious awareness, the past he experiences is as fluid in terms of meaning as is the present. This is what marks the difference between man and beast in relation to time: man does not merely undergo his past, he constantly shapes and reshapes it. Because he can symbolize it in awareness, his past is not fixed but flexible.

REVOKING THE PAST. In *The Human Imperative* (1972), Alexander Alland, commenting on Harlow's work, states: "Human beings equipped with the symbolic process can do something which Harlow's monkeys are incapable of. They can repeat their childhood and symbolically reformulate their personalities" (p. 50). Indeed, if it is meaning rather than fact that matters to the symbolic animal, man has wide control over his past. First, because of his reflective ability, he can look backward, contemplate the timescape of his life, and restructure it in terms of new knowledge, values, goals, and perspectives. What may have been experienced in the past as loss, defeat, or error may appear to the present as opportunity and asset. Second, this restructuring of his *intentionality* (May, 1969) permits him further to alter the past (in terms of its potential effect upon his future) by channeling the symbolization (his memories) of it according to new guidelines. In fact, to the extent that such restructuring is effective, a modified past is bound to ensue, for man constantly "intends."

ONLY THE LIVING PAST.   Man's capacity to evoke, to reevaluate and, in the process, to modify the past is largely what psychotherapy is about. For the past, as perceived, can be either growth hampering or growth promoting. Psychotherapeutic liberation is accomplished, not solely but to a significant extent, by altering the symbolic structure of the patient's (or client's) past and the power which that structure exerts on him. This view of the therapeutic process applies even to such nonhistorical approaches (those that do not focus on the distant or proximate past) as client-centered, or Rogerian, therapy, which does not deliberately and systematically deal with the *chronological* past. It does, however, deal with the psychological, existential past in that it considers all material that arises spontaneously in the client's awareness as significant—that is, as alive—irrespective of whether that material pertains to the most remote or recent past.

From the onset, client-centered therapy thus made an implicit, although systematic, distinction between the chronological past and the existential past that is incorporated into the present and is at least potentially available to awareness—hence amenable to modification.

Exploring the patient's past systematically (to the point of following a chronological order!), as traditional approaches frequently do, amounts to dealing with a mixture of deadwood and live material without benefit of a criterion for differentiating between the two. The distinction between the chronological past, with its verifiable facts, personages, and events, and the psychological past, with its subjectively assigned values and meanings, should contribute significantly to the elimination of experiential deadwood in therapy and improve and accelerate the therapeutic process.

Some Fallacies About Time

Because man is apt to confuse physical and psychological time, he is also apt to become entangled in all kinds of unreal and therefore insoluble problems. One of the most common is the age gap that separates the generations and often is perceived as unbridgeable. In fact, the gap is not necessarily or essentially chronological but experiential. It is a gap in communication, interests, activities, and in mutual regard widened by a social philosophy that results in what Urie Bronfenbrenner calls the "split-level family."

As long as the problem is regarded as a matter of calendar time, the gap cannot be bridged, since people, unlike tape recorders, cannot be given the "replay" or "fast forward." Conversely, when dealt with as a lack of common experience, the problem can in principle be resolved. Communication and reciprocal empathy can go a long way toward bridging supposed or real distance.

Another fallacy about the role of time in the dynamics of human behavior is the belief that it heals—especially symbolic wounds. Time may be a condition for the forces of health to accomplish their work, but the same can be said for the forces of destruction. Recovery from emotional injury depends on the subject's capacity and opportunity for experiential renewal, his effective use of this capacity, and the nurturing influence of a supportive environment. Rapid recovery is the hallmark of mental health. But it is not accomplished, only gauged, by time.

Reinterpretations of the past do not imply changing the facts of the past. Physical evidence cannot be changed or abolished without violating it. This does not, however, detract from the plasticity of its meaning. What counts for the Symbolic Animal is not usually the facts or events as much as their significance for him as a person, a symbolic universe.

The symbolic universe of man is intimately interwoven with man's temporal consciousness. However, man as a historical animal would be mute before the passage of time if it were not for his language. Let us now turn to a consideration of the meaning of language in man's symbolic universe in order to assess the inestimable value of this most human of attributes.

In Summary

At its growing edge, current thinking on the subject of time reveals this: Time, in the psychological sense of duration, is pure quality, not measurable extension. The latter is technological time, an artifact designed for practical purposes in an organized society.

Because of our inclination to think in elementary categories of quantity and extension, we confuse time with space. We spatialize instead of temporize existence. We reify time; that is, we reduce it to an object, a frame in which existence is enclosed. The reduction of time to space prevents us from experiencing time as intrinsic to our being and from realizing its relation to freedom, fully functioning, and the meaning of life.

Modern man's continuous and ubiquitous reliance upon clocks and calendars obscures his grasp of the nature of time and, hence, of existence. Repression of his awareness of the finitude of time—that is, of his awareness of death—further removes and estranges him from the essence of his Being.

The emergence of insights of this kind gives us an intimation of what the science of psychology will be when it will have liberated itself from the mechanistic fallacy that views man according to the model of the tangible, space and motion determined object, the machine.

II Culture Maker

All animals have a nature. Their nature defines their basic needs and, in the case of nonhuman animals, provides the mechanisms for the direct satisfaction of those needs. Only man has the kind of nature that allows him to devise an endless variety of means for satisfying his needs and wants. The whole of the alternative ways and means whereby a human community attempts to satisfy the needs of its members is its culture. It is one of the most striking differences between man and other species.

Among the many behavioral components that contribute to the emergence and perpetuation of culture three are central: language, technology, and law. *Language,* as here used, must be understood not only as a means of communication geared to survival, as is the case with nonhuman "languages," but as a medium of intellectual, descriptive, normative, and esthetic expression as well as a practical tool. Similarly, *technology* is more than its modern, highly sophisticated, and specialized forms. It encompasses the fascinating variety of tools and products created by man throughout time and space. It is a process that extends from the shaping of crude tools to the invention of machines that make tools that make tools *ad infinitum;* from harnessing fire to harnessing electricity; from cleaving rocks to splitting atoms; from roasting on spits to cooking in microwave ovens; from living in caves to dwelling in modular houses. In sum, technology is like mind made visible and tangible. The notion of *law* here includes not only the formal, codified modes but also numerous regulative expressions, tacit as well as explicit. Law is embedded in countless social, political, economic, tribal, familial, and international contexts. Its expressions range from the regulation of games to the control of crime, and its aim is, ultimately, freedom—since there is no freedom where there is no law.

Common to language, technology, and law is their instrumental quality, their culturally "architectonic" function as means to communication, livelihood, and freedom—basic conditions for the actualization of man as a person.

4 The Talking Animal

While the most fundamental characteristic of man is his symbolic capacity, the most striking expression of this capacity is, of course, language. Just as man and only man is capable of handling symbols and not merely signs, so he is capable of speech, not only communication. These two functions differ markedly. Communication is not necessarily verbal; it can be physiognomic (facial, vocal) in its means and visceral in its understanding. But visceral communication stands in the service of nature. Language proper is a manifestation of culture capable of serving man's quest for truth, beauty, and human progress as well as his elementary needs. This unique capacity is, of course, also serviceable in the pursuit of the antithesis of these values. Language can be made to conceal as well as to express thought. For every one of man's capacities is double-edged.

Animals do communicate, of course, and do so in a variety of sensory ways—by expressive cries, grunts, and calls; by scent; and by many kinds of body language. In some species these sense modalities have a broader range than they have in man—for example, the dog's sensitivity to high-frequency sound waves or his extraordinary olfactory sense. Each species communicates effectively according to its nature, sometimes using astoundingly intricate patterns—not all of which have as yet been fully decoded by researchers.

Nevertheless, animals do not have language in the human sense of the word. Their spontaneous, unconditioned utterances are limited to expressing either internal, visceral states or external concerns that essentially pertain to survival of the individual or the species (food, mating, gregariousness, play). Human linguistic ability, on the other hand, ranges far beyond survival-oriented communication to the highest reaches of disinterested abstraction. It comprises the capacity for making declarative statements; that is, propositions whose truth or falsehood can be verified and is, consequently, independent of the subjective, organic state of the agent uttering them.

Speech, then, represents a capacity that far outreaches the functions of animal communication and that differs from the latter in structure, purpose, origin, flexibility, and multiplicity of dimensions. Speech is found in even the most primitive of human communities—and not in the sense of a limited vocabulary tossed out as one-word sentences (after the fashion observed in young children). Even primitive (in the sense of preliterate or nonwritten) languages represent orderly syntactical systems involving consistent, lawful ways to modify and arrange words so as to convey differentiated meaning. There is no evidence of human communities whose members communicate solely by inarticulate sounds or by physiognomic expression.

However, *it takes a human environment for man to develop his specifically human potentialities.* Thus, children severed early in life from adult human contact are incapable of expressing themselves orally (vocally) in any way other than by inarticulate utterance. Nevertheless, such supposedly feral children, their handicap notwithstanding, still prove strikingly different from the most intelligent nonhuman animals in the astounding speed with which they latch onto, and catch up with, the language of whatever human community they are adopted by—unless, of course, the neurobiological basis of the child's intelligence is severely impaired, as was the case with the celebrated Wild Boy of Aveyron (Malson, 1972).

So crucial is syntax in human language that the physically insignificant variation in *locus* of one or two monosyllables may result in crucial semantic difference:

You don't know how much I have for you to do.
You don't know how much I have to do for you.

While the former conveys a neutral fact, the latter is likely to affect most interlocutors as reproachful or critical. Yet practically everyone except the very young and the mentally deficient prove able to observe these syntactical rules without giving them much thought.

Greenberg's appraisal of human language concisely expresses the focus of this chapter:

Language is unique to man. No other species possesses a truly symbolic means of communication and no human society, however simple its material culture, lacks the basic human heritage of a well-developed language. Language is the prerequisite for the accumulation and transmission of other cultural traits. Such fundamental aspects of human society as organized political life, legal systems, religion, and science are inconceivable without that most basic and human of tools, a linguistic system of communication. Language is not only a necessary condition for culture, it is itself a part of culture. It, like other shared behavioral norms, is a complex process of learning. Like other aspects of human culture, it characteristically varies from group to group and undergoes significant modification in the course of its transmission through time within the same society (1961, p. 1).

Meaning and Validity

Man communicates mainly with words, and these are symbols, not signs, though they can be used as signs (Exit, Fire, Shelter, and so on). In and of themselves, the sounds that make up words have, of course, neither meaning nor validity. They acquire these attributes by consensus; that is, by implicit or explicit social-cultural agreement. Meaning alone, however, is not enough; it must be validated, especially by those who are in a position to endorse meaningfully—for example, scientists, lexicographers, educators. For instance, *Piltdown Man,* which refers to a supposedly pre-Neanderthal man, or the *Vinland Map,* a piece of forgery presumed to be a pre-Columbian Viking map, are terms that no longer have any validity (except in reference to hoaxes).

Under the influence of such events and conditions as scientific discovery, cultural ups and downs, fashions, and so forth, certain words may lose their cultural endorsement or validity. Take, for example, *ether, hero,* or *politics.* In their original sense, these words are now empty or near-empty vessels either because of the acquisition of new knowledge or a shift in affect value or because of the widespread denaturation of the thing represented by the word. For example, *politics* no longer means the practice of reason but the practice of power. Many such words are mouthed in certain rhetorical contexts, but their meaning lacks currency.

Man and Sentences

Human language further differs irreducibly from animal communication in that it is propositional in character and syntactical in structure. Man's verbal utterances consist of organic units of speech whose meaning, depending upon word sequence(s), can be diametrically opposed.

The die-hard reductionist might object that what is here called syntax has its equivalent in variations of tone, pitch, and modulation of animal calls and possibly in other modes and overtones of communication (what LaBarre terms "phatic communication" [1961, p. 57]). Indeed, birds, bees, dogs—possibly all animals—use variations of tonal pattern, rhythm, and intensity in their species-proper idioms. Such variations, however, correspond only to the vocal patterns and intonations that man also uses.

That nothing in the "language" of animals corresponds to the rules of grammar and syntax that govern the elements of human speech should be obvious even from this simple example taken from Susanne Langer's (1967) remarkable treatise on the different stages of syntactical formalization.

I knew you would not do it is a syntactically legitimate sentence, though it is not a declarative statement that can be proven either true or false. It is too indefinite for that. By attaching a determinant to one or more of its elements, we make the sentence more definite.

I knew you would not do it.
I, George, knew you would not do it.
I, George, knew you, John, would not do it.
I, George, knew you, John, would not cheat at cards (p. 91).

Only when every pronoun is determined, as it is in the final sentence, do we have a proposition. Only such a proposition can be verified. There is no evidence of anything in animal "language" that suggests a capacity to juggle "vocabulary" to achieve even a remote approximation of the precision involved in even the simplest declarative sentence.

THE CASE OF THE DANCING HONEY BEE. This fascinating naturalistic gem is often referred to in connection with the propositional, declarative, intentional type of language that is the prerogative of man. Vercors poetically describes the honey bee, which soon after hatching is capable of communicating to other bees the location of a tree in blossom, doing so with the precision and the sense of direction of a sea captain grown white-crested at the wheel (1950).

According to Thorpe (1965, p. 99), the dance of the honey bee constitutes an exception to what is otherwise assumed to be exclusively human linguistic behavior. Initially, Thorpe seems to have a case. The behavioral stunt of the honey bee consists of a patterned dance with which it communicates to other bees the exact direction and distance of a food source. This instance of communicational behavior, then, is not expressive of a subjective, visceral state but seems to satisfy all the external requirements of a declarative utterance (the content of which is *verifiably* either true or false independent of the emotive state of the reporting animal). Therefore, according to Thorpe, the dance of the honey bee constitutes an exception to what is classified as exclusively human linguistic capacity.

Upon closer examination, however, it seems that Thorpe's declaration that the uniqueness of man's propositional language has "been abolished by the dance-language of the honey bee" is somewhat premature. Indeed, he continues by adding the significant specification that "although no animal appears to have a language that is propositional, syntactic, and at the same time, clearly expressive of intentions, yet all these features can be found *separately* (at least to some degree) in the animal kingdom" (1965, p. 99).

Even if the features that Thorpe regards as indicating propositional and syntactic modes of communication were what he claims them to be—which they are not, as we will see—their *separate* existence could not compare with the composite, Gestalt-like manner in which they operate in man. But there is much stronger evidence to show that however fascinating the case of the honey bee, it is only a case of parapropositional language.

GENETICS AND CULTURE.   That the "sentence making" of the honey bee is not a case of propositional language is clear from its species-wide dissemination—its intraspecies ubiquitousness. It is performed identically by bees that have never had contact with one another. In other words, the dance "language" of the honey bee, contrary to human speech, is genetically—not culturally—determined. Human languages differ from one another almost in direct ratio to the distance separating the communities in which they originated. Adler, summarizing Bennett (1964), has the following comment on the "sentence making" of the honey bee: "If the honey bees were to make the statements they do make, not by instinct, but as a result of learning, calculation, and inference, they would need a brain as large as a man's and would possess a degree of intelligence well above the human average" (1967, p. 312). Therefore, until evidence to the contrary is provided, it seems we may conclude with Adler that "this fascinating process of communication on the part of these insects is a purely instinctive performance"; that, contrary to Thorpe's statements, it "does not represent, *even in the slightest degree*, the same kind of . . . linguistic performance that is to be found in human speech" (p. 114; Adler's emphasis).

The total communicational repertoire of a given animal—that is, his own repertoire, unaffected by human conditioning—is rigidly determined by the genetic code of his species. Mutations may occur, but this, of course, is beside the point, since mutations themselves are a function of gene modification, not of individual creativity or cultural influence. As for the minor variations in communicational behavior that may be observed where a species appears under significantly different geographical conditions, they represent essentially mechanical adaptations explainable in terms of environment.

Speech, on the other hand, is a culturally determined phenomenon. Its modes vary according to the communities in which it develops. (The total number of human languages now known to exist is estimated by the American Museum of Natural History at about 2,800). The adult can choose the language he wishes to use, either by moving to a different environment or using books and other technological means (that is, in a symbolically once-removed fashion).

The *potentiality* for speech is, of course, genetically determined: all humans, regardless of time and place, have the capacity for it, barring impairment of their nervous system or speech organs. But the actualization of that potentiality is a function of cultural conditions. Man can be bilingual or multilingual; more important, he can invent new nonverbal (Morse, semaphore) or computer languages. Not so the animal. Although the mockingbird can imitate the calls of other birds, he is limited to those calls he has actually heard.

> If we play recordings of normal songs to a socially isolated white-crowned sparrow or a chaffinch in sufficient quantity and at a very particular phase of the life-cycle, differing from species to species, normal development will result. The song that the young males produces shows evidence of actual imitation of the model presented. . . . There is evidence for chaffinches and white-crowned sparrows that if the young male is presented during the appropriate critical period with playback not only of his own species song but also that of other species, he will selectively learn the conspecific example. This was demonstrated with two male white-crowned sparrows, one presented both with white-crown song and song-sparrow song for example, learning only the former. Male white-crowned sparrows presented with song-sparrow song alone during the same period, from about ten to fifty days of age, rejected the models and developed in much the same way as an untrained bird (Marler, 1973, pp. 301–02).

SELF-EXPRESSION VERSUS NEED REDUCTION. Human language and animal communication differ not only in their structure and origin; they also differ functionally. Animal communication is quite obviously instrumental in the biological or biosocial realm—feeding, mating, breeding, mutual protection, and gregariousness. What is it that allows us to say that their language serves no other purpose than the preservation of the individual and the procreation of the species? The answer is the same as for any scientific conclusion: the absence of evidence that would allow us to infer that animal communication serves nonsurvival purposes.

Conversely, man's speech is seldom aimed directly at survival. In a highly organized society, few words are exchanged with outright reference to biological purposes. Instead, human speech serves mainly to express matters concerning the self rather than the organism or to describe objective purposes and their pursuit. ("Objective" is used here to designate the [an] orientation away from the subject's primary needs: for example, the expression of ideas about things, events, and situations, or relations among these.)

Moreover, when man's verbalizations are aimed at satisfying biological needs, they are usually articulate and selective. Except in conditions of extreme deprivation they aim, for instance, not merely at food but at certain foods, not at beverages but at certain beverages. As Julian Huxley observes, "Plenty of animals can express the fact that they are hungry, but none except man can ask for an egg or a banana" (1943, p. 3). Huxley's stand is confirmed in the work of Wolfgang Koehler, which probably remains unsurpassed in thoroughness and extent. Koehler tried assiduously to teach his clever parrot, Geier, to say "food" when hungry and "water" when thirsty. Geier, however, did not "cross the species line" (cited in Lorenz, 1952). Nor has any other talking bird been successfully trained to associate even one of those two simple words with the basic survival state it designates. In other words, no animal capable of uttering articulate sounds has proven capable of effectively using even so elementary an (existential) symbol.

In summary, man's linguistic ability *selectively* serves the purposes of *self-expression* and *self-transcendence* as well as *self-maintenance*.

P.S.: Machine Languages

A new concern is the electronic "language" of computers. With respect to the uniqueness of man's linguistic ability, we must distinguish here between computer "language" and another type of symbolic language, not actually available but mathematically conceivable (at least in the mind of the late A. M. Turing).

Computer language does not seem to pose a problem in regard to the uniqueness of human speech. Computers and their languages are devised by man. They can be programmed in such a way as to be creative (in the limited sense, that is, of being allowed to engage in unpredictable goal-directed activity). What does pose a potential challenge to man's exclusive linguistic capacity is a model synthetic language envisioned by Turing.

Computers need programming; Turing's machine does not (that is, it would not if it existed). It is a robot requiring only a minimum of "infant programming" at the start. More remarkable, it is conceived of as a robot capable of *learning an ordinary language and using it conversationally;* that is, with all the variations in meaning, affect, and key—from humorous to sarcastic, from playful to serious—in which one and the same statement can be made. These two properties, then—the ability to learn an ordinary human language and the conversational (though not the vocal) use of it—are the characteristics that distinguish Turing's machine from all existing systems. The robot would demonstrate this capacity by playing Turing's parlor game as well or almost as well as humans.

Although exciting to the imagination, Turing's game is not about to become a reality. But it is an interesting theoretical challenge to the thesis that man's linguistic ability is unique. Strictly speaking, the challenge is relevant first and foremost to the question of man's unique ability to engage in conceptual thought, but it is pertinent here since conversational language is the visible expression of conceptual thought.

Until Turing's dream materializes, let us not lose sight of the basic principle of right reasoning, according to which the status of an issue must be appraised in light of the evidence that is actually available at the moment of appraisal. Considering the current explosion of knowledge we must, of course, keep an open mind about future possibilities. But we must be careful not to mistake an open mind about the future with a confused mind about the present. There is for the present no evidence to challenge the uniqueness of man's capacity for speech.

5 Man
the Toolmaker

Ever since the term *homo sapiens* was first coined, epithets for man have proliferated—each one proclaiming a distinctly human attribute. Most fundamental, if most recent, is *homo symbolicus.* Many other designations, which in the last analysis are reducible to the latter attribute, remain aptly descriptive in their own right: thus, *homo politicus,* the lawmaking organizer of community life; *homo ludens,* the playing animal; *homo economicus,* Bentham's concept of man as the "pleasure machine" and Marx's view of man as the "production machine"; and *homo ridens,* the laughing animal, creator of humor, farce, and fun.

When the post-Renaissance naturalists first turned a scrutinizing eye on man as part of the natural world, they viewed his capacity for making artifacts as that which most distinctly set him apart from the rest of the animal kingdom. Hence, in the idiom traditionally used for such purposes, they coined the expression *homo faber:* man the artisan, the animal who fashions the countless objects of his ever-expanding needs and of his most fertile dreams. So representative is man's toolmaking capacity that the late anthropologist Louis Leakey, who in 1964 discovered the most ancient of all hominid fossils found up to that time, labeled his epochal find *homo habilis* (dextrous, skillful man), basing this designation upon the presence of stone tools found on the sites of *habilis* and testifying to his hominid status.

Is Toolmaking Uniquely Human?

Recent findings by ethological researchers pose an apparent challenge to man as *the* toolmaker. The findings of Jane van Lawick-Goodall for example, who studied wild chimpanzees in their native forest near Lake

Tanganyika, lead one to wonder whether this long-established distinction is still justified. She reports and photographically substantiates that chimps are capable of activities that can indeed be regarded as crude instances of tool *fashioning*.

The rudimentary capacity of certain primates for using as tools certain objects lying within their immediate vicinity has long been established by Kellogg and Kellogg (1933), Yerkes (1925), and Köhler (1925). If we define toolmaking in its most elementary sense as the modification of certain objects for use to achieve certain goals, then it would seem prima facie that van Lawick-Goodall has a case. She says of one chimp, named David Graybeard, that "he didn't just make use of any old bit of material lying around. . . . He actually modified stems and grasses and made them suitable for his purpose" (1967, p. 32). She further reports on David's ingeniousness in securing food (through the roof of a shed presumed to be chimp-proof). Commenting on the latter observation, she speaks colorfully of the chimp's activity as "ripping a hole in a roof—and in a theory" (p. 30).

Granted, however, that certain primates can fashion certain—admittedly crude—tools, it remains that those tools are 1) fashioned exclusively out of materials directly within the animals environment and reach; 2) fashioned only, as far as present evidence goes, in the service of the most elementary of life-maintaining activities (food seeking). Neither of these goes beyond the level of perceptual associations. The means-to-end relation perceived by the chimps is, then, purely sensory. There is no evidence as yet that in the absence of immediately given and relatively suitable means (grass, vines, stems, and so on) the animal would be able to fashion ersatz tools—a feat of which man is eminently capable as he demonstrated, first in the Iron Age and currently as a matter of course. Also, the tool-fashioning capacity reported by van Lawick-Goodall consists only of the act of trimming—in this case, of removing the parts of the raw material (grass or vine) that interfere with its effectiveness as a "tool." In other words it consists in modifying, more than creating, a given object as it is perceived as a tool. One may wonder whether this modification is as novel as it is made to appear or whether it could be a function of the researcher's mental set. Indeed, something akin to this search for facilitating a goal-directed operation can be observed in the behavior of dogs, even puppies, playing with a rolling object or gnawing a slippery or otherwise recalcitrant bone. When given the opportunity to tackle the thing on either a slippery or a carpeted floor, they manifest an immediate (operational) preference for the facilitating effect of carpet underfooting. The limitations of the chimps' toolmaking activity—the fact that they are reduced to *removing* parts of the "natural tool" (blades of grass or vines) —stands out even more clearly when one contrasts it with attempts to make the tool more effective and more lasting through *construction;* for example, fashioning it out of several blades, matched for size, tied together, and perhaps coated with some gluey substance secreted by surrounding plants, as man would tend to do.

As for the chimps' capacity for using rocks as weapons—aside from the fact that it is a case of using, not of fashioning—it is indeed analogous, but not identical, to man's first use of weapons. There is as yet no evidence of animals going out to search for particularly effective, sharp rocks, sharpening whatever rocks are available, collecting and keeping them in strategic places for future use, and returning them to the "arsenal" after use—all of which are common elements of man's use and manufacture of tools.

Van Lawick-Goodall deals briefly with one of these aspects of the tool concept: "Some authorities suggest that only when an implement is kept for future use is the toolmaker showing forethought; for this reason people often ask whether the chimps ever save the tools for reuse. This would have little point, since most of the objects would shrivel and become useless if kept" (1967, p. 33). On the surface, her point is well taken, but it seems to imply that the chimps themselves are aware of this limitation of their raw materials—an important point that remains to be proven. A more parsimonious explanation for the once-only use of these tools—but one that reduces "toolmaking" to trimming—might be that grass blades can be secured any time from the immediate environment. Van Lawick-Goodall reports that Leakey, discussing her observations on the toolmaking activities of the chimps, replied, "I feel that scientists holding to this definition are faced with three choices: They must accept chimpanzees as man, by definition; they must redefine man; or they must redefine tools" (p. 32).

Can this comment be regarded as valid? Possibly. The modification or refinement of basic definitions is one of the potential yields of all research. For example, in regard to the larger issue here at stake—the difference of man—the concept of language became differentiated into communicative language and syntactical language and name-using ability was removed from the list of criteria differentiating the linguistic ability of man and other primates (Bronowski and Bellugi, 1970). These changes were the result of philosophical analysis and research findings. But to conclude that either man or toolmaking stands in need of redefinition because of the observations gathered on chimps' blade-trimming (and potato-washing) activities (van Lawick-Goodall, 1971) seems, so far, a bit premature. Finally, there is as yet no evidence, as van Lawick-Goodall freely admits (1971), of an animal's capacity to make tools that make tools—perhaps the most essential characteristic of man's toolmaking activity. Indeed, aside from weapons, most of man's tools are designed for the making of other tools, especially utensils, instruments, and the construction of shelters.

Matching His Grasp with His Reach

In the context of a discussion of man's extraordinary repertoire of attributes, one might suspect his technological capacity to be a rather uninspiring and pedestrian topic. Actually, even the briefest inquiry into its history leads one to marvel and delight at the tangible evidence of the species' inventive genius. Especially fascinating is the prehistoric phase, when every tool and utensil was not only self-made but conceived "from scratch," with little or no heritage of accumulated knowledge and experience for the early craftsman to build upon. No other evidence testifies as tangibly to man's urge to move forward and upward than the history of his technological capacity. Tools and artifacts are truly man's genius made visible and reveal a veritably power-driven itch for extending his natural reach in every direction.

TRANSPARENT TOOLS. When viewed as witnesses of human unfolding, tools and other artifacts lose the heavy, mute character they tend to assume in their workaday capacity. They become luminously transparent, revealing their maker's inexhaustible genius for visualizing means to ends, overcoming obstacles, protecting himself, and enhancing his existence. While perhaps not the loftiest of his achievements, man's technological accomplishments are doubtless the most spectacular proof of his uniqueness. At this juncture of history, one can debate the reality of his ethical, social, and esthetic progress; but his technological achievements are compelling and are indeed universally acknowledged—though not, as we will see, uncritically.

Mind Made Visible

Eons ago, at the dawn of hominid existence, man had to implement his quest for survival by using whatever the environment provided and in which he could recognize some technological potential. Thus, he used caves for dwellings, hides for clothing (fig leaves for modesty, as sacred myth tells us); for food he relied on raw fruits and roots fortified by whatever game he could catch and kill either with his bare hands or with whatever was laying around: sticks, rocks, pebbles, and clubs.

For perhaps thousands of years, man contented himself with the means provided by nature. But when he began chipping his first rudimentary tools, the results were so functional they became the model of the very handtools that remain basic to modern man's toolbox. A survey of the development of man's technological epos is, of course, out of the question within the compass of this book. But a few lines about the earliest and most recent of his toolmaking achievements may help to dramatize the immense distance man has covered since he first glimpsed the possibility of improving his material condition.

The evidence that reaches farthest into prehistoric time is that of the hammer. From its origin until the present, this elementary tool has remained basically the same—a two-part, head and handle combination. The early hammer was an outgrowth of our Stone Age forbears' attempt to lend greater hitting power to his all-purpose club by outfitting its striking end with a stone secured by strips of hide. This primitive arrangement was greatly improved by shaping the stone head so that the handle might be attached more firmly and the blows be made more effective. Interestingly, the earliest wooden handle was commonly bent around the stone, which was grooved to receive it—altogether something of a tour de force by modern standards of manual dexterity.

As soon as a new and harder kind of stone was found, the hammer lead to the stone ax. Sometimes a hole was drilled through the stone head of a hammer or ax to receive the handle. This feature soon became standard and remains basically unchanged. (In this connection it is interesting to recall that when the 1973 Skylab crew wanted to "unjam" that most intricate of man's cybernetic stunts, they finally had to fall back on the earliest and most elementary tool, the hammer.)

The history of the other common tools is an equally fascinating testimony of the unfolding of intelligence in the rough. These tools, however, like metal hammers, came on the scene only after man acquired a mastery of the most momentous of technological means, fire.

Lucky Strike

The tool quality of a given object or force is, of course, a function of the perceiver. Animals perceive as well as humans, but prove incapable of conceptualizing the nature and potential of the particular object. A fascinating example of this capacity to recognize an object's multiple means-value is early man's intimation of the constructive possibilities of a spectacularly destructive phenomenon. Fire was around long before the emergence of man, caused as it was (and still is) by a variety of natural forces and events: volcanic eruptions; sunlight hitting the concave surfaces of glassy substances; heat generated by branches rubbing against each other and reaching the ignition point; and so forth. The major and ubiquitous source of fire is, of course, lightning, and it is estimated that approximately 10,000 thunderstorms occur daily throughout the world.

Early man originally must have been terrified by the awesome spectacle of electrical storms. But he and he alone proved capable of overcoming his terror and systematically reflecting upon the most dramatic of the storms' effects. Watching the consuming and transforming power of fire, he proved capable of recognizing the potential uses of this force for the improvement of his physical condition and set out to capture and bend it to his needs. As usual, he was successful. Thus, hundreds of thousands of years ago, Peking Man used fire. Better, the evidence shows he must have controlled it to the point of being able to tend it in his caves and take it with him when he moved, transporting it in the hollow of horns or burying a spark of it in an ingenious contraption made of twisted bark called "slow matches" by the archeologists.

The next step in the development of man's command over fire was production—a step that spanned thousands of years. Not until Neolithic times is there evidence that man could actually produce fire. How he first brought it about remains a mystery, but that it occurred serendipitously is almost certain—probably by a chance spark produced while hitting a pyrite substance with a flintstone or through friction while drilling a hole in dry wood with a flint. Anthropologists do not know for certain how the event occurred, but since they found these objects in Neolithic camps or sites, their hypotheses are highly plausible. Having acquired full mastery over fire, making it at will, man soon discovered the countless uses of his revolutionary source of power. From then on, technological progress—that is, the industrial arts—developed apace. We of the atomic age know to what threshold this development led.

Getting Things Rolling

What got things literally rolling not only with regard to transportation but also with regard to the diffusion of culture, was, of course, the wheel. Interestingly, according to historian William Culican (1972), the wheel, like the alphabet, seems to have been invented only once, that is, in *one* locality from which its use spread all over the world. One basis for this interpretation is the knowledge that the tools of an advanced, metal-using community were necessary for processing the wood in such a way as to produce a serviceable wheel. This technological fact, supported by archeological inference, points to ancient Mesopotamia as the cradle of the wheel.

The earliest specimens of wheels known to archeologists go back to the fourth century B.C.; hence these wheels belong to the Neolithic period. The potter's wheel was apparently first conceived, with vehicle wheels "soon" to follow. The latter were originally solid; spoked wheels do not appear on the scene until around 2000 B.C. An interesting fact testifies to man's metaphysical as well as technological concerns: the earliest wheels were found in graves (at Kish and Susa in Iran). The idea of death as a journey to another world—still a common metaphor, but originally taken literally—was apparently widespread. Indeed, in Kivik, Sweden, an area that by prehistoric standards was extremely removed from Mesopotamia, a carving was found on a chieftain's grave dating back to about 1000 B.C. and representing a chariot supported by a four-spoked wheel.

The archeological literature about the evolution of the wheel is a veritable epic of human ingeniousness. The early solid wheel, the idea for which was probably sparked by the sight of rolling logs, was followed by the spoked wheel, the rims of which were originally formed with incredible manual skill from a single piece of wood bent in full circle by heat. These basic patterns were followed by a succession of improvements in the hoops fitted around the rims, starting with the iron tire (shrunk onto the wood while the metal was still hot—again, a feat of extraordinary dexterity) and ending with the modern inflated rubber tire.

A particularly ingenious and appealing detail in the story of "man the wheelmaker" concerns the earliest ball bearings, discovered in the hubs of a Celtic wagon preserved in the bog at Dejbjerg, Denmark. To avoid wear, the hubs of certain types of wheels featured inside channels outfitted with little rods of wood revolving between hub and axle—"spare parts" that could be replaced easily and economically. One may feel "all thumbs" and unimaginative reading of exciting do-it-yourself improvements like these, conceived without benefit of schools or how-to manuals and executed with the crudest tools.

Tools That Make Tools That Make Tools

Ever since the dawn of technology, man fashioned his tools in his own (functional) image, after his own capabilities. First he aimed to enhance and magnify his muscular and skeletal capacities by devising the tools for hitting and throwing; tearing, breaking, and crushing; prying, taking apart, and reassembling; carrying and moving; and weaving. Over the centuries, these tools grew in number, variety, and complexity, but the basic design and especially the process of their production remained basically unchanged until the nineteenth century. Then technology took a dramatic leap with the invention of the super producer of tools and other man-made goods—the machine, first steam and later electrically powered. The effect of this technological feat upon the economic, social, familial, and even value orientations of working-class life was so sudden, profound, and devastating that the period was appropriately labeled as revolutionary. With the Industrial Revolution Man the Artisan, autonomous creator of finished products, became Man the Attendant—the first step in a process of increasing subordination to lifeless agents that make tools that make tools *ad infinitum*.

The Leap into Cybernetics

Before this burst of mechanical development, man had begun to extend and enhance his sensory equipment as well. This process would lead him to a vastly expanded vision of both the micro- and macrodimensions of his universe and would gradually affect all areas of his knowledge and activity and their philosophical correlates. After the invention of the microscopic lens by Leeuwenhoek in the early eighteenth century, the development of man's capacity for sensory expansion and penetration advanced with increased momentum. Invention of the microscope was followed by that of the telescope, photography, telephone, telegraph, radio, X-ray, television, radar, laser beams—the whole of it extending, sharpening, and refining man's sensory and symbolic sight, hearing, and penetration.

In an epochal burst of ingeniousness, man leaped over these summits of mechanical achievement and landed foursquare in the cybernetic phase of his technological development, creating the paragon of all man-made devices, the computer. This time he modeled his creation so closely upon his own functional self that it outperformed countless functions that long had been considered uniquely human: systematically memorizing and retrieving; associating and categorizing; calculating; forecasting; organizing; monitoring; translating; decision making. In the computer we seem to find the all-purpose superman—the "thinking" machine, as it is popularly known, the tool that is apt to take over if man fails to watch, not just it but also himself.

Tools That Shape Man

As can be seen from even the preceding thumbnail sketch, man's technological history represents an unceasing quest for enhancement either of power—first muscular then symbolic—or of sensory and conceptual acuity or of speed, precision, and all-round mastery of his environment. Similarly, it represents a process of delegating either power or function to animate or inanimate others. All or part of the activities that used to be performed by the leader, owner, originator, or otherwise directly interested parties are gradually transferred to subordinates—an arrangement that liberates the former to enjoy or occupy themselves in personally more enhancing ways through creative work or leisure, play, education, contemplation, and the like. At first, routine functions were delegated to subordinate fellowmen. But increasingly they are being left in the "hands" of mechanical substitutes. Thus, legions of "servants" have suddenly sprung upon the scene to relieve every man from menial duties (and manual skills) in every sector of daily life. They are fast, docile, clean, "cool," punctual, performing at the flip of a switch, the press of a button, unconditionally, without argument or bargaining—the ideal servants that Pygmalion might have wished.

The Mechanical Servant Turns Master

At the present juncture, the relationship between man and his tools is no longer a simple, one-way process. It has become a transaction. For tools now shape man no less than he shapes them. In fact, it may be justifiable to say that they are now taking the lead in the programming. The effects of this transaction (or reversal) are of a magnitude and complexity that cannot be detailed here. But their implications for mankind are so profound they cannot be left unmentioned in a text dealing with man's uniqueness. Indeed, an essential feature of this uniqueness is his near-infinite plasticity or adaptability. This property allows him to survive under vastly diverse conditions, but it also exposes him to the denaturing influences of his new mechanical environment; that is, to influences capable of interfering with the exercise and development of his *specific* nature, which is not biological, not mechanical, but symbolic. At the present time, the overall effect of technology on the human condition is both enhancing and diminishing. Before we examine these effects, however, let us glance at the manner in which the model became reversed.

As the products of his technological genius grew in complexity, the trend toward a reversal of the modeling process became more visible. For man started functioning increasingly after the characteristics of the cleverest of his tools: strictly time regulated; efficient and achievement oriented; objective, uninvolved, and impersonal. His lifestyle, values, and even his philosophy of life were being modified according to the mechanical model.

Paradoxically, the first, most enduring, and most radical agent in the reversal was "not the gargantuan steam engine but the lilliputian clock" as Roszak aptly phrases it. "For even the steam engine had no industrial significance until it became part of a regulated system, a production process, a system which ran like 'clockwork'" (1969, p. 228). What is there about the "lilliputian clock" that lends it this extraordinary power? According to Mumford (1967) and Matson (1964), as well as Roszak, it is the capacity of clock-regulated automation to achieve the ultimate in routinization, control, and concentration. The objectivity that the clock introduces—the totally nonsubject quality of performing the tasks assigned, with no possibility of distraction, involvement, or the liabilities of feeling, preference, and value stances—is the key to its remarkable effect on man's life.

Dazzled by his stunts, man the inventor could not help musing, "If muscle power can be replaced by a mechanism, how much more desirable to replace the mind behind the muscle with a mechanism. . . . Why should we not invent machines that objectify thought, creativity, decision-making, moral judgment, etc.?" (Roszak, p. 228)—all of which he promptly and gleefully proceeded to attempt. Whenever he hit upon human functions that could not be duplicated, he would get around the difficulty by trimming these functions to a reproducible minimum. Thus, as Roszak writes:

> If we discover that a computer cannot compose emotionally absorbing music, we insist that music *does* have an "objective" side, and we turn

that into our definition of music. . . . If we discover that computers cannot teach as teaching at its most ideal is done, then we redesign education so that the machine can qualify as a teacher. If we discover that computers cannot solve the basic problems of city planning—all of which are questions of social philosophy and aesthetics—then we re-define the meaning of "city," call it an "urban area," and assume that all the problems of this entity are quantitative. In this way man is re-placed in all areas by the machine, not because the machine can do things "better," but rather because *all things have been reduced to what the machine is capable of doing* (pp. 230–31; italics added).

There is no doubt that the computer is a powerful new element on the human scene. However, its power lies not in the computer per se but in man's attitude toward it, arising from a strange combination of people's near-religious awe and a naive fondness for technological gadgets. This attitude foreshadows Aldous Huxley's prediction that man would not only accept, but embrace, his subjection to the machine.

If man insisted upon using his technology as a servant rather than a master, the two could form an unsurpassable team for the advancement of the process of hominization. For there is no doubt that the primary condition for the civilization of *mankind as a whole* requires an advanced technology that frees man from the burden of subsistence work and allows him the time for rest, leisure, and play that must accompany his education as a citizen and as a person, the guardian of the future as well as the past.

6 Lawmaker, Lawbreaker

As a topic for contemplation, law is, at first, about as attractive as the multiplication table. But to those who aren't put off easily it offers an illuminating focus for studying the specificity of man. Indeed, lawmaking draws sharply upon several distinctly human functions. First of all, it draws on reason in its unique capacity for grasping a situation as a *Gestalt,* or structured whole, whose elements are interdependent in such a way that change in any one part alters the whole (for example, the law establishing equal rights for women affects not only women but the spheres of labor, economics, politics, the family, housing, credit, and so on). Second, lawmaking draws upon man's extraordinary capacity for foresight; that is, for projecting into the distant future not only one chain of possible events involving countless variables but several chains, which he analyzes, weighs, compares, and decides upon.

In addition to the high-order intellectual functions it brings into play, lawmaking at its best presupposes a penetrating existential awareness and concern about the problematic nature of life; the unpredictability of the future; and the precariousness of man's condition in terms of life and death, good fortune and misfortune, the fickleness of power, and the oscillations of human impulse. Lawmaking, then, presupposes a keen ethical sensitivity and, paradoxically, a high respect for the value of freedom.

The Capacity to Say "No" to Himself

All healthy organisms (unless they are parasites, like mistletoe, or behaviorally stereotyped, like ants) express an urge for independence. But only man is capable of curtailing that urge in himself—capable and, in variable measure, inclined to do so. But man aims beyond physical and social independence. To the extent that he matures as a person, he strives beyond independence toward autonomy—independence tempered by reason, care, and concern. This is one more dimension that sets him distinctly apart from all other life. In the entire animal kingdom, man alone has the capacity to go deliberately (which implies rationally) against his inclinations. People's effectiveness in striking a relatively satisfactory accord between the pull toward independence and the awareness of a need to check that pull constitutes a remarkable balancing act. Remarkable, at least conceptually. Practically, this capacity often has to be activated and enforced by external agency, since practice generally lags behind principle where human behavior is concerned.

Man's characteristic capacity for behavioral restraint of self and of others is expressed in the universal phenomenon of law:

> A system of ordered relationships is a primary condition of human life at every level. More than anything else, it is what society means. Even an outlaw group, a pirate ship, a robber gang, a band of brigands, has its own code of law, without which it could not exist. The picture of the "lawless savage," running wild in the woods, is wholly fictitious. The "savage" is never lawless, he clings to his own laws more tenaciously, more blindly, than does the civilized man. Only the completely *déraciné*, the man torn from his social environment, or the extreme sophisticate, or the tyrant who emerges in a time of confusion, can be described approximately as lawless (MacIver, 1960, p. 379).

Not even the jungle is lawless. It is regulated by something more orderly than what we understand by "the law of the jungle"—as we learn from recent studies (Ardrey, 1966); (Schaller, 1964); (Morris, 1968); (van Lawick-Goodall, 1971).

Lawful Versus Law-Abiding Behavior

That every human society has laws, written or unwritten, is not a matter of dispute. The fact is that laws have been recorded throughout history and across cultures. The question is whether law exists in the human realm *only* and whether the whole universe does not behave lawfully.

The answer is that everything in nature is as lawful as a falling apple. The apple falls in a predictable direction with predictable velocity and impact. It "obeys" the laws to which it is subject, although it does not choose to obey. Apples have no alternative. Falling apples, like rising moons, are lawful enough, but only man can choose to follow the law: "Purpose is unacceptable as an explanation for the behavior of inanimate matter (no one today would think of explaining the fall of a stone by saying that it is moved by an impulse to rejoin its mother Earth)" (Fuller, 1968, p. 179).

A step above the rigorously necessitated behavior of inanimate objects is the drive-regulated behavior of animals. These forms of behavior, however, are identical or nearly identical throughout the species. Hence their origin is biological not, like human law, cultural.

Regulated Behavior Versus Rule Following

There is a crucial difference between regulated social behavior among animals and law-regulated or rule-following behavior in man. First of all, only man *institutes* law and does so *by convention*. (The arbitrary and coercive dictates of tyrants do not properly qualify as law.) Also, only humans subject themselves to the very laws they themselves create and/or enforce. Furthermore, "the rule of law requires that the source of law itself, the state, respect a lawfulness that is not of its creation" (Fuller, 1972, p. 151). None of these characteristics are found in the regulated social behavior of animals.

The absence among animals of political activity—that is, of behavior regulation instituted by way of convention—is common knowledge and confirmed by both ethological and psychological research. True, certain "arrangements" reminiscent of implicit law among humans have been observed among animals. Most widely known among these "laws" are territoriality and leadership. Such regulated behavior may exist between individual animals or within the structure of a group when, for instance, one animal asserts himself as the leader while the others validate this role by adopting a more or less complementary role. Adoption of these roles is quite likely conditioned to some extent by such factors as differences in physical size or force among individuals, especially between males and females, but its species specificity shows that it is essentially biological, that is, genetic in origin.

ONLY MAN CAN BREAK THE LAW. Another key difference between law-regulated or rule-following behavior in humans and drive-regulated behavior in animals lies in man's capacity to break the rules to which he is subjected by law. "For a creature to be correctly said to have a rule it is necessary that it should be able to break the rule" (Bennett, 1964, p. 17). Applying this principle to the celebrated case of the honey bee, Bennett notes:

> Normal, well-constructed honey bees do in fact break the rules by performing the "wrong" dance or flying in the "wrong" direction after observing a dance; yet this further detail about their behavior still leaves one unwilling to say that they are guided by rules. It does remove the impression that the bees are in the grip of the rules, but not by showing that the rules are in the grip of the bees. . . . We cannot say that bees

have rules unless they somehow manifest an awareness of their rules as rules (pp. 17–18).

There is no evidence to show that bees have such awareness—hence they have no awareness of breaks of the rules *as* breaks of the rules. "It does look on the face of it as though we can say of honey bees that their dancing behavior is covered by rules, but not that honey bees have rules according to which they dance. Or in other words, although the dancing behavior of bees is regular, it is not rule-guided" (pp. 15–16).

Familiar cases of *apparent* rule breaking may be observed in domestic animals. Anyone who owns a dog can observe certain maneuvers that look as if the animal were weighing his chances of getting away with something against which he has been more or less successfully conditioned. Actually, the animal's "deliberation" can be explained as an association-based oscillation between his conditioned and natural responses, with an outcome resembling a compromise. Thus, an apartment dog may try to prolong the short outings he is granted by repeatedly lifting a hind leg—literally an empty gesture—because he knows that as long as the appearance of draining operations is maintained, his master will let him stay outside a little longer.

As for deviations from lawful behavior in wild animals, it is true that a fox, naturally geared to snatching chickens or the like, may fail to exhibit this inclination on a particular occasion. This does not imply, however, that his abstention is deliberate. It may be accidental, the result of some chance event, either internal (biochemical upset) or external (perception of danger). Therefore, such behavior must be regarded as a *happening* rather than an *action,* to use Peters's (1958) apt distinction between involuntary, unreflected events and conscious, intentional behavior.

Certain ethologists (van Lawick-Goodall) and certain writers who deal with such research (Ardrey) report or describe behavior that they consider to be significant modifications of species-specific patterns. These variations in social behavior, however, represent only slight departures from the patterns of behavior characteristic of the particular species. Moreover, conclusions based upon ethological fieldwork—deep within the natural habitat of the animals observed—need careful empirical checking and the examination of alternate premises. What comes to mind here is the shift of the interpretative pendulum in the field of anthropology from the early stance of total relativism to the current trend toward a carefully ascertained universality. The likelihood of such swings of interpretation in the area of ethology appears even greater since the observations involve not just *intra*species differences between observer and observed but the vastly more hazardous *inter*species differences. This interspecies difference is one reason that Alland, in *The Human Imperative,* considers Morris's popular *The Naked Ape* "successful only as a prolegomena to the study of man and . . . a dismal failure when it comes to the essentials of human history" (1972, p. 150).

Finally, when an animal's behavior deviates from its customary pattern in a clearly novel and goal-directed way, it remains that only *one* alternative is involved. This makes the action vastly different from the process of human deliberation. For one thing, deliberation involves awareness of two or more alternatives, complete with their respective consequences. What is more, several or even all the alternatives may be *novel forms of behavior,* which places the whole operation on a distinctly conceptual, not an associative, level. Such deviations usually consist of complex symbolic activities calling into play an array of extremely intricate patterns and sequences, not merely a single and familiar variable. Law-abiding behavior, then, is a uniquely human phenomenon—and so, is conscious lawbreaking.

Most significant, perhaps, among the differences between regulated behavior in animals and its counterpart in humans, is the law-abiding citizen's willingness to obey laws of which he disapproves. Note especially here the key term *willing.* It emphasizes the fact that man is *capable* not only (grudgingly perhaps) of obeying laws in which he does not believe but of being willing to recognize and espouse the value not of the law but of the principle. This is precisely what characterizes law, government, and the political process—constant variation in ingredients but identity in substance. By comparison, animal behavior exhibits the structure of a nearly closed system in which the constitutive elements change only under drastic environmental or even genetic mutation (Alland, 1972).

Finally, while human laws are instituted for the purpose of enhancing rather than merely maintaining life, animal rules are survival oriented or are perceptually and concretely associated with the mechanisms that mediate survival.

Cultural and Hereditary Factors

The difference between rule following, specifically human behavior, and regulated animal behavior is, of course, rooted in the difference between culture and genes—in spite of the fact that these two determinants are not absolutely compartmentalized:

Genes are responsible for man's capacity to acquire culture. They are also responsible for the basis of other capacities, the potential for a wide range of behaviors. The expression of these traits depends upon the environment in which maturation takes place. Different human populations may have somewhat different potentials, particularly small isolated populations living in extreme environmental conditions, but it must be borne in mind that while genes may produce different probabilities for behavior they do not produce the actual behavior itself. Thus different environmental conditions (including education) can produce the same behavioral results on different genetic backgrounds. Individuals with very similar genetic backgrounds can be very different. . . . *This does not exclude the possibility that culturally based behavior patterns affect genetic structure and that alterations in genetic patterns may facilitate cultural adaptation to specific environments* (Alland, 1972, p. 151; italics added).

We may assume that regulated social behavior in animals is genetically determined because of its striking uniformity and rigidity, its resistance to external modification in the sense of development toward greater differentiation, and the absence of cumulative transmission. Conversely, one of the intrinsic characteristics of human legislative behavior is its variety, flexibility, and capacity for change and repeal.

Furthermore, because human laws are culturally determined, they vary through time and space like culture itself. They are amenable to sometimes slow and sometimes dramatic modification, and change and adaptation are at the core of legislative activity. By contrast, regulated behavior among animals (for example, ants, termites, and cockroaches) may remain fixed through geological time. Granted, certain animals adapt to their environment, within relatively narrow limits. However, such changes are not meant to enhance their existence but occur under rigorous survival pressures. Most human laws, on the other hand, are instituted not primarily for the purpose of individual survival but for the enhancement of the community or some of its privileged or handicapped members.

Law, then, is an ongoing and open-ended process. As such, it manifests all the characteristics of the open system that general systems theory defines as a whole that is not only more than the sum of its parts but different from that sum in that the ingredients that make up the whole are constantly being replaced. In the phenomenon of the flame, for example, the combustible ingredients disappear successively while the flame is maintained.

Law and Ethics

Over and above the behavioral evidence of the uniquely human character of lawmaking, there is the evidence of ethics. Man's political and legislative activity consists of more than the striking of power balances described in *The Territorial Imperative* and *The Naked Ape*. As Fuller reminds us, "Unless we think of a striving toward justice as a part of the concept of law itself, we cannot distinguish between a state where 'the rule of law' prevails and a tyranny in which what are miscalled rules of law are mere objects of selfish manipulation by those who control the government" (1972, p. 151).

That ethics are uniquely human is one area of general (if implicit) agreement among all scientists and philosophers dealing with these questions. More precisely, the agreement concerns the absence of an ethical dimension in animal behavior. True, a few authors, Skinner at the helm, dismiss a meaningful ethics altogether, since they dismiss the condition for ethics, freedom, as a mere epiphenomenon derived from "the fallacy of the inner man" and, therefore, "good riddance" (1972, p. 191). But the works even of researchers who adhere to a substantial (as distinguished from an epiphenomenal) view of ethics contain no evidence of any attempt to train their animals in even the rudiments of ethical behavior.* Operationally, then, there seems to be unanimity on the question of ethics as a human, and exclusively human, dimension. In fact, the key figure of comparative psychology, B. F. Skinner, writes eloquently and at length on ethical training (*Walden Two*, Chapter 14). And there is hardly a more intense manifestation of ethical concern than his very own sustained (though in my view, mistaken) efforts to save mankind from chaos and annihilation.

If social scientists in general and comparative psychologists in particular do not regard ethics as a uniquely human prerogative, then one must wonder why they are so intent upon using words that are devoid of referents: conscience, justice, rights, fairness, and so on. This whole vocabulary is reduced to sheer rhetoric the moment we deny the reality of ethics. Lawmaking and obeying the law are inconceivable without the presupposition of an at least potential ethical dimension within the individual. Where the agent has no ethical prerogatives, he has no ethical rights or obligations; hence he cannot engage in lawmaking—that is, setting up rules that must be sanctioned, directly or indirectly, by the community and made binding for all members. This proposition is supported (at least behaviorally) by all social scientists, insofar as none, apparently, is capable of speaking about law without resorting, in the last analysis, to the language of ethics.

Rules, restrictions, and obligations are part of every culture, but their substance, even when pertaining to the same issue, may be diametrically opposed, depending upon the culture within which they appear.

> The content of substantive law varies tremendously among primitive societies. Two features, however, are almost universal; homicide within the group in one form or another is legally punishable everywhere;

* In their experiment on the ability of male rhesus monkeys to raise baby monkeys, Mitchell, Redican, and Gomber (*Psychology Today*, April 1974, p. 66) report that because they were concerned about the safety of the infants, they "familiarized the animals with each other" before leaving the babies in the care of the adult males. This process was not (and was not intended to be), however, a process of ethical training of the adult monkey but protection against the risk of infanticide occasionally observed in adult monkeys. The ethical element in this situation was part of the experimenters', not the subjects', behavior.

adultery, with a few possible exceptions, also comes universally within the scope of legal action. It should be realized, however, that just what constitutes illegal homicide and adultery varies with the culture. For example, among the Eskimo infanticide, senilicide, and invalidicide are legally privileged if committed by a relative or a close friend. Among these peoples coitus between a married woman and a man to whom she has been lent by her husband is not illegal adultery; on the other hand it is most definitely illegal without at least the husband's implicit permission (Hoebel, 1972, p. 822).

In concluding this brief discussion of the relation between law and ethics, it should be emphasized that the roots of man's legislative activity and of his notions of rights and obligations lie not in mere power balances sealed by social contract but in the very soil of ethics. Implicit confirmation of this is found in the fact that no social scientist claims that animals have rights, though all would probably agree—at least in theory—that man has obligations toward them. Fortunately, if duly observed, such obligations amount, in practice, to the same benefits for the animal as those that would flow from the corresponding rights.

Thus, while man has a moral and, in organized society, a legal right to use any animal, to control the proliferation of some, and even to exterminate rats or other vermin, he is not granted the right to make even noxious animals suffer *needlessly* or for his own preverse pleasure. The Act for the Prevention of Cruelty to Animals stipulates no exceptions whatsoever, and it aims thereby at not only protecting animals but at protecting man from himself. Indeed, cruelty harms *not only the victim but also the agent,* and only man has the capacity for cruelty. Animals may be aggressive and even prey upon one another (though very few animals prey upon their own species), but they are not capable of cruelty. Cruelty, being deliberate and calculated, presupposes conceptual capacities that animals do not possess.

Furthermore, cruelty in whatever form, is incompatible with the dignity of a being who has the capacity for reflective thought, for generalization and empathy; that is, the capacity to symbolically put himself in the place of another sentient being. More important, since man is the sum total of his experiences, hence of his actions, cruelty constitutes a hazardous thread in the fabric of his being.

Law in Time

Since my aim is to present man as *inherently* competent and creative rather than programmed solely by cumulative cultural forces (whose effect, of course, merges with those of his own initiative), I am once more reaching back in time to provide a longitudinal glance at a uniquely human capacity.

According to the *Encyclopædia Britannica*, the oldest tangible evidence of law in the ancient world is the famous Code of Hammurabi, King of Babylon (c. 2100 B.C.), consisting of 3,600 lines of cuneiform writing carved on an eight-foot stele found at Susa, Iran, in 1901 and now at the Louvre. Because of its remarkably humanitarian spirit, Hammurabi's Code has earned the reputation of being the greatest among ancient legal systems, despite the fact that it featured retributive punishment. Its substance is so rich, so encompassing, articulate, and wise that it cannot have sprung full-fledged from the mind of a single legislator; rather it must be assumed to have been drawn in large part from earlier "codes," as the legal prescriptions that antedated Hammurabi were somewhat ambitiously called. No direct evidence of these earlier codes is preserved, but we can infer their existence from references found in ancient documents.

For their time, many of the stipulations of Hammurabi's Code are remarkably sophisticated. For instance, it abolished the barbaric rules of blood feuds, of private retribution, and of marriage by capture—all of which were deeply rooted in ancient tribal custom. The Code was particularly rigorous in regard to those who defrauded the helpless and is marked throughout by a deeply rational and human concern. One is struck, however, by the savage *lex talionis,* or law of retribution, that runs through this admirably articulate and human document. Note the imaginative—if gruesome—combination of symbolism and literalism in the following excerpt from the Code's section on criminal law.

> Loss or mutilation of an offending member was inflicted according to the nature of the offense; e.g., the hand that struck a father was cut off; the eye that pried into secrets was put out. . . . The notion of "a life for a life" extended to such correspondences as the execution of a creditor's son for having caused the death of a debtor's son while holding him as a pledge (Gadd, 1972, p. 43).

The "eye for an eye" principle, however, was not applied indiscriminately. The law took pains to specify in what cases its precepts did or did not apply and reveals a genuine concern about the commensurateness of penalty with offense in cases where the evidence was unclear. "Accidents, and any injuries beyond reasonable possibility of prevention, were not generally imputed as offenses. . . . The owner of an ox that gored a passer-by was responsible only if it was known to be a vicious beast. . . . On the other hand, carelessness and neglect were severely punished. A clumsy surgeon might lose his hands as the penalty for a maiming operation; a veterinary had to repay part of the value of a beast that died through his treatment" (Gadd, p. 43).

Particularly interesting with reference to our concern with man as man rather than man in one of his many roles is the legislation concerning the family. No less interesting is the evidence that almost four thousand years ago, the problems of the family were basically the same as they are now.

Adoption, which was regulated by several laws, was common for the purpose either of perpetuating a family or of securing the continuance of a business. . . . The control of a father over his children was unlimited until their marriage; he could dispose of their labour and even of their persons for his profit. Daughters could be freely given either in marriage or as religious votaries or as concubines. . . . Marriages were arranged by the parents. . . .

A man might divorce his wife at will, but must restore her dowry and provide for her maintenance and that of any children; if there were no children, he both returned the dowry and paid her a sum equal to the bride price. But in order to receive these benefits the wife must establish that she had not failed in her duties, for in this case she might be divorced without compensation and even lose her children. For her own part a wife could obtain judicial separation for cruelty or neglect; but she sued at her peril, for if the fault was found to be on her side, she might incur the penalty of death by drowning. . . . For adultery both guilty parties were liable to drowning, but if the wronged husband pardoned his wife the king might do the like for her paramour (Gadd, pp. 42–43).

NOTEWORTHY STONE.   For those whose mind has an imaginative bent, the stone carrying Code of Hammurabi is of some interest. As was mentioned earlier, the Code was engraved on an eight-foot-high stele. The kind of stone chosen for this monument—the most significant in Hammurabi's realm—was igneous rock, formed from the crystallization of molten magma from beneath the solid crust of the earth. The name of the particular stone, *diorite*—derived from the Greek *dior*, meaning "observe, take note of" and *ite*, meaning "stone"—evokes the idea of notable or noteworthy stone, a singularly appropriate appelation for a rock that carries the precepts regulating the behavior of a nation. Even if "dior" may not have been coined at the time of the conquest of Babylon by the Greeks (after the Persians, 538 B.C.), the intimate but coincidental correspondence of the meaning and the name of the stone remains fascinating.

Leaping from the remote past to the distant future, Stanley Kubrick's film, *2001*, based on Arthur Clarke's novel of the same name, repeatedly featured a large, stele-shaped monolith to mark the major stages of the evolution of life—first on earth, then on other planets. The message contained in the *name* of the stone bearing the Babylonian code is aptly evoked by the *size* of the monolith in Clarke's futuristic world: each in its own way compels attention. Both the form and the size of the monolith are aptly conceived to symbolize the awesome centrality of the law as the pivotal element of civilized society. Towering above the creatures at its base—first apes, then astronauts—the monolith effectively symbolizes the enormity of the law dominating the ongoing, forward-moving process of human destiny, its vicissitudes and its contingencies. The inviolability and unapproachable sanctity of the law is symbolized, also, by the fact that the monolith gave off an intolerable sound that kept man at a distance.

DOING BETTER THAN HE KNOWS. The exact function and meaning of the monolith in Kubrick's powerful canvas of the human epic are not made clear in either the film or the book. No doubt it can be interpreted in many ways. The idea of the centrality of the law in civilized society may not have occurred at all to either the producer-director or the author, but the fact that it was not intended does not mean that it was not expressed. As Thomas Aquinas recognized long ago, "A teacher may teach better than he knows."

III Toward Delight: Play, Love, and Beauty

Play, love, and beauty, three significant areas of human expression, share a strangely underdeveloped status in the field of psychology. Common to each of these manifestations of human specificity is that they aim not at means values but at end values. Ideally, each is pursued for its own sake. So essential is this "gratuitous" dimension that play, love, and esthetic enjoyment lose both their identity and their psychological benefits the moment they are used to serve ends other than the gaining or giving of joy.

In their fullest expression, play, beauty, and especially love represent the summit of man's creativity. Not only are they relatively independent of material props and media but they generate "being" in him who experiences and expresses these values. Play, love, and beauty open a perspective upon that toward which man is forever aspiring—the presence of joy, which is a quality of experiencing, indeed of being, so pervasive that it is compatible even with hardship, pain, and other such "roughage" that make up much of life's daily fare.

7 The Playing Animal

All animals apparently engage in that excited, random, and unfocused kind of activity we call play. But only man exhibits the peculiar phenomenon of regulated play conventionally known as games. Remarkably identical in their basic pattern, games are found in all cultures, whatever the stage of their evolution. For games are not essentially a matter of complex props and rules. They are a function of the kind of psychological processes engaged in the structure of the game, and these processes, as we will see, exist in even the most rudimentary games.

The universality of game playing is intriguing because games serve no observable survival function or otherwise utilitarian purpose, either for the individual or for the species. Nobody has to play, strictly speaking, unless he turns professional, in which case his activities retain the structure but lose the meaning of play. Nor does a culture need games to qualify as a culture (Huizinga, 1949). It is precisely because playing is totally free from necessity (though not necessarily free from considerable effort) yet so ubiquitous a behavior that it is exceptionally revealing.

The following pages are aimed at giving a brief sketch of the nature and function of game playing and at ferreting out some plausible hints as to the significance of the phenomenon for the actualization of man's specific potential as a person, especially as a social animal.

What's in a Game?

To qualify as a game, an interpersonal activity must have a basic structure or minimal framework. In its simplest expression that structure comprises at least three externally observable requisites. First, since games are organized social activities, there must be an orderly arrangement of *roles* for the participants to perform. Second, games require a *goal* toward which the activity is geared. Without a goal, the players would have no way of knowing when the game is over and who won it. Third, and most characteristically, games presuppose mutually agreed upon *rules* regarding the ways and means of reaching the goal. Where there are no rules, there are no means to evaluate the performance and, hence, no game—it's "tennis without a net" in Robert Frost's words. The particular nature and arrangement of roles, rules, and goals, plus the kind of props, if any, are what lends a game an identity of its own.

Not necessarily part of the game concept are *competition* and *stakes*, in the sense of material rewards—though some sort of symbolic stake, winning or losing, is inherent in all competitive games. Where heavy stakes are involved, competition may be so high that it denatures the psychological meaning and function of the activity—turning play into work or, at least, into a means rather than an end in itself and eliminating thereby one of the chief characteristics of play.

Whether a game also qualifies as play depends on the psychological variables, motives, values, and attitudes that are consciously or unconsciously involved. Among these, two experiential attributes are recognized as indispensable: first, the playing must be freely engaged in; it may not be coercive no matter how worthy the reason for imposing it on self or others. Second, it may not serve utilitarian or other ulterior purposes. It must be gratuitous, self-purposive, autotelic, and "disinterested," in the sense of not seeking any gain other than fun.

A third requisite for play was recently formulated by Hein, who regards it as "more definitive" than the preceding two attributes. She feels that the "unreality" of play, its "detachment from reality"—which she recognizes as implicit in the other two requisites—should receive independent emphasis. She does not deny, of course, that play activities are real in the sense that they exist in the real world. "A football game involves real people and real objects as much as an auto accident does" (1968, p. 70). But the football game is "unreal" in that it is accompanied by "the consciousness that it is 'different' from 'ordinary life'" (Huizinga, 1949, p. 28). Hein's formulation of this third quality of play is especially helpful with reference to play as a model for life (discussed later in the chapter).

New Meanings

Until fairly recently, *game* referred exclusively to activities that—though often strenuous, competitive, and governed by a matrix of rigid rules—were practiced essentially for their own sake, that is, for the enjoyment they promised. In current usage, however, the terms *game* and *game playing* designate phenomena that are removed by various degrees from the original meaning of the term.

GAME THEORY.   One of these new usages derives from the introduction of the game concept into social science research. "Game theory" here designates a currently favored approach to the analysis of social phenomena—usually conflict situations—which are regarded as if they were games and in which the "players" are assumed to proceed rationally and to utilize calculations of risk. The researcher then applies a system of mathematical operations to these transactions in an effort to derive information about the basic structure of complex sociological phenomena. Thus, the application of game theory revealed that many interpersonally significant phenomena formerly unexplored and vaguely characterized as charm, power, dependency, or ignorance, have in fact a structure reminiscent of the game. The structure is tacitly observed by the participants even though they may be only partially aware of acting according to patterns and rules.

PSYCHIATRIC USAGE.   Another departure from the original meaning of game playing has arisen with the adoption of the term in psychiatric discourse. By a greatly expanded use of the term *game* (borrowed from *game theory*), Berne popularized this usage in *Games People Play* (1964), an examination of complex, essentially deceptive, often neurotic, interpersonal activities. Characteristic of Berne's use is the fact that the patterns of interaction he describes are games only in the sense that they can be analyzed according to the structure of competitive games. They are distinctly not games in the sense that they are not played for the sake of playing—that is, for sheer fun. Instead, they are focused upon a surreptitious gaining of dominance or of secondary gratification.

COLLOQUIAL CORRUPTION.   In line with an increasingly cynical use of terms that were originally either neutral or more or less lofty, the meanings of *game* and *game playing* have been altered in the public mind to the point of confusion. Indeed, unless the context clearly points to the contrary, these terms are now widely used in ordinary speech as euphemisms for manipulation, deception, and exploitation.

Types of Games

Among the transactional activities that, on the basis of their structures, can be regarded as games, we can distinguish two basic categories: fun games, and life games. Depending upon the nature and preponderance of the experiential variables involved—awareness, intentions, calculations, values—life games may be further differentiated into object games and metagames. Object games are those in which the aim is relatively clear-cut and limited in the sense that it revolves around either material gain or ego indulgence. Metagames are activities whose objectives are such intangible values as education, altruism, self-actualization, agape, salvation, and the like.

PLAY FOR PLAY'S SAKE. Fun games, then, or games proper, are play for play's sake, not for the sake of profit, prestige, fund raising or therapy—for which, according to Walter Kerr's witty but serious reflections in *The Decline of Pleasure* (1962), they are increasingly being used. Granted, such common practices as golf for business, bowling for health, cards for charity, and of late, ping-pong for "diplomacy" are harmless and well-meant endeavors; nevertheless, they represent subtle corruptions of the game as a source of fun.

One thing almost certain to change the nature of a fun game is the presence of high stakes and, hence, stiff competition. These elements go counter to the requirements of a carefree losing of the self in the fabric of the playful game. Incidentally, if the fun game is to be scored or otherwise evaluated, it should be done as much or more in terms of style than of outcome. "What counts should be the shooting of the arrow rather than the hitting of the target," as the Oriental sages would put it. For the target may be hit by chance, while the shooting is a measure of the player's skill, which is, in turn, a measure of himself. When style is disregarded and outcome is all, the game becomes a contest and loses its psychologically regenerative, recreative quality.

Stephen Potter's charming little work on *The Theory and Practice of Gamesmanship* (1947) is an attempt to deal humorously with the "winning" motivations generated in all game playing. With great subtlety he reminds us of the fine line between fair play and unfair advantage, which is an important determiner of whether one is engaged in the competition of a fun game or the competitiveness of life games.

Of course, cultural attitudes about the goal of games vary. In *Patterns of Culture* (1951), Benedict reports that the Zuni Indians of the Southwest think that a higher value attaches to the boy who lets his competitor "win" a race.

Games are an important way in which a culture inculcates its values. The competition of the free enterprise economy no doubt accounts for "winning" as a goal and sports as an industry in our culture.

The varieties of the fun-game transaction across cultures and history are innumerable. Like his search for beauty, man's yen for fun reveals his inherently creative nature in an abundance of forms.

WHAT'S THE OBJECT? "What people really need or demand from life," according to Szasz, "is not wealth, comfort, or esteem, but games worth playing" (de Ropp, 1968, p. 11). Life games are interpersonal processes that have all the structural elements of a game without being recognized as such by the participants and without yielding the affectively stimulating, recreative rewards of the fun games. This category of game is described with great insight and gusto by Robert S. de Ropp in *The Master Game* (1968), my source for much of the following.

In the hierarchy of life games, object games occupy the lower level. As de Ropp classifies them, those most commonly played in our culture come under three headings, phrased in colorful if somewhat barbed terms. The most elementary form of object game he calls "Hog in Trough"; its grossly material aim consists of "getting one's nose in the trough as deeply as possible . . . elbow[ing] the other hogs aside as forcefully as possible" (1968, p. 14). "Cock on Dunghill" is played for fame; it is "designed primarily to inflate the false ego. Players . . . are hungry to be known and talked about. They want to be celebrities whether or not they have anything worth celebrating" (p. 14). Deadliest of all the object games is the "Moloch Game"* "because it aims at glory and is achieved at the cost of human lives" (p. 14). Fortunately, this variety is not open to everyone because it requires access to considerable power or a command of specialized techniques used in the presumed service of great causes.

If we grant validity to the Moloch Game, it would seem to find expression in not only the grand scale of war and political, economic, or financial strategies but also the ruthless manipulation of individual by cunning individual—as illustrated in literature by such figures as Becky Sharpe in Thackeray's *Vanity Fair* or Scarlett O'Hara in Mitchell's *Gone with the Wind*. The antisocial quality that pervades the Moloch Game achieves a degree of disregard for human life and well-being that may become criminal.

As for the less demeaning object games—those that are legitimate, constructive, and even necessary, such as making a living and raising a family—de Ropp classifies these, somewhat condescendingly, with the name "Householder Game."

Metagames are aimed at ideals, at science, art, religion. Their rules are symbolic, point to other rules, and presuppose, therefore, a higher level of psychological organization. (While all animals are generally considered incapable of playing games, they are definitely incapable of playing metagames.)

A succinct example of the difference between object and metagames is Patrick Henry's "Give me liberty (metagame) or give me death" (object game). Another example, less dramatic but more related to everyday life, is the complex phenomenon of romantic love, which can be aimed either at sexual gratification (object game) or at personal fulfillment for either or both parties (metagame). The variety of metagames is obviously as vast as the variety of ideals that man can set for himself.

The distinction between goals and ideals, which relates to de Ropp's

---

* Moloch was a god of the Ammonites and Phoenicians to whom children were sacrificed by burning.

games, is that goals tend to be tangible, and ideals symbolic. Consequently, goals are more within the realm of the object game, and ideals motivate the metagame. Ideals are, by definition, beyond full attainment, and because they require continued striving and growth, they are eminently suited to metagames. The intriguing utopian scheme presented by Herman Hesse in *Magister Ludi* (teacher of the game) (1959) is a good example of the metagame. Hesse's novel proposes an ideal society five hundred years hence in which an elitist subculture is organized entirely around an annual game that has only ideal ends.

NEUROTIC GAMES. Falling somewhere in between true metagames and object games, as de Ropp defines them, are Berne's *Games People Play* (1964).These games lack the plainness of goal and the single-minded, often ruthless, pursuit characteristic of the object games. They fall within the category of the metagames because their stakes are usually intangible, for example, defense or boosting of the ego, and because the players prove capable of using metarules—that is, they possess a degree of awareness of what they are doing and a capacity to deceptively modify their rules to fit diverse situations. They are, however, of a low order of metagames in that they lack—even in principle—the exalted quality of the metagame. Their aim is invariably tricky and self-serving, as for instance in cases of perverted pursuit of knowledge, beauty, or salvation. Characteristic also of this type of game is its exploitive character or, paradoxically, its self-punitive outcome, exemplified in the following transaction:

> *Salesman:* "This one is better, but you can't afford it!"
> *Housewife:* "That's the one I'll take" (Berne, 1964, p. 33).

At face value, the salesman simply states two valid but incompatible facts. In actuality, he is using an intimidating strategy aimed at stinging the customer's ego, which he suspects retains some immature features. Indeed, instead of replying, as Berne suggests, "You are correct on both counts" and minding her pocketbook, the customer chooses to strike back at the salesman's arrogance and to "teach him a lesson"—for which she pays. The score is 1–0 in favor of the salesman.

The author of *The Peter Principle* has proposed the "Peter Principle Game" (*Psychology Today*, October, 1973, pp. 94 ff.) to illustrate the losing-by-winning promotions that take place in hierarchical organizations. When, at last, a person wins promotion to his highest level of incompetence, he loses all the satisfactions of productive and creative work that he formerly enjoyed at lower levels of the organizational scheme. Lawrence J. Peter has caught the neurotic character of much hierarchical organizational life. Winners lose and losers win.

SPORT. While competitiveness is a perfectly legitimate ingredient of even fun games, it has gradually acquired such overpowering proportions that the play quality has been lost. Nowadays, as soon as a high degree of prowess is achieved, it is considered too valuable to be "wasted" in fun and must be turned into an economic resource. The player can no longer afford to play for play's sake. What used to be a source of enjoyment tends to turn into a grim enterprise climaxing in professionalism. From "gentleman," as he used to be, the professional sportsman turns "player," as the British pointedly describe the difference.

Game playing, even by the nonprofessional, seems to move further and further away from the play sphere proper until it becomes something that yields the benefits of neither play nor work. The player approaches the game in the puritanical spirit of discipline, perfectionism, and pursuit of success. Since about the turn of the century, when this attitude began to surface, rules have assumed increasing importance and records have zoomed to incredible heights. After "play" became "sport," sport became a fully remunerative occupation or a preparation for such while its management developed into big business.

In its basic structure, professional sport has all the trappings of fun games. But from the point of view of psychological dynamics, professional "playing" is as different from actual playing as leisure is from real-life work. It lacks the psychological-emotional attributes and the kind of reward that accompanies play for play's sake. Instead, professional play yields high material gain—or the promise of such—and is earned at a correspondingly high emotional cost. Although the aim of professional sport is ulterior to the means, it does not qualify as a life game because the participants are clearly aware of the structure of the game and observe rules that are explicitly stated, identical, and accepted by both sides.

THE NO-GAME LIFE.　Finally, there is what de Ropp calls the "no-game" life-style whose nonplayers are unable or unwilling to find a game worth playing. They either are unable to make a choice or, having made one, are incapable of sticking with it. Like Szasz, de Ropp regards such individuals as usually affected by or progressing toward serious psychological disturbance.

The Human Condition in a Capsule

At the beginning of this chapter, I pointed out that the analysis of game playing holds particular promise for an understanding of man, the only animal that engages in a kind of activity that is free, yet at the same time, regulated. What is referred to is, of course, the prototypical fun game that is played spontaneously, for the sake of playing, without ulterior concerns, and with full awareness of the fact that the contest is make-believe (Hein, 1968).

When we look into the dynamics of games as play, we find that they involve the simultaneous exercise of a number of contrasting, actually antagonistic forces and tendencies—much as does life itself. Game playing, then, is likely to contain certain cues as to the manner in which human needs can be harmonized and resolved in a way consistent with the direction of the good life.

COOPERATIVE ANTAGONISM.   Games are the prototype of that interpersonal behavior that Riesman (1958) calls "antagonistic cooperation." The roles are antagonistic but the overall design of the activity is synergistic. The participants are cast in opposing roles or camps, and unless they consent to fight each other—and work at it—there is no game. People who play lackadaisically or who deliberately role play their part (as when adults "compete" with a child to whom they want to give the pleasure of "winning") are not playing the game. Not to offer resistance to one's legitimate opponent is to cheat him and oneself out of the fun of the performance. Paradoxically, then, unless the players consent to oppose each other for the purpose and duration of the game, they are not players. Correlatively, neither are they players if they do not stop their antagonistic behavior after the game is over.

People do like and need cooperation, for it represents a mild form of love. But they apparently also like to struggle for or against something. And maybe they need to engage in struggle lest they deteriorate. Thus considered, the uphill struggle that, for most people, is life can be regarded as an opportunity for developing a number of strengths rather than as a frustrating, senseless thwarting of impulse.

NEED FOR FREEDOM AND RESTRAINT.   Most striking about games is the combination of freedom and voluntary restraint incorporated in the rules —freedom to play or not to play; to choose one game rather than another; to modify the rules, provided it is done by common consent. But however it is exercised, this freedom always involves the acceptance of limits and the submission to sanctions if the limits are not observed.

In this era of scepticism about self-discipline and the concept of the law, the felicitous combination of freedom and restraint illustrated in game playing would seem particularly worth pondering with respect to the pursuit of the good life. Also worth pondering is the fact that there is safety in the restriction of freedom; rules are restrictive and protective. But their protection must be earned lest this asset become a liability. For people usually feel entitled to strike back harder for foul play in a situation governed by rules than in one in which each party acts according to his own peculiar ways and views.

SAFETY AND RISK.   Everybody prefers victory over defeat. Where ego demands are strong, sensitivity to defeat may be equally strong. Where the outcome of a transaction is unpredictable, as it is in games, the player runs a certain risk, if only symbolic and ego involving. But the player who is equipped for the challenge, not only in terms of skill but also in terms of attitudes, is bound to enjoy the game regardless of whether he is winning or losing. Thus, if a player's opponent is weak, he has the satisfaction of winning. But in that case the satisfaction is hardly exhilarating because the outcome was practically known in advance, and the very certainty kills most of the fun of playing. If, on the other hand, both players are strong, the loser as well as the winner can draw satisfaction from the very strength of his opponent. Indeed, whatever the outcome of the game, opponents are each other's claim to fame: their skill or competence is defined in terms of one another.

One of the individual's needs is, no doubt, safety. But another one apparently is the need to confront risk with the tension and effort and perhaps the anxiety that go with that experience. One may wonder whether enough attention has been given to the desirability of allowing the growing individual to satisfy that particular need. Too much emphasis upon safety and too much protection from anxiety may well be at cross-purposes with the requirements of growth. May expresses his keen awareness of the necessity for "protecting" the growing person from too much safety.

> Granted that shyness can be pretty painful (surely neurotic shyness should be gotten over) and that everyone no doubt feels himself too shy, yet is it so good that normal shyness should be entirely erased? *Is not shyness the growing edge of new relationships?* And does shyness not have its normal constructive function, to be sure possibly painful on one side, but zestful and exhilarating on the other, of opening up new areas of experience? Indeed, is not shyness in its normal degree the most *personal* of all emotions. I for one would be very dubious about the pleasure of spending many evenings in circles where no one was ever shy. . . . (1967, pp. 43–44)

> It would be irrational for the student, or any of us, *not* to be anxious in the kind of world we live in. "Anxiety is our best teacher," wrote Kierkegaard. And he went on: "I would say that learning to know anxiety is an adventure which every man has to affront if he would not go to perdition either by not having known anxiety or by sinking under it. He therefore who has learned rightly to be anxious has learned the most important thing" (p. 49).

Erich Fromm, however, has hypothesized an opposing consideration. The situation of anarchistic uncertainty can create a need to "escape from freedom" (1941). Thus, a balance between safety and risk (or uncertainty) would seem to be an optimal desideratum for human fulfillment.

TENSION AND RELAXATION. A most enlightening observation about play is that is explodes the notion that work (as disciplined exertion of body or mind or both) is a curse because it may be hard and exhausting. Playing may involve extreme exertion of the entire organism. Curiously, it maintains its appeal despite—and maybe because of—the challenge.

Work can certainly be burdensome and tiring. But this is not necessarily due to the associated physical or mental expenditure. Rather, it may be due to the attitudes (often unexamined) with which work is approached. When it is regarded as the exercise of one's chosen activity, as one of the things with which one wants to occupy oneself, work can hardly be claimed to be a heavy burden—even though it may be exhausting. For the performance of a self-chosen task has the earmarks of play rather than of work. It follows then, once more, that man lives essentially in a symbolic world—a world of meaning rather than objective fact.

When work is not demanding, when it becomes repetitive and dull, as on the modern assembly line, the whole object of workers may be focused on higher pay for only so long. Then the objective becomes getting out. "Thirty and out" has become the autoworkers' goal to escape the bitter dehumanizing effects of work that is neither challenging nor meaningful.

THE GAME OF LIFE. George Herbert Mead (1955) has analyzed social development in terms of play and the game. He suggests that the child's imaginative play is his "work" of self-becoming: he takes on the role of others as they react to him. This objectification of self is the essential process of reflective activity required for selfhood. When the child plays "doctor," he takes the attitude that a grown-up has toward him as a child going to the doctor. Thus he "sees" himself in one little part by this seeming play activity.

When the child becomes old enough to play in a game, he further develops his ability to hold the attitudes that others have toward him. To play first base, one has to be able to take the attitude of every other player on the field toward oneself as first baseman. Larger social participation is the natural development of such game-development of roles. Playing one's role (first baseman) in the game (baseball) is the means for organizing concurrent sets of social roles and attitudes in which one takes one's own place. This "play" and "game" activity in children throughout all cultures is a preparation of the person for social participation in the adult culture.

Play as a Model for Life

"What then is the right way of living?" asked Plato in the *Laws* (vii, 796), and he answered, "Life must be lived as play, playing certain games, making sacrifices, singing and dancing, and then a man will be able to propitiate the gods."* It may be ancient wisdom, but is it not a little cheap to regard all human activity as play?

* No doubt "making sacrifices" refers here only to the fact that much of the ancient Greeks' play was carried out on ritualistic occasions.

It would be cheap if one considered play merely as pastime, but Plato is known to have considered that "play and seriousness are sisters." Play need not be frivolous. Its psychological characteristics enumerated above do not preclude it from being serious and involving great effort, sometimes even anxiety. Nor does the seriousness of an endeavor preclude enjoyment.

Without trivializing the business of living, it is both possible and advantageous to view it not only according to the *structure* but the *spirit* of game playing; that is, in terms of the attitudes underlying play in its purest creative and recreative sense. Dumazedier's statement about leisure fully applies to play:

> The prime condition of leisure is the search for a state of contentment; it is enough to say "That interests me." This state can consist in the denial of all tension, study, or concentration; but it can just as well consist in voluntary effort or even in the deferment of gratification. Whether the avocation involves battling against the elements, against a competitor, or against oneself, the effort of perfecting one's performance or one's wisdom can be greater than that spent on one's regular occupation and may even approach the intensity of religious discipline. But it is an effort and a discipline that is chosen voluntarily, in the expectation of an enjoyment that is disinterested (1968, p. 251).

The last sentence vividly expresses the significant parallel that can be drawn between leisure and life. Both can be regarded as an effort and a discipline, chosen freely in the pursuit of disinterested enjoyment and, in the last analysis, in pursuit of the good life along the most direct route.

WORK AND LEISURE: POTENTIALLY IDENTICAL.   It would seem, however, that the absence of choice precludes the possibility of modeling life after play or leisure. Life is not optional; it is imposed upon us. We are, as Heidegger put it, "thrown" into existence. Biologically, all this is true. However, what counts here is not man's biologically determined state but his symbolic capacity. Symbolically—that is, from the point of view of how we think about life, how we value it, and what attitude we take toward it—existence is optional. Biological determinism is but the condition for man's option to fashion his personal existence in such a way as to either affirm and espouse or deny and undergo life. This is the adult's primary option, and he has no choice but to exert it—though many seem to do so by default.

It is precisely upon this similarity between life and play that Adler (1970) bases his proposition that the distinction between work and leisure can be obliterated by virtue of the subjective attitude with which one envisages and approaches each. If one chooses work that is performed out of interest—that is, for its intrinsic rewards rather than for its subsistence value—then the larger part of one's life (commonly taken up by subsistence work) is actually spent in leisure. The same applies if, short of choosing one's subsistence duties, one succeeds in viewing them as activities one wants to perform because of the challenge, the humanitarian value, even the self-disciplinary opportunity, or, in some way, the symbolic rather than the utilitarian meaning of the activity. This redefinition of work and attendant reorganization of attitudes is possible for the symbolic animal, capable of freeing himself from the concrete stimulus situation and its one-way meaning.

REALITY: INTERPRETATION AND ILLUSION.   But what about the condition of unreality or detachment, the "as if" quality of play that was mentioned above as perhaps its most characteristic element? If life itself is not to be regarded as "real," then what is? On the surface, this is a much tougher objection than the question of the freedom to engage or not to engage in play, to affirm or to negate life. The question is tougher, at least, in the framework of Western thought. Not so, however, in Eastern thought, especially in Zen Buddhism, in which the unreality of the world is expressed in one of its most basic concepts, *maya,* an illusion through which reality is interpreted to man by his social institutions. "The *maya* or unreality lies not in the physical world but in the concepts or thought forms by which it is described . . . *maya* refers to social institutions—to language and logic and their constructs—and *to the way in which they modify our feeling of the world*" (Watts, 1961, p. 47; italics added). A concise and clear description of the concept is offered by Wood, who also relates it very aptly to contemporary Western thought.

> An old Hindu, and especially Vedantic teaching, referring to the creation of all manifest things, of both the mind and the body, from ignorance (avidya), through the two processes of (1) veiling (avarana) the reality, and then (2) building on the basis of the veiling by projection (vikshepa). The product—the whole world of body and mind—is then called a maya. The word maya is often translated "illusion" which is not to be confused with "delusion."* Strictly, in modern terms, it seems very closely related to the idea of relativity or relative truth, which is never *really* correct (1962, p. 80).

This idea of the perceptual unreality of life has traditionally been profoundly alien to the Western mind. Even now, despite intellectual knowledge to the contrary, Western man still clings to a "realistic" outlook based on phenomenologically correct but ontologically unfounded beliefs; for example, that matter is solid, that sense observation yields incontrovertible facts, that facts are somehow intrinsically true, and that what is not amenable to sense observation is intrinsically "not there." This lingering belief in objectivity—not in the limited sense of consensus, sincerity, or

---

* "Illusion" is here taken in the sense of a misperception that is a function of normal conditions; for example, optical illusion, existential-phenomenological illusion: time seems longer when waiting eagerly. Conversely, "delusion" is taken in the pathological (clinical) sense; for example, delusions of grandeur or of persecution.

fairness but in the absolute (and absolutely fallacious) sense that so-called objective knowledge offers undistorted access to the intrinsic nature of things—is perhaps the most visible case of Western man's illusion about his world.

However, as some of the insights of modern theoretical physics that are pertinent to the subject become part of general education and as phenomenology supersedes the earlier physicalism in psychology, the educated citizen of the West moves—uneasily indeed—toward a world view devoid of the earlier comfortable (if unexamined) beliefs in the solidity, the permanence, and the certitude of things that were implicit in the materialistic nineteenth-century view of the universe. The educated person becomes aware of the fluidity, the plasticity, the open-endedness, and, indeed, the mystery of the universe he inhabits. At the same time, it begins to dawn upon Western man that, contrary to his intellectual forbears of the last two or three centuries, to whom everything seemed clear, structured, and as determined as clockwork, he is at liberty to interpret "reality" in alternate ways and to choose the interpretation most meaningful to him without hampering his thinking by "hard" facts and "final" explanations.

It is from this emerging point of view, intimated more convincingly by theoretical physics than by any other source of knowledge, that the possibility of conducting life according to the model of play makes sense; that is, *freely* (the strictures of our daily physical, social, and economic life do not preclude the attitudinal freedom here referred to); *gratuitously* (devoid of ulterior motives); with *detachment from "reality"*; and *in pursuit of contentment*. In a world in which the crucial variables (death, illness, accidents, and other blows) may strike anytime; in which the blessings of love, wealth, and reputation carry no guarantee; in which truth, beauty, and virtue are matters of controversy; and in which meanings and values have to be supplied by the individual himself—in a world of this sort is it farfetched or irresponsible to envisage and engage in life in the "as if" manner of play, performed according to the proper rules?

A genuinely playful, detached approach to life would have the further advantage of freeing man from the crushing burden of wanting to control the uncontrollable—life itself—and its countless, unpredictable, protean manifestations. In such an approach—as in play—winning and losing do not mean intrinsic gain or loss. For even he who loses a game is the richer for having played it, since the loss cannot undo the delight gained in playfully doing what he wants. Thus viewed, it becomes clear that what counts is not who the winner is but how the game is played.

8 Interpersonal Creativity

There is no question but that man is the social animal par excellence—social not in the sense that his feelings and behavior toward his fellowmen are always cooperative, constructive, or altruistic but in the sense that man typically engages in more diverse relationships with his congeners than members of any other species do. This chapter and the following deal with the most satisfying, most joyful of these relationships—with those whose affective nature qualifies them as manifestations of love.

If love is the attractive topic of this chapter, one might ask why it is not clearly announced in the title. For one reason, the word is usually taken in too narrow a sense, evoking only the romantic type, while this chapter deals with a variety of affective involvements. Second, and more significantly, an important fact needs to be emphasized: love, especially in the sense of care and concern, represents the highest and most fertile expression of creativity: "Love signifies the creation of personality" (Kagawa, 1929, p. 109). The prevailing underestimation of this kind of creative power has to do in some measure—probably much greater than we realize—with our failure to label as creative such personal expressions as kindness, concern, warm regard, good will, patience, affection, and love. Yet what more effectively achieves constructive and beautiful change in people?

Correct labeling plays an important role in the quality and effectiveness of our existence, as Dollard, Auld, and White (1953) have shown with respect to clinical problems. For instance, we all know that activities labeled as "leisure"—strenuous though they may be—are experienced as relaxing and desirable, while certain activities that have all the earmarks of pastimes are experienced as work if they are thus labeled. Hence the importance of highlighting the joyfully creative capacity of love.

Interanimation: Building Persons

We all tend to give priority to those behaviors that we see as most enhancing. If we fail to see the full measure of enhancement of certain actions, we usually fail to allocate them a high priority in the ordering of our daily pursuits. Everybody values creativity; that is, every healthy and well-functioning person likes to think of himself as creative and feels enhanced when he is recognized as such. Unfortunately, our concept of creativity is usually limited to the realm of things, especially of things for which there is no compelling need—decorative objects, clever hobbies, practical ideas, do-it-yourself projects, and the like. All of these are useful and enjoyable enough, but fall short of tapping the most precious and powerful expressions of man's creativity. The channeling of so wondrous a power along such diminutive lines cheats both the creative agent and his countless potential beneficiaries of the joy that flows from building, enlivening, repairing, and beautifying not just things but persons.

One of the most expressive words ever put together to capture the essence of this capacity to joyfully affect others, and with mutual benefit, was coined by John Donne: *interanimation.* With *anima* (meaning life, soul, spirit) as its core, flanked by a suffix that denotes action and a prefix that lends reciprocity, the word captures precisely that which stands out among the numerous, often nebulous properties common to the experience of love; namely, its capacity to awaken and vivify, to arouse from a state of inert potentiality to a state of enlivening actuality that emotionally, spiritually, and even physically enhances the parties involved.

Remarkably consonant with the idea of interanimation is May's observation (1969, pp. 313–14) that love generates being by enriching one's sense of participation and belongingness, heightening his powers of constructive imagination, and developing his latent affective sources. Love does all this first by stimulating, then by deepening and strengthening the capacity to give and take and thereby to merge creatively with others.

When affective exchange—companionship, friendship, and other forms of love—is recognized as an expression of creativity, instead of a merely existential frill, people will tend to engage in such exchange with more zest and mutual reward.

The Nurturing Staple

There is a growing realization of the value of two basic attributes of love (in the sense of care and concern). One of these attributes is its "staple" nature, its nurturing quality. It is essential yet commonplace—like bread, salt, or milk, for which there is a steady need—something that is (or ought to be) close at hand in one form or another and whose absence, if prolonged, constitutes real, noticeable deprivation. The other attribute is the healing and rehabilitating power of love. So essential is this attribute that it is difficult for a mature, healthy personhood to develop in the absence of joyful identification with others who care. From these significant others, the individual selectively draws the features of his uniquely personal gestalt.

Fortunately, some measure of love is part of the fabric of all but the most hapless lives. In fact, it is so intrinsic to ordinary human experience that some of its best brands may go unrecognized by the beneficiary because of their inconspicuous everyday character. Thus, much of love's goodness may be lost on those to whom it comes in a steady flow and who tend, therefore, to take customary blessings for granted (in accordance with the law of adaptation and its unavoidably dulling effect upon experience). Such persons may not realize the vital role of love in the economy of their lives until they have lost it.

Acquiring Academic Respectability

Before it rose to its present status, the *concept* of love went through some lean years, obliterated as it was by this century's heady "discovery" of sex. Around mid-century, at the height of the reign of reductionism in academic psychology and of psychoanalysis on the popular scene, love was stripped of its specificity and reduced to a sublimated derivative of sex: a cultural by-product of a biological function. The whole vocabulary of love was carefully shunned in psychological circles because a mechanistic ideology had imposed a taboo on referring to the subject by name (Bloom, 1967).

Some readers may feel that no such prohibition ever came to their attention, but the fact that the taboo remained unspoken was precisely one of the reasons for its effectiveness. Adams remarks in his well-documented chapter in *Love Today*: "A dominant ideology is embodied not only in the abstract formulations of learned authorities but also in the everyday life of the members of the society. . . . For example, a learned and dignified treatise reducing all of man's impulses or thoughts to the basic drives of hunger, sex, dominance, etc., is congruent with much cruder expressions of the same belief in everyday life, such as a sneering laugh, or, in a heartier vein, a loud guffaw. . . ." (1972, p. 35). A familiar case of the effectiveness of unspoken taboos can be found in families where nothing whatsoever having to do with sex is ever brought up for comment, question, or discussion. Where the topic of love was concerned, this same climate of deadly silence prevailed in academic psychology little more than a decade ago.

Love could be referred to only by esoteric abstractions such as cathexis, identification, narcissism, symbiotic attachment, oral or anal eroticism, and genitality. The vocabulary of love, tenderness, affection, communion, ecstasy, longing, and happiness was shunned as naively sentimental, an attitude reminiscent of the introductory pages of Huxley's *Brave New World,* in which parenthood is presented, in some subtly inverted way, as obscene. To speak of love—by name—would have amounted to discrediting oneself as a tough-minded member of the academic community.

The first, in my experience, to plainly use the word *love* in a distinctly academic context was Carl Rogers. In one of his groundbreaking films on client-centered therapy (1952), he commented upon the change that had occurred in a client during the period of his interaction with her, adding that he attributed the progress to her "experience of being loved" by her counselor. From the comments I happened to overhear, I gathered that the effect of his explanation upon the audience was something of a shock. The term *transference* would have been acceptable, since it was a thoroughly aseptized, neutral term, but the use of the word *love*—in a serious, academic discourse was a practice that his listeners clearly did not support.

Considering the former status of love within American psychology, the bridgehead it has recently established on the field must be regarded as a momentous development. A detailed account of the rise of this subject from its underground past to its present standing would make a fascinating story that cannot, however, be offered within the compass of this book. For the epic leads through a variety of fields that ranges from pediatrics to, of all things, cosmology—the whole of it recently celebrated with a postage stamp! To lend some insight into the emergence of humanistic psychology as a whole, however, a token history of love's journey from obscurity to near eminence seems too essential to be completely overlooked.

Interestingly, that journey was not a planned and massively promoted event as was, for instance, the ecological movement. Love surfaced on the academic scene in essentially serendipitous ways; that is, in the margin of the pursuit of other endeavors. Researchers and scholars in a variety of fields, working on diverse topics, found themselves confronted time and again by situations that could not be explained according to existing empirical, logical, or quantifiable paradigms. At first gingerly and euphemistically, but gradually more boldly, academics began to advance the idea of love as a significant variable in the human economy. The creative power of love soon revealed itself with unsuspected vitality and universality to researchers in several fields.

INFANT CARE AND CHILDREARING. Probably the first to call professional attention to empirical evidence of the literally vital effect of love was pediatrician Margaret Ribble. In *The Rights of Infants* (1943)—which was a widely read book in the early forties—she reports on her work with institutionally raised children of whom a significant percentage developed *marasmus* (general physical decline) despite adequate physical and medical care and whose death rate was significantly higher than that of infants raised in homes. Ribble identified the problem as a severe lack of affective-social stimulation or, as she put it, "adequate mothering"— rocking, stroking, cuddling, and similar manifestations of care that parents tend to lavish on young children. In the typically understaffed institutions where the infants (foundlings and orphans) were boarded, this emotional nurturance was not provided.*

Ribble, however, attributed the infant's vulnerability to social-emotional deprivation to the unstable organization of the primary bodily functions in the early months of a child's existence (Watson, 1958, p. 224). Subsequent research has revealed, however, that her physiological explanation must be sharply separated from its psychological counterpart. Indeed, her assumption about the unstable physiological organization of the infant was forcefully challenged and successfully disproved by Pinneau (1950) and others and was soon totally discounted in pediatric circles.

But her insight into the importance of adequate mothering was never discredited. Rather, it was confirmed by a number of empirical studies (Rheingold, 1956; Bantam, 1950) and is now part of established thinking on the subject. To this day, Ribble's recognition of the importance of social-emotional nurturance is emphasized to the point of overgeneralization; for example, "An infant dies without love" (Otto, 1972, p. 9). In summary, as Kubie (Kubie and Ribble, 1945) aptly concluded, Ribble was right, but for the wrong reasons. Incidentally, my own interpretation of such unfortunate cases, confirmed by Kagan (1973, p. 1), is not as pessimistic or deterministic as that of many authors. The human being is so extraordinarily flexible, so basically oriented toward health and growth that past handicaps can be surmounted provided subsequent conditions offer the individual a wedge of opportunity to "catch up with himself" in the damaged areas.

In retrospect, it is strange that Ribble seemed to find it necessary to call upon a shaky physiological explanation to buttress her remarkably accurate insight into the emotional dynamics of infancy. Such a detour is a graphic example of the reluctance with which professional and academic circles approached the function of love in the human economy. It brings to mind Maslow's comment about one of Ribble's contemporaries, anthropologist Ruth Benedict, who revealed similar wary caution toward using the vocabulary of affect to explain some of her observations. Maslow reports that while he was studying under her, "she kept struggling with words which she did not dare to say in public in her capacity as a

---

* For the benefit of the reader who feels distressed at this state of affairs, I should add that, largely as a result of the public's response to Ribble's book, children's hospitals started programs using volunteers to supplement the children's physical care with social-emotional stimulation.

scientist, because they were . . . involved rather than cool, words that could be said over a martini but not in print" (1971, p. 200). Ribble, too, must have sensed that explanations that hinged solely upon the role of love would probably be dismissed as purely sentimental—as the projections of "a feminine mind lacking intellectual toughness."

SOCIAL SCIENCE AND PHILOSOPHY. Both terms here refer to a wide variety of writings that transcend the categories of social science and philosophy in the narrow, academic sense. These writings constitute major testimonies from authors who have attained eminence in their respective fields of endeavor and who, at the height of their careers, speak from the dual perspective of scholars and observers of the human condition.

Leading the procession of these contributions is existential philosophy and its typical, viscerally intense interest in such humanly relevant matters as freedom, love, commitment, and death. Among the authors who identified love as the crucial dimension of human existence were Kierkegaard (*Works of Love,* 1946), Marcel (*Du refus à l'invocation,* 1950), Heidegger (*Being and Time,* 1962), and especially philosopher-theologian Buber (1958) with his notion of I and Thou. In *I and Thou,* he describes the difference between the attitude man has (or ought to have) toward other persons and toward things. These attitudes represent the basic matrices of human activity: the world of persons and the world of objects. The former is a world of *community* in which the I approaches, meets, or encounters the other as a Thou and entertains *with* him a dialectically meaningful relationship, one changing the other. The It, on the other hand, is a world of *organization* and manipulation; it involves only one center of consciousness, the I, which appropriates, handles, and acts *upon* the It according to a strictly unilateral agent-to-object, utilitarian, and even exploitive model of behavior.

From the late fifties on, peaks of interest in the subject of love were aroused recurrently by widely read books by psychologists (Fromm, 1956; May, 1969), psychiatrists (Menninger, 1951), sociologists (Sorokin, 1950, 1954, 1959), anthropologists (Montagu, 1953), theologians (D'Arcy, 1947; Lepp, 1963), and men of letters (C. S. Lewis, 1960) dealing with the subject of love in a realistic, unsentimental, and well-documented manner. Most widely known among these works are, no doubt, Fromm's *The Art of Loving* (1956) and May's *Love and Will* (1969). The latter work courageously focuses upon two concepts that until very recently were anathema in academic psychology. For both love and will were regarded as pure epiphenomena, that is, as by-products of neural processes, devoid of reality or efficacy. Love was thought of as an illusion arising from idealistic notions about sex being accompanied (and redeemed) by some lofty intangible called love; and will was seen as a self-aggrandizing interpretation of man as having a say in his behavior and destiny.

Without making it the central topic of their writings, countless other modern and contemporary authorities were instrumental in revealing the reality and centrality of love in human existence: Bertrand Russell (1967), Loren Eiseley (1970), René Dubos (1962), Dietrich Bonhoeffer (1967), and Teilhard de Chardin (1965), the scientist-philosopher who, in his renowned *The Phenomenon of Man,* concludes that the ultimate evolution of man will be marked by the fullest development of his capacity for awareness and his potential for love.

CLINICAL PSYCHOLOGY.   Buber's I-Thou model of human interaction immediately calls to mind Rogers's concept of the person-to-person relationship that pervades his work as a whole and that he implemented on a remarkably consistent basis in his approach to counseling and therapy. Although Buber's concept was evolved long before Rogers articulated his almost identical concept, Rogers arrived at his conclusion independently and without knowledge of Buber's work.* Indeed, Rogers developed his paradigm of constructive human relations inductively from his observations of client-counselor interaction. Conversely, Buber's notion of the same type of relationship was evolved in a clearly deductive manner, associated as it was with the relation between God and man.

The effect upon clinical psychology as a whole of Rogers's determined emphasis upon the affective rather than the cognitive economy of the client eventually resulted in a radical substitution of a relationship-centered approach to therapy for the earlier, insight-centered approaches. His discovery of the healing and growth-releasing properties of positive affect over the intellectually clarifying powers of interpretation and explanation was soon confirmed by others and consolidated into a powerful trend.

> The curative power of love is also increasingly emphasized by the recent studies in psychiatry. The investigations of K. E. Apple, F. E. Fiedler, C. Rogers, V. E. Frankl, H. J. Eysenck, G. W. Allport, R. Assaglioli, E. Straus, and other[s] . . . show that the *main* curative agent in the treatment of mental disorders is not so much the specific technique used by various schools of psychiatry as the establishment of the rapport of *empathy,* sympathy, kindness and mutual trust between the patient and the therapist and the placing of the patient in a social climate free from inner and interhuman conflicts (Sorokin, 1959, p. 8; Sorokin's emphasis).

At present, it would be hard to find a single brand of psychotherapy that does not incorporate as a central part of its approach the notion of

---

* In 1950, two other foreign postgraduates, Dr. Walter Smet and Peter Securius, and I introduced Buber's work (which in Europe was already at the height of its fame) to Rogers who, at the time, had not heard of it. Interestingly, and despite the excellence of the translation, Rogers's comments on *I and Thou* revealed that he did not at first recognize his own thinking underneath Buber's typically solemn and verbose German style.

love; that is, of love as positive affect and warm respect for the client's residual capacity to judge and to initiate and for his nascent forces of self-rehabilitation that become operative in a maturely satisfying relationship.

COMPARATIVE PSYCHOLOGY AND ETHOLOGY. Even strictly experimental psychology joined in to usher the subject of love to center field—to wit, Harlow's celebrated work on the affective behavior of primates. His widely known experiments show the preference of young chimpanzees for the "cloth mother" over the "wire mother" and the differential effects of such affective experiences on the animal's further social development.

In connection with my earlier reference to the hidden taboo on the vocabulary of love, the appealing title, *Learning to Love* (1971), under which Harlow chose to report his observations on animals offers an almost amusing example of changing academic fashion. Also instrumental in promoting the topic of love are the observations and vivid pictures by Jane van Lawick-Goodall and her photographer husband of the humanlike affective behavior of wild chimpanzees.

Curiously, while the climate of the 1940s did not allow Benedict and Ribble to use the word *love* in a human context, the pendulum has since swung so far in the opposite direction that the term is now being used even in the fondly metaphorical sense of the pet lover's language. This is a charming but, strictly speaking, misleading use of a term that refers to a spectrum of affective phenomena so extraordinarily varied that it must be regarded as uniquely human; for example, the numerous varieties of love differentiated by Orlinsky (1972) and the even more numerous forms or phrases recognized by Bloom (1967) in his description of love as a lifelong phenomenon. The use of the term *love* to refer to animal affectivity—a very real phenomenon reflecting the rudiments of human affectivity and eminently worthy of study—is an interesting case of reverse reductionism.

Forms of Love

What the word *love* readily brings to mind is one particular type of love: the celebrated romantic type involving partners of opposite sex and typically blossoming in the spring of life. Because eros, or romantic love, is the form of love most commonly known and most intensely pursued, it is here the object of a chapter all its own. The forms of love, however, can be as varied as the individuals involved. Nevertheless, patterns are discernible within this diversity.

Orlinsky (1972) and Bloom (1967), in fact, have matched particular types of love with the needs of each stage of life. In their respective studies, Orlinsky distinguishes eight and Bloom seventeen phases of life (see Table 8–1), which they connect with corresponding modalities of love. The outcome of their work reveals an affective spectrum that potentially covers a lifetime. Not every individual, of course, has the good fortune to encounter each variety of this affective range. But he potentially qualifies, in many ways, for either receiving, giving, or exchanging this vital ingredient of existence. Missing out, then, on one or more of these forms does not mean missing out on love altogether.

More widely known than the preceding more or less academic differentiations of the love spectrum are the classical types of love identified by the ancient Greeks: *eros,* or romantic love; *philia,* or friendship; and *agape,* which originally designated the love of God for mankind but now commonly refers to humanitarian concern for mankind as a whole. Less celebrated but no less vital is parental love and its filial counterpart. Another variety of affective experience that certain authors regard as irreducible to any other form is companionship: a mild, unselective, undemanding, mutually tolerant enjoyment of human fellowship. A discussion of the most commonly recognized forms of affective engagement other than romantic love (the object of the next chapter) follows.

PARENTAL LOVE: THE NEED TO BE NEEDED.   Most forms of loving are reciprocal: the parties involved validate their relationship with feelings that are essentially similar. Parental love, by contrast, is perhaps the only form that endures without expectation of equal return. Parents can offer seemingly limitless affection and care and, ideally, respect for the child, while the latter responds with feelings that go through several phases: from dependency and unquestioned confidence through relative withdrawal, if not rejection, toward warm appreciation and realistic esteem, culminating ideally in a reciprocation of care and concern. Filial love seems to be a process whose stages were aptly tagged in an epigram attributed to Mark Twain: at seven years of age the child believes Daddy knows everything; at fourteen, he knows nothing; at twenty-one, it's amazing how much the old man has learned.

Rooted as it is in a biologically determined tendency to help the young and to cherish them, parental love is a humble, down-to-earth yet sublime form of attachment geared mainly to protection and service. Nevertheless, it is a relationship that is recognized as seminal with respect to future intimate relationships. Individuals whose childhood has lacked this sort of affective bond (either with natural or adoptive parents or with effective substitutes) are believed to be seriously handicapped as far as sustaining deeply satisfying relationships in adulthood. On the whole, this belief, founded upon inference (not, of course, upon experiment), seems to be sadly valid. Yet the effects of such deprivation are not absolutely fatal and irreversible. Indeed, if the individual can feel challenged to overcome them, his handicaps can constitute a powerful stimulus to extraordinary performance.

TABLE 8–1

LIFE SPAN DEVELOPMENTAL FRAMEWORK AND CORRESPONDING DEVELOPMENTAL STAGES OF LOVE*

Biological/Social Problems (developmentally serial)	Developmental Foci: The focal relationship of properties of actor systems (inputs, outputs, and persisting structures) and psychosocial spheres (individual, micro-, and macro-social)	Forms of Love (developmentally cumulative)
0. [Pregnancy—a problem for others. Cf. stage 6]	[Prenatal equilibrium]	[A form of love for others. Cf. stage 6]
1. Birth and Survival	Physiological inputs into the proto-personality of ego	Hedonic feelings
2. Self-differentiation	Physiological and psychological outputs from the proto-personality of ego	Affection (for sentient being) Attachment (for non-sentient beings)
3. Age/Sex Differentiation and Self-Identity	Emergence of the personality of ego through the equilibrium of affective investments	Romantic-Idealism
4. Education (formal and informal)	Person's increasing input into dyadic or proto-primary group relations	Reciprocal Friendship and/or Nonreciprocal Modeling
5. Procreativity and/or Creativity	Person's increasing involvement in the output from the dyadic or proto-primary group relations	Orgastic Love and/or Sublimations
6. Marriage and Progeny, and/or Products	Emergence of a primary group through the equilibrium of affective investments and interpersonal relationships (creating a persisting micro-social structure)	Contractual or Married Love, and/or Sublimations

* Bloom defines love as *"the patterned affective investments* between the loving person, or persons, other sentient beings, things, and abstractions. The *affect is positive or favorable;* the investment process *involves real or symbolic interaction* and possible mutual enhancement; and the *pattern is a social structure* based on a common definition-and-evaluation-of-the-situation between the loving persons" (1967, p. 248; italics added). He concedes that some of the forms of love that he distinguishes may at first surprise the reader, but contends that each contains the conceptual properties that, in his analysis of love, are regarded as basic. Taken from "Toward a Developmental Concept of Love," *Journal of Human Relations* 15, no. 2 (1967): 249–50.

TABLE 8–1 continued

Biological/Social Problems (developmentally serial)	Developmental Foci: The focal relationship of properties of actor systems (inputs, outputs, and persisting structures) and psychosocial spheres (individual, micro-, and macro-social)	Forms of Love (developmentally cumulative)
7. Occupation and life in society	Contributions (made by individual-as-involved-in-micro-social group) to input of the macro-social system	Symbolic Loves: The Virtues (or the Religious-Moral Virtues)
8. Assumption of Power and/or Death of ego's Parent generation	Contributions to the outputs of the macro-social system	Symbolic Loves: The Powers
9. "Atman Experience"	Emergence of an "I-Eternal Thou" total experience. . . .	Mystic Love
10. "Climacterics"	Contraction from highpoint of macro-social system output contributions, but with the appreciation for what ego created/contributed in the past as being applicable to present and future	Respect Love (Filial Piety)
11. Contraction from occupational roles or equivalent	Contractions from making inputs into a macro-social system, but with the respect for what ego contributed in the past for its own sake	Experience Love or Wisdom
12. Development of grandparent and/or patron role	Emergence of indirect micro-social membership through affective investments and interpersonal relations with others as main actors	Romantic-Immortality Love
13. Conservation of Resources	Ego decreases his range of micro-social output contributions	Love of the Familiar (conservation love)
14. Preservation of Resources	Ego decreases his contributions into primary groups and focuses only on the most important of these groups	Integrity Love (putting into order)

TABLE 8–1 continued

Biological/Social Problems (developmentally serial)	Developmental Foci: The focal relationship of properties of actor systems (inputs, outputs, and persisting structures) and psychosocial spheres (individual, micro-, and macro-social)	Forms of Love (developmentally cumulative)
15. Death of spouse, friend, relative, significant other	Reemergence of the individual through the equilibrium of symbolic affective investments (toward deceased objects)	Memory Love
16. Contraction of the Personality System	Ego's increasing dependence on others for making psychological and physiological outputs on his own behalf	Appreciation Love
17. Contraction of the Physiological System	Ego's increasing dependence on others for providing physiological and psychological inputs on his own behalf	Existential Love
18. [Death] cf. stage 8	[Death as final equilibrium for ego and as a temporary disequilibrium for others. This equilibrium is controlled by factors external to deceased ego—physiological-chemical factors—and to others related to ego—social-cultural factors.]	[cf. stage 8]

COMPANIONSHIP. The caring that typifies companionship, or comradeship, is mild and casual, tolerant, and undemanding. Though companionship is loosely referred to as friendship, the two are not synonymous. It is true, however, that "friendship" has grown wildly inflationary in contemporary society and has gradually assumed a more casual form. This should not be taken to mean that our contemporaries are less appreciative of the seasoned and comforting type of relationship that is friendship but that the conditions of life—the extreme physical and social mobility characteristic of technologically advanced cultures—are not conducive to the growth of such deep and lasting associations between essentially independent parties.

Like parental and filial love, companionship is a plain, everyday sort of affective tie but one that provides welcome lubrication to social contacts and proves remarkably sustaining. Were it not for these humbler kinds of love, we would probably never ascend to the peaks of eros, philia, and agape. Also, since we cannot maintain ourselves for a very long time in the rarefied air peaks, we would have nothing to fall back on. Fortunately, companionship, that comfortable all-purpose relationship with our fellowmen, offers plenty to fall back on that is affectively satisfying, obtained at little cost, and wears well. The social-emotional gratification derived from casual good fellowship with a wide variety of people may be commonplace, but, like a loaf of bread, it is the mainstay of many affective diets.

It appears that even a well-functioning adult cannot remain normal in prolonged conditions of social deprivation. Common sense testifies to this, and research confirms it. A vast amount of literature deals with experiments on social deprivation (Haythorn and Altman, 1967; Mullin, 1960; Nardini, 1962; Rohrer, 1961). Some of it deals with animals, some with adult volunteers; much of the latter has been conducted in relation to the NASA programs. The conclusions derived from these experiments unanimously substantiate the tenet that severe sensory deprivation and social isolation (affective deprivation) result in psychological deterioration. These findings are further confirmed by diaries and other testimonials from explorers or veterans of otherwise lonely ventures. Whatever it is that we call "mind" atrophies when severed from human contact.

The major condition for the development of companionship is physical proximity. Therefore, classmates, roommates, teammates, job mates, neighbors, colleagues, and the like are the raw materials for this easily tied, easily untied relationship. Unimposing and unpretentious though it is, companionship is of great social signifiance. Its unselective, non-exclusive, casual, and tolerant properties seem destined to play an increasingly integrative role in a densely populated community in need of truly egalitarian, mutually appreciative, and accepting attitudes.

Like eros and parental love, companionship is biologically determined. To see this, we must broaden the concept of biology to encompass not only *survival* of individuals or species but also *development* of their particular nature; that is, in the case of man, his intellectual, ethical, esthetic, technological, and social potential. Even after childhood, man could hardly actualize himself as a person without considerable contact with numerous and varied people and without countless—perhaps minimal, often subliminal—give-and-take transactions provided by companionship.

FRIENDSHIP. Friendship is here taken in the classical sense, referring to a deeply meaningful bond, not a casual acquaintanceship. It is a warmly personal relationship rooted in a commonality of significant values and interests and, at least at some phase of its history, of shared time or activities. It is a relationship marked by an exceptional degree of authenticity and loyalty, combined with a high respect for each other's individuality and freedom and enjoyment of each other's presence. Usually it is a durable relationship that spans a sizeable portion of one's existence. The friends' delight in each other is seldom erotic in nature; seldom, that is, at least since antiquity, when friendship commonly involved a culturally sanctioned erotic element (exemplified by the friendship between Socrates and Alcibiades, and Alexander and Haipheston).

Friendship was once confined to partners of the same gender; for example, the biographically celebrated cases of Goethe and Schiller, Emerson and Thoreau, Roosevelt and Hopkins, and Stein and Toklas. But now that the overall relations between the sexes are undergoing marked change, this gender-determined feature is on the wane and seems destined to disappear. Whether friendship flourishes best between partners of the same or of different genders—or whether gender is a significant variable—the future, perhaps the near future, will tell. This is indeed the first period in history to provide the conditions for friendship between the sexes to develop freely without fear of social disapproval or biological consequence.

An Evolved Relationship. Friendship may be less exhilarating than romantic love and is definitely less easy to come by than companionship. But it is a far more evolved relationship than these, both ontogenetically and phylogenetically; that is, from both the point of view of individual development and evolution of the species. But what is meant by "more evolved"?

Where growth and personhood are concerned, "more evolved" always implies more fully actualized, more differentiated, more autonomous; hence, less determined by external circumstances—genetic or cultural— more reflective and, therefore, more integrated with the total self. Unlike romantic love, friendship is not a matter of glandular pressure enhanced by cultural enticement. Nature, that is, biology, does not lure us into friendship the way it lures us into romantic love. Nor is friendship a necessity, as is parental care, human fellowship or companionship. Man can survive and adequately develop without the kind of intimately personal relationship that is friendship. But he is then missing out on something very precious.

Friendship is wonderfully free from side effects. It does not tend to turn into a one-way (or even a two-way) possessiveness, symbolic enslavement, or subtle exploitation as romantic love is apt to—or was apt to before marriage became genuinely optional for both male and female. Nor does friendship suffer from the torment of jealousy, for it does not aim to monopolize. Granted, this type of affective relationship is limited to small circles—the most celebrated instances of it consisting of only two parties.

Why is friendship thus limited? First, the chances of meeting persons that mesh with the self on the level of reality—as distinct from illusion or perception—and that offer an *authentic encounter* rather than a *role relationship* are not abundant in our society. Second, for a relationship to be "tested" for comfortable and durable wear and for it to consolidate into friendship, it must extend over a suitable length of time. Third, since friendship is an active sharing, not some fond remembering or exaltation of a brief encounter, it requires—to stay alive and productive or, if you prefer, creative—a certain continuity or maintenance, hence a certain investment of time and effort.

More than any other affective relationship, friendship is an expression of the self and the principle of individuality. It rests not on body magnetism, random proximity, or interlocking roles but on affinities of the "self-structures": configurations of values, interests, capacities, and attitudes that form the core of personality. The uniqueness of the person, then, is the foundation of friendship.

Precious Yet Gratuitous.   Friendship, then, is truly a matter of choice, hence a genuine expression of self. Because it is so completely gratuitous, so luxuriously free from biological and social pressures, friendship can afford to be highly selective. Indeed, while we are our brother's keeper, we are not duty bound to be his friend. And although we have obligations and responsibilities toward our friends, they seldom exact a serious psychological toll. For instance, friendship does not require us to give up our most cherished existential pursuits or accept crippling compromises—as is the case with mature love between the sexes or with parental devotion—in order to maintain either or both our self-respect and the affective bond. Even companionship may, in some cases, make heavy (though illegitimate) demands upon one's privacy and prerogatives (see, for example, "The Web of Friendship" in Whyte's *The Organization Man*). In fact, rather than restricting the parties' freedom, the bond of friendship enhances it, for freedom, or at least the exercise of it, is a function of internal strength and confidence—both of which are augmented by friendship— and may derive further support from the manifold assets that are apt to flow from a loyal and secure bond.

The Transparent Bond. Friendship presupposes psychological equality. More precisely, to be friends people must consider each other as having equal worth regardless of economic, social, educational, and age inequalities. For the function that more than any other characterizes friendship is meaningful communication of views, hopes, concerns, joys, and sorrows, marked by an exceptional degree of genuineness. Rogers aptly conveys this particular quality of friendship when he speaks of "transparency." Transparency does not imply that friendship requires total communication, or scrutinizing of the parties' past and present experience as if they were each other's analyst. Either directly or indirectly, such a requirement might cause a measure of hardship to one or the other. For instance, loyalty to third parties may require a degree of reticence even between close friends—a limitation that is implicitly understood and respected by mature persons. While friends are deeply interested in and devoted to one another and while they are fully receptive to anything either one offers for sharing, they are not mutually inquisitive. This mindful and undemanding yet intimate character of friendship is one reason it is so eminently enjoyable.

In summary, what I refer to by transparency is *complete openness* rather than *complete coverage*. Whatever is said or remains unsaid between friends is free from those self-protective distortions, embellishments, and subtle calculations or deviations that tend to preside—not always inappropriately—over communications with people in general. Spontaneity combined with respect defines the boundaries. The clarity and unadorned simplicity of communication between friends inspired C. S. Lewis to one of his typically vivid images: "for eros, naked bodies; for philia, naked minds" (1960, p. 103).

AGAPE: TRANSCENDENT LOVE. This form of love is the most evolved expression of man's affective repertoire. Originally, the term was reserved for reference to the love of God. Through the ages, it has come to stand for an unconditional love of man for his fellowman—a rare but nevertheless real phenomenon. Agape is found in persons who have grasped in some way, not necessarily verbal, that spiritually the individual mode of being is an abstraction; that it is, in Augustine's words, "a center without a periphery," merging with all being to form a vast symbolic fabric, a "mystical body" in which each element affects and is affected by the whole, either raising or lowering its level of health, strength, and grace.

If the word *philanthropy* were not preempted, it would be quite appropriate as a definition of agape since its roots, *philia* and *anthropos*, mean love and man respectively. From the point of view of its usage, however, the word is clearly unsuitable. In our culture, philanthropy usually takes the form of organized, large-scale support, material or physical, administered by hired personnel and dispensed to people in a qualified state of need. On the affective and spiritual level, it tends to be sterile because it is usually void of personal involvement on the part of either giver or receiver.

Another difference between philanthropy and agape is that the former specializes, so to speak, in the care of the needy, the poor, and the weak—such is, indeed, its function and its greatness. Agape, however, sets no requirements nor does it necessarily aim at helping out in concrete ways, even though it often has this effect. Agape reaches out spontaneously, a welcoming hand to whoever is willing to grasp it. Agape can be compared to the Taoist notion of the Way of Life and is aptly symbolized by water, Lao-Tsu's favorite symbol of the Way: "Man at his best, like water,/ Serves as he goes along" (Bynner, 1944, p. 29). The same is true of agape.

Not a Hunger But a Fullness. Agape is entirely free from biological need and essentially independent of cultural determinants. Unlike eros, it is not a hunger but a fullness; unlike philia, it is not dependent on affinities of character, interests, and values; unlike companionship, it is not dependent upon the proximity of its objects. For it encompasses not only those immediately present but also those unknown, far away in space or time; those in the past toward whom it feels grateful; those in the future for whom it feels responsible. Toward all of these it feels compassion, realizing that all partake of the human condition.

Agape manifests itself as an even and durable but inconspicuous capacity for care and concern without desire for reciprocity, reward, or control. It is a welcoming, life-affirming attitude that does not imply naiveté. People capable of agape are not holy innocents; they recognize phoniness, deceit, and manipulation. They may be willing to die for their fellowman, but they are not willing to grant him his every wish. It is one of the characteristics of this kind of love that it resists, tactfully but firmly, whatever tends to lower the level of personal functioning. Agape, then, can say "no." It can speak hard truths, though it does so reluctantly and for the sake of something more valuable than the safeguarding of merely pleasant relations.

Nor does agape wear a pious face or affect sublime airs. On the contrary, elements of this love can be found in the most unlikely personalities. Thus, taking a couple of examples from fiction, McMurphy, the Dionysian rogue in Kesey's *One Flew Over the Cuckoo's Nest* revealed time and again a surprisingly keen strand of this type of love for his fellow inmates, especially for the weak, the rejected, and the fearful. His ultimate gesture of joining the "Chief" in the electroshock treatment is in keeping with the most celebrated cases of agape. So was the behavior of the humble, misshapen, and ostracized artist Rhayader in Paul Gallico's magnificent short story, "The Snow Goose." So also the native priest, Kumalo, in Alan Paton's *Cry, the Beloved Country.*

Agape, like its name, is a rather unfamiliar phenomenon. Man's potential for it has not been actualized on any scale worth boasting about. In its full-blown, clearly recognizable manifestations, it is in fact so rare that some people may wonder whether the name actually corresponds to anything real. Therefore, describing it makes one feel as if one were asking people to admire the emperor's new clothes.

Yet agape does exist. If you carefully scan your experience, direct or indirect, that is, gained either from personal observation or from reports, you are almost bound to glimpse instances of behavior that contain at least a strand of this self-transcendent form of love. History is studded with outstanding instances of it. We have Dorothea Dix, the nineteenth-century schoolteacher who was tirelessly instrumental in liberating the mentally ill from their incarcerated conditions, and in our own century, Dr. Dooley, the physician who conceived and implemented the idea of the ship *Hope,* the floating clinic for those in underdeveloped countries in need of medical attention. There is the luminous symbol of self-forgetful care for the poor of seventeenth-century France, St. Vincent de Paul; and closer to us in time, Florence Nightingale, the indomitable reformer of hospital care; Albert Schweitzer, the missionary-doctor of Lambaréné, and the frail but plucky Vinoba Bhave, Indian apostle of land reform who, under the singularly apt motto, "I will loot you with love" (*Time*, May 11, 1953), journeyed barefoot across his vast country, urging the landowners to share their property with the disinherited. And overarching all these is, of course, the figure of Christ, whom Jung identifies as the archetype of the transcendent "self" and whom true Christians revere as the supreme model of love.

Persons animated by this type of love are probably the happiest among men and the least exposed to neurosis because their concern, though emanating from self, is neither focused on nor confined to their own gratification in the affective exchange. They know that what matters is the active state—loving, not just being loved. As Anders Nygren puts it: "Eros recognizes value in its object—and loves it; agape loves and creates value in its object" (1969, p. 210).

Usually Subliminal, Sometimes Dramatic. Agape does not typically assume spectacular forms, although every period in history has its heroic harvest of this uniquely human behavior. One dramatic instance is the following, taken from Ernest Gordon's *Through the Valley of the Kwai*, a participant's account of a period in the lives of World War II POWs. Captured by the Japanese, the men were forced to work on the marathon construction (Operation Speedo) of the Burma Railroad, cutting hundreds of miles through the dense jungle of tropical southeast Asia. Among many others is the story of a POW whose name is not even recorded in Gordon's book, possibly to avoid the traumatic effect the story might have upon the relatives of the victim. To prevent the reawakening of old hostilities and prejudices, the scenario of this shockingly brutal case should be introduced by a few words about the circumstances under which it occurred. Admittedly, however, no circumstances could excuse such outrageous and fatal actions, whatever the orders under which the agent was operating.

Throughout the book the author, who was an engineer before the war and later became a chaplain at Princeton Theological Seminary, manages to depict the inferno of the Kwai without lapsing into bitterness or hostility toward the former enemy. Indeed, with understanding and forbearance for those who were, essentially, the instruments rather than the cause of the torture, he attempts to convey something of the inhuman conditions to which the Allied POWs were subjected by their Japanese guards. Of the latter he writes that they themselves were severely punished by their superiors for any lapse in their odious duties; hence they could not be expected to treat the prisoners with tolerance and understanding. The author presents the ignominious treatment of the POWs as part of the inherent horrors of war, not as characteristic of the Japanese alone.

> The day's work had ended; the tools were being counted. When the detail was about to be dismissed, the Japanese guard declared that a shovel was missing. He insisted someone had stolen it to sell to the Thais. He strode up and down in front of the men, ranting and denouncing them for their wickedness, their stupidity, and most unforgivable of all, their ingratitude to the Emperor.
>
> Screaming in broken English, he demanded that the guilty one step forward to take his punishment. No one moved. The guard's rage reached new heights of violence.
>
> "All die! All die!" he shrieked.
>
> To show that he meant what he said, he pulled back the bolt, put the rifle to his shoulder, and looked down the sights, ready to fire at the first man he saw at the end of them.
>
> At that moment, the Argyll [a Scotsman] stepped forward, stood stiffly to attention and said calmly, "I did it."
>
> The guard unleashed all his whipped-up hatred; he kicked the hapless prisoner and beat him with his fists. Still the Argyll stood rigidly at attention. The blood was streaming down his face, but he made no sound. His silence goaded the guard to an excess of rage. He seized his rifle by the barrel and lifted it high over his head. With a final howl he brought the butt down on the skull of the Argyll, who sank limply to the ground and did not move. Although it was perfectly evident that he was dead, the guard continued to beat him and stopped only when exhausted.
>
> The men of the work detail picked up their comrade's body, shouldered their tools, and marched back to camp. When the tools were counted again, at the guardhouse, no shovel was missing (1962, pp. 104–05).

Such events stand tall on their own; no further commentary seems necessary. Yet quite a few people are unimpressed, indeed, distinctly critical of such cases. They reason that the life of the victim may have been of greater value to humanity than that of the men for whom he sacrificed it. This speculation is quite possibly valid but misses the point—man's capacity for love and the clear manifestation of this capacity. In certain cases, such manifestations may quite possibly go unnoticed, but that again is part of their meaning. Self-sacrifice is a supreme gamble, not a bargain. It may go unnoticed by the human community; then again, it may resound through the generations, edifying and inspiring some among us to a transcendence of self that needn't be total but needs to be kept alive.

True, few of us would genuinely *wish* for an opportunity such as that accepted by the anonymous POW. But *wishing* for an occasion to prove one's devotion to mankind and being *willing* to seize the occasion should it arise differ from one another as much as sickness differs from health.

Does Agape Have a Future? It is probably safe to assume that the current generation will bring forth, as well as any other, that limited number of individuals who will seize the ultimate opportunity illustrated above. They will seize it, not necessarily in a direct and dramatic manner but by setting themselves a life task in which the total gift of self may loom as a possibility or even as a near certainty, as it did, for instance, in the case of a Martin Luther King. It is undeniably a tremendous path to choose, one in which death may be more life confirming than existence itself.

If I read my students' attitudes and aspirations correctly, it is indeed quite probable that there will be men and women whose lives will express agape to a high degree. Nevertheless, the probability seems lower now than in the past when such actions were almost invariably regarded with admiration and unhesitatingly honored as noble and heroic. By contrast, growing numbers of people today are apt to regard such behavior as stupidity on a heroic scale and as a manifestation of neuroticism, a martyr complex.

Assuming that this negative attitude toward self-abnegation is real, how is it to be explained? From the psychologist's vantage point, I perceive two probable elements. One is the tendency of established psychologies to interpret all that rises above biology as a function of social conditioning and *nothing else*. It is the latter clause, of course, that is significant. For it is a platitudinous truth to say that both biology and conditioning are involved in human behavior. Even such elementary biological functions as eating and copulating are sociologically and symbolically conditioned.

But these necessary conditions do not exclude the operation of other less obvious variables. Reduction of a phenomenon to its necessary conditions is neither rationally nor empirically justified and is, moreover (if we take theoretical physics as a model), entirely obsolete. In the human realm, such a practice amounts to a truncation of the person. Again, the elaboration of reductionistic theories of this sort and their propagation among the nation's college population is no doubt done without malicious intention. But the effect amounts, nonetheless, to a debunking of man in his most generous and self-transcending attributes. Although man's view of himself and his kind bounces back in due time, nevertheless, it has been said that, with respect to effective action, time is quickly running out.

Another way in which clinical and personality psychology seem to be responsible for the decline of man's readiness to engage in self-abnegating behavior lies in what Maslow calls the tendency to pathologize everything that differs from average behavior, regardless of the direction, upward or downward, in which it differs (1968, p. 48). Granted, seeking pain and self-immolation for the sake of pain and self-immolation or for secondary gains is morbid. One may wonder, however, whether the inability to recognize value in a person's willingness to risk his life for his fellowman is not also tinged by a certain morbidity.

As I know them, our young people are at least as generous, concerned, socially conscious, and committed as any at any time. But if they are made to feel neurotic and preposterous when inclined to embrace a situation that they regard as worthy of risking much—maybe everything—they will leave the opportunity for those who are "foolish enough."

True, psychology should not present an idealized and magnified image of "the unfinished species" as Teilhard de Chardin aptly characterizes mankind. The task of psychology, like that of any discipline, is to discover the truth about, not to exalt, its object. Aside from representing a departure from that task, the presentation of exalted images might induce certain impressionable individuals to attempt to actualize themselves after such ideologically based models and in the process immolate themselves. By the same token, psychology must not depict man as less than what he is lest mankind as a whole be imperiled.

9 Beyond Sex
to Love

Like life itself, love looms larger than language. It is, therefore, not particularly amenable to description, much less to explanation. Nor does it need to be, for love must be known from living encounters. More than anything else, such encounters tend to reverberate through our awareness, inviting contemplation. And, as America is beginning to realize after long engagement with frantic activity, contemplation is not an idle thing. It heightens our awareness and enjoyment of a good already ours or ours to become, brings design in the ineffable complexity of experience, and lends perspective to the epic of existence. All this applies, in variable measure, to each type of affective involvement. But it is particularly true and felt in the case of romantic love.

Eros, or romantic love, is the most celebrated and most dramatic form of love. It is what every young male and female yearns for. Consciously or unconsciously, rightly or wrongly, they regard it as the most valid measure of human happiness: the universal dream come true, the pivot around which everything turns. More than anything else, eros is capable of firing the imagination and mobilizing the energies. And longer than anything else, romantic experience reverberates through man's memory and, beyond words and images, through his whole being.

The remarkable intensity that this form of love tends to assume has to do with the fact that the mutual attraction of the sexes characteristic of romantic love has its roots in biology, or more poetically, in "life's longing for itself" (Kahlil Gibran, 1964, p. 17). Vital forces are, either subtly or forcefully, in charge. In the service of these forces, romantic love has performed with extraordinary eagerness and durability—and, perhaps, with more fertility than mankind can afford. Even when lovers do not actually aim at procreation or physical intimacy—indeed, are actually seeking to avoid either one—they nevertheless feel driven by an urge that is often beyond their capacity to channel into lasting satisfaction.

Love versus Sex

Because of the universality of the romantic phenomenon and the fact that it is the prototypical form of love between partners of opposite gender, the popular eye tends to view love and sex as, indistinguishably blended. True, sex lends a forceful and exquisitely obsessive edge to this variety of love. But while romantic love and sex are intimately intertwined in the concrete, they have significantly different foci. Love is essentially a symbolic process unfolding on the level of imagination, thought, and sentiment; sex, a glandular, biochemical involvement boosted by strong emotional correlates.

Lowen goes so far as to declare love and sex "independent and to some degree unrelated" (1972, p. 17). Theodore Reik, in *A Psychologist Looks at Love* (1944), stated that the two differ in both origin and nature. He defined sex as a biological function geared toward pleasure and reduction of physical tension, and love as a cultural phenomenon aimed beyond pleasure at happiness, through an intimately personal relationship. Campbell (1970) confirms Reik's view when he characterizes sex as the response of the organism to the call of the species and love as the individual's longing for confirmation of his worth as a unique being. These characterizations seem valid as long as one does not lose sight of the fact that in the case of full-fledged romantic love, both forms of attraction and gratification are twin experiences.

THE CALL OF THE SPECIES. Several important parameters differentiate sex from romantic involvement. *Phenomenologically*—that is, as subjectively experienced—sex, at its best, is the most intensely pleasurable experience of man's hedonic repertoire. *Biologically*, it represents the mechanism of procreation and survival of the species. *Physiologically*, it is the function of an organ system. *Biochemically*, sex involves the endocrine system, and its effects, therefore, are diffused throughout the organism in a manner comparable to drugs and with similar "habituating" effects—hence, perhaps, the heroin addict's description of his high as "an orgasm of the whole being."

Authorities agree that sex is a far less evolved, less complex, and less differentiated phenomenon than love. Despite all similarities in organs and function, however, human sexual activity (in the sense of genitality) cannot be equated with its counterpart in the animal realm—no more than feeding, as a psychological phenomenon, can be equated in man and in animals, regardless of the near identity of the biological functions and anatomic structures involved. Except in cases of severe deprivation, both sex and feeding in humans are culturally ritualized and socialized phenomena.

In the case of sex, the source of this difference reaches much deeper than cultural conventions. The critical difference is neurologically based.

It resides in the fact that sex in humans is cortically regulated and consequently under voluntary control. This neurological fact entails the momentous psychological consequence that humans, contrary to animals, are not powerlessly subjected to the sex drive. They can regulate, postpone, or sublimate sexual activity. More important, from the point of view of human relations and personal happiness, this cortical basis allows man to be selective with regard to partners. It also allows him to control the timing and conditions of sexual expression. Because of the heavy endocrine involvement, however, control weakens at the same pace that sexual expression becomes habitual.

Cortical control, then, far from restricting the potential yield of sex, actually enhances it. In Lowen's view, "This focus upon a single individual raises the level of sexual tension, for it inhibits the tendency to discharge the tension indiscriminately" (1972, p. 18). Clearly, the higher the level of tension, the more gratifying its release or, as Gilbert observes, "abstinence makes the heart grow fonder" (1948, p. 81).

Sex and Sexuality. Pansexualism is the Freudian view that all human behavior and experience can be reduced to manifestations of the libido, understood as a life force that is ultimately oriented toward sexual pleasure. For several decades, phasing out somewhere in the late fifties, this view dominated psychological thought about human affectivity. After the initial effervescence of this "revelation" subsided, it gradually became obvious that Freud had vastly overreached his grasp. At present, few social scientists subscribe to Freud's early, radically reductionistic views. Without denying the power and pervasiveness of the sexual dimension, prominent authors with extensive scholarly and/or clinical knowledge of man affirm the necessity for less rigid, less biologically determined views of the forces at work in the mutual attraction of the sexes. One result of this new trend is the distinction between the concepts of *sex* and *sexuality*.

Technically speaking, the meaning of the term *sex* is increasingly confined to erotic phenomena and relationships of a predominantly genital nature. *Sexuality*, on the other hand, has acquired a vastly more comprehensive meaning associated with a more diffuse and symbolic sphere of appeal than the psychological reverberation of organ systems; it conveys a generalized erogenous sensitivity and responsiveness to the sensuous quality of human contact, real or symbolic. Thus, the meaning of sexuality relates to the psychological characteristics traditionally labeled "masculinity/femininity"—as distinct from the biological notions of "maleness/femaleness."

Differential labeling of these phenomena—the specifically genital and the diffusely erogenous—is definitely useful. Semantically, however, the distinction between *sex* and *sexuality* can be difficult when the context is unclear, because the two words share the same adjectival and adverbial forms.

Dionysian Man. The new concept of sexuality—as distinct from sex—is related to the revival of the Freudian concept of *polymorphous sexual perversion.* This rather awkward label, which refers to neither perversion nor promiscuity, was originated by Freud to characterize the undifferentiated capacity for pleasurable excitability of the young child.

Polymorphous sexual perversion has been brought back into focus by Norman O. Brown (1959, 1966, 1970), Herbert Marcuse (1955, 1964, 1968), Paul Goodman (1956, 1963), and others, who affirm the existence of this tendency in repressed form within the adult personality. In their presentation of the new Dionysian Man—erotic, playful, poetic, joyful—these authors champion the idea that expression of this tendency should be encouraged and cultivated as a way of affirming certain vital capacities that technological civilization is presumed to have deadened. The suggestion was eagerly adopted by the counterculture, whose followers made a colorful and bold, though perhaps somewhat overzealous and therefore transient, attempt to revive man's primal capacity for an abundant and joyful contact with nature and his fellowmen.

This Dionysian view of life and of human relations would seem to be associated also with the emerging exaltation of the sense of touch—kissing, hugging, embracing, holding—that has recently become noticeable. It is also in line with the current psychoclinical tenet that direct physical contact has a certain healing and reviving potential.

In sum, and in their broadest sense, the concepts of sexuality and polymorphous sexual perversion refer to the assumption of an almost undifferentiated human potential for pleasurable sensitivity and responsiveness. This sensitivity is assumed to be oriented toward nature as a whole and, especially, to the human other—regardless, in principle, of sex, age, status, or other cultural and biological variables. These concepts refer, then, to something like an intermediate phenomenon between the bodily involvement of sex and the symbolic involvement of love.

A PERSONALIZED ASPIRATION.   While sex is basically the response of the organism to the call of the species, love is essentially the expression of individual aspiration—an attraction that is focused not in organ systems but in selves. Therefore, love aims not at the satisfaction of a *particular* need but an overall good that transcends the solely emotional level and reaches deep into the total experiential structure, lending a different perspective to self and life.

Romantic love is a symbolic process of an erotic nature, a state of mind, of imagination, and of sentiment. For it has to do mainly with the image of the other. The image may be accurate or distorted by projection and wishful thinking; nevertheless, it is the object of exhilarating contemplation.

Once they have experienced this exhilarating state of mind, lovers are determined to pursue its course, if necessary, at the cost of hardship, deprivation, even death—as illustrated in the great works of literature and not infrequently in everyday life. Their view of love's course, however, is often something of a mirage based, as it tends to be, upon projections. Indeed, unmitigated romantic love frequently fails to result in happiness in the ordinary sense of an enjoyable, emotionally, spiritually, and physically gratifying life. A number of authors, among them the insightful C. S. Lewis (1960), contend that (at least unconsciously) lovers do not aim primarily at happiness but at mutual belonging—which is not necessarily the same thing at all. Indeed, even when clearly shown that their conjoined future is heavily stacked against them, romantically involved young people are apt to enter into a binding covenant with one another. In fact, the very adversity of the situation seems to intensify the attraction. What they perceive in one another, correctly or mistakenly, is the complementary portion of their self-structure. Apparently no other prospective assets and benefits can outweigh the value attached to this feeling of unique complementarity. Lovers see each other literally as each other's fulfillment.

Love's Trajectory

Romantic love always unfolds as a story. Often it's a short story, sometimes it is lifelong—at least it may echo throughout a lifetime. But always and by its very nature, romantic love is a thing of change. Of course, since man himself is a changing being, other affective bonds change also. But compared to the movement occurring within romantic love, their vicissitudes are mere ripples on otherwise placid waters.

In other types of affective relationships, changes are usually due to external circumstances—physical distance, work pressures, or a widening of the affective circle or the life space in general. Romantic love, on the other hand, is inherently subject to transformation. It is apt to exhibit wide-ranging oscillations and, paradoxically, declines or dies in the process of evolving into a fuller and richer but unavoidably less exciting relationship—a symbolic parallel to the biological death of the spawning salmon. These unavoidable changes tend to perturb the partners, especially those unenlightened about the nature of this particular type of affective bond.

Especially in the present age of rapid change, it would be very bold to trace a hard and fast paradigm for processes as utterly unique as romantic involvement. Nevertheless, it seems possible to recognize something like a widely varying, fluid pattern in eros's journey from the time of its first spark to that of its fulfillment. In those cases in which romantic attraction outlasts its trial-and-error phase and reaches fulfillment in a mature and viable relationship, it typically proceeds over three stages that gradually shade into one another: a forceful budding, glorious blossoming, and quiet fruition—metaphors that lack originality but are hardly surpassable in their evocative power. These stages are more commonly known as falling in love, being in love, and loving—understood as a way of life rather than solely a way of feeling.

This traditionally observed pattern, though basically unchanged in its loosely structured three-part sequence, seems to have assumed, however, a different profile in recent years. The identity of each phase is less pronounced and, on the whole, less dramatic than it was in the past. Currently, the whole process seems to be telescoping in a rather undifferentiated, rapid, and often abruptly ended fashion, issuing in either a breakup or marriage (or similar bond). There is no hard evidence on the matter, but a number of cues suggest that the conditions of modern living have altered the process in the following ways: the first phase—falling in love—does not reach the peak of excitement that it used to exhibit; the second phase—being in love—is shorter; and the third more rarely reaches its full fruition. On the whole, the process seems to be less intense, less durable, and less successful—at least in terms of lasting results. (The plasticity that biological determinants assume within changing cultural contexts is here confirmed once more.)

Despite the current fluidity and ambiguity of the romantic phenomenon, I will try to outline the characteristic features of each of its phases as they were traditionally observed, while attempting at the same time to point out the features that differ most noticeably from the classical pattern. Since the phases are less marked than they used to be, however, the following presentation will unavoidably amount to something of a magnification of the process. Also, the picture that emerges from it will necessarily be more paradigmatic than idiographic, since any attempt at segmentation and "averaging out" of so untidy and fluctuating a development as romantic love is bound to violate the uniqueness of the particular case. Despite these drawbacks, I trust that the following sketch of love's trajectory has enough reality value to make it meaningful to the present.

FALLING IN LOVE. Falling in love is the most exquisite and intoxicating, but also the most ephemeral, phase of the romantic venture—unforgettable, but as unrecapturable as the popping of a champagne cork. If it is the real thing—that is, if it is romantic involvement and not mere sexual craving—it often starts with an emotional bang: a bursting forth of forces that have pressed for release yet take one by surprise. The story usually opens with some happening: an exciting event, unplanned, unreflected, and usually experienced as something close to "esthetic arrest," as Campbell (1970) calls it, rather than glandular reflex. Although the partner may not be of unqualified beauty, he or she is experienced for a time as an eminently "beautiful person."

The term *falling* is an apt characterization for this first phase. Interestingly, the same expression is used in many languages to refer to the same phenomenon. "Falling" evokes the suddenness, the precariousness, and the impermanent nature of the experience. The falling may be hard or soft, depending upon the partners' personal bent and the paths they choose to walk. Thus, the individual who is incapable of delayed gratification is likely to fall hard, where less impulsive and more reflective types may come down softly. How one falls, however, is not wholly determined by the way he is temperamentally "weighted." It is affected just as much by the circles he chooses to move in. As for the type of person one falls in love with, it is usually the one who happens to cross one's path at the moment that both imagination and emotion combine into a climax of psychological readiness. Consequently, while one hardly chooses the person with whom one falls in love, one does have a say on the hunting grounds.

In this initial stage, the love-struck man or woman goes through a state of inordinately high affective excitement and psychological involvement. Falling in love is the "many-splendored thing" par excellence, a peak of ecstasy. The center of gravity of one's being and significance seems to shift abruptly from oneself to another person. James Baldwin offers a vivid illustration:

> Pretend, for example, that you were born in Chicago, and have never had the remotest desire to visit Hong Kong, which is only a name on a map for you; pretend that some convulsion, sometimes called accident, throws you into connection with a man or a woman who lives in Hong Kong; and that you fall in love. Hong Kong will immediately cease to be a name and become the center of your life. And you may never know how many people live in Hong Kong. But you will know that one woman or man lives there without who you cannot live. . . .
> If your lover lives in Hong Kong and cannot get to Chicago, it will be necessary for you to go to Hong Kong. Perhaps you will spend your life there, and never see Chicago again. And you will, I assure you, as long as space and time divide you from anyone you love, discover a great deal about shipping routes, airplanes, earthquakes, famine, disease, and war. And you will always know what time it is in Hong Kong, for you love someone who lives there. And love will simply have no choice but to go into battle with space and time and, furthermore, to win (Baldwin and Avedon, 1964).

At this early stage, romantic love is not necessarily accompanied by sexual craving (C. S. Lewis, 1960), although love and sex have become inseparably linked in the contemporary mind. True, the essence of young love (at any age) is made up of desire. But it is a desire for something related to the other *as a person* rather than the reverberation of one organ system yearning for another. The first act of the three-part romantic drama, therefore, is—or used to be—played out largely on the level of imagination. Love at this stage is symbolic delight, the "magnificent obsession," an experience that alternately drains and increases the energies of the love-struck.

The often irrational intensity of the romantic urge is founded at least in part on the fact that the process usually coincides with the peak of the parties' physical fitness. It also coincides with maximal exposure and openness to stimulation from such environmental media as music and song, theatre, and reading—most of which are focused upon romantic themes. The combined effect of the internal urge and the environmental inducements frequently goads the young into sealing their precarious relationship with bonds whose closeness is soon apt to be felt as restrictive of freedom and individuality.

Cosmetic Partners. During this brief but highly emotional phase, the object of excitement usually is not the real but the perceived partner; that is, an embellished version sometimes as unrelated to the substance of that person as his or her telephone number. The image is apparently conjured up from the depths of the individual's longing for fulfillment and confirmation as a male or female. Each of the partners tends to project upon the other the image of his fondest dreams. And each tends to validate the other's projection by unconsciously enacting the image and role of the ultimate "beautiful person." Thus, each of the two finds his counterpart utterly satisfying and self-enhancing and wants to regard it as the "real" she (or he) "whom nobody else knows"—a belief that is often more literally true than the parties realize but not in the sense that they assume. What adds a particularly gratifying edge to the experience is the self-enhancing belief that this precious uniqueness reveals itself only to the one who is capable of awakening it by virtue of an equally precious and hidden uniqueness.

This mutual embellishment, while supremely gratifying, is, of course, mutually misleading, though it is not intentionally deceitful. On the contrary, in this first, enchanting phase, the partners often *feel* they are experiencing and expressing their most authentic selves. Nevertheless, "this pretty pose cannot be maintained," as El Gallo comments in *The Fantasticks,* a play about precisely the kind of cosmetic images with which eros entices its emotionally intoxicated subjects.

But sooner or later, the make-up melts, cracks, or fades away, gradually baring the planes and angles of the underlying reality. At this juncture, the romantic venture tends to assume a new character. The relationship may be strengthened by the discovery that the other is somewhat less extraordinary than was thought at first glimpse—a sobering discovery but one that allows each partner to reveal his own ordinary self. On the other hand, under the spell of *feeling* loved and of loving in return, something of a small miracle may occur: the person's real self may gradually transform to blend with the cosmetic self. This is particularly apt to occur if the relationship outlasts the first phase and merges into the second.

Animus and Anima in Search of Each Other. The apparently mysterious yet common tendency for lovers to build a glorified, cosmetic image of one another has been so widely observed throughout the ages and the cultures that it presses for explanation. One source of insight into the origin and forcefulness of this phenomenon can be found in Jung's (1969) theory of archetypes. As he conceives of them, archetypes are unconscious primal models of certain vitally significant existential objects that the human being is striving to encounter. These symbolic objects have their remote origin in the cumulative unconscious experience of the human race. They refer to experiences that are not exactly cognitive but more in the nature of idea-feelings; in other words, they represent a blend of affectivity, cognition, and conation, sensitized to particular categories of objects. Archetypes, then, are models of which we are not consciously aware but which presensitize us to certain encounters with existential reality. They are believed by some to exert a guiding influence in the ongoing search in which man, as the symbolic animal, the reflective thinker, and the questing beast, is bound to engage.

Among the various archetypes proposed by Jung, two are relevant here. They are the *animus,* or principle of masculinity, and its counterpart the *anima,* or principle of femininity. Together they constitute what Jung calls the "soul image." (The similarity of these concepts to the Zen Buddhist concepts of the *yin* and the *yang* is striking.) Each of these archetypes is thought of as a latent force that is constantly though unconsciously stirring within humans, longingly scanning their world in search of its corresponding other. When animus or anima, presensitized to its counterpart, encounters its object, incarnate in the person of, respectively, a female or male, its latency is apt to become energized with primeval force.

Animus and anima, unconsciously operating principles of search and direction, are mentioned here with a view to throwing light upon the surprising readiness of the young (although not confined to just the young) to be sparked into a romantic state of mind by often premature impressions of having encountered the uniquely corresponding partner. These archetypes also lend meaning to the frequently observed tendency of males (and we assume now also for females) to harbor a latent Don Juan— in the case of females, a Messalina—complex that keeps involving them in what D'Arcy (1947) calls "chain loving"—or at least keeps them watching for the ideal partner even after long and gratifying attachment to their spouse.

Exquisitely Addictive. Just as anger and fear energize the body for "flight or fight"—unless they freeze and momentarily paralyze the synapses—so pleasurable emotions, too, have their chemical counterpart. Either they make for joyful excitation, followed by pleasurable exhaustion, or they lead to a relaxed state of exquisite abandon.

The intensity, rapture, and liabilities of romantic love are heavily conditioned by the body chemistry. At the height of involvement, it is possible for the mere sight, indeed the mere thought, of the loved one to trigger an overall pattern of physiological response (hence, the blushing of maidens stirred by nascent love, as the traditional stereotype would have it). Blushing may be disappearing from the scene—no doubt a result of the changed conditions of boy-girl commerce—but underneath a skin grown thicker, the physiological effects apparently continue to be felt. In the first stages of the process, especially, when sexual involvement is apt to be incomplete, the partners are aroused by vivid anticipation. Because of this diffuse yet intensely organismic involvement, romantic love at its peak has a quasi-addictive quality. This is especially the case when the relationship assumes genital expression. When the stage is thus set, a single enrapturing encounter may "hook" one or both partners—if not necessarily to one another, then at least to the gratification derived from the experience.

Naturally, we are not speaking here of the kind of physical addiction resulting from the use of hard drugs. However, Blau ventures a very graphic comparison by proposing that the effect of love is "very much like a narcotic or substance addiction. In the presence of the substance, there are feelings of euphoria, worthwhileness, greatness, fullness, richness, capability, action, warmth, tenderness, peace, and the intense feeling of wanting to do something tremendous and being capable of this" (1972, p. 162).

Indeed, sex being a biochemical as well as an emotional event, its effects upon the organism are remarkably similar to some of the effects of hedonic drug use. That is, it bonds one to experiences that are felt as supremely gratifying, sought with compulsive eagerness, and apt to cause adverse reactions when gratification is interfered with or withdrawn.

Because of the disruptive effects that may accompany intense romantic involvement—at least in the cases of insufficiently mature partners—Casler's pronouncement that romantic love is pathological is not entirely inappropriate. Nevertheless, I strongly resist applying this label to the whole process of romantic love, the most exquisitely intense of all emotions and one that countless individuals prove able to distill into fruitful bonds sustained by treasured memories.

BEING IN LOVE. While the first phase of the romantic venture is typically triggered by an exciting and often long-remembered happening, the second phase is gradual and initially imperceptible. Time has elapsed since the first encounter; hence mutual and common experience has accumulated, providing a broader and more realistic basis for the relationship. The effervescence subsides, the "peak experience" slopes down toward a plateau with widening perspectives.

What explains the relatively early decline of that most prized attribute of the nascent relationship, its enchanting quality? Paradoxically, it seems largely due to the partners' passionate attempts to retain the exhilaration and intoxication of early love that it eventually begins to elude them. Indeed, they try to be together as much as they can. They forget, or do not know, that because of the inescapable law of adaptation, the excitement of an experience stands in inverse relation to its incidence. The more frequent the pleasurable event, the less pleasurable its yield (as we know from experience in any area of enjoyment). As a result of increased contact and the correlative adaptive process, the wilder flights of imagination are curbed, and infatuation begins to ebb. The partners gain the opportunity to acquire a more down-to-earth view of one another and thereby a firmer hold on their relationship. Each becomes gradually acquainted with the other as an individual rather than as a powerfully magnetized, complementary object. Mutual attachment becomes more realistic, reflective, and personalized, and tends to move toward stabilization.

The Joyful Apprenticeship. This is a phase of mutual discovery and transformation. Given extended time and realistic conditions—that is, not only leisure and entertainment—this phase may well be the most creative period of the romantic process. Limitations and divergences in each other's make-up begin to be perceived. Quarreling is not uncommon, but both the quarrels and their resolutions, because they reveal the individual, are beneficial. On the whole, differences are easily integrated within the dyadic relationship because both partners anticipate rich returns from their relationship if it can be carried to maturity. Therefore, the give-and-take of compromise is felt to be well worth the cost. One of the outstanding merits of the process at this stage is the near painlessness with which the desired outcome—that is, growth in each other's image—can be achieved.

During this wide-ranging process of mutual identification and adaptation, the relationship remains highly enjoyable. The immediate goal of the partners seems to lie in maintaining this high level of mutual enjoyment. Succeeding in this attempt is felt as supremely rewarding. While their thoughts are no longer obsessed with one another, lovers remain at the center of each other's preoccupation. The needs of the other tend to have precedence over those of the self. Each prefers to bask in the reflected glow of the other's happiness rather than to have his own way.

Whether they are physically in each other's presence or not, they now attend to one another in the sense that they engage in a sort of mental consultation with one another on how and what the other would like him or her to do or be on such and such an occasion; on what the other would say, feel, or do about any of the countless problems and opportunities that arise in the course of everyday existence. Imperceptibly, this mutual model results in the development of common attitudes, a tendency to feel and react in the same direction. The beauty of it all is that this converging process unfolds, on the whole, effortlessly, indeed, eagerly.

But is this not an exaggeratedly positive picture of what is apt to take place during this phase of the relationship? What is here being described presupposes certain conditions. As mentioned earlier, the relationship must extend over an adequate length of time, and it must afford an opportunity for a variety of shared experiences. More significantly, the relationship requires a certain structure in order to be conducive to optimal learning. Such learning presupposes that the partners have not yet committed themselves totally to one another in the way characteristic of the closing stage. This means that each can still feel free to break the gathering tie and each is aware of the mutuality of this prerogative. This awareness and attendant concern introduces an undeniable though productive tension in the relationship. It is productive in that it tends to alert the partners to the fluctuations and dynamics of their relationship and to the feelings being bared—their own and the other's. Apparently, this margin of incertitude is precisely what makes this phase of the relationship so eminently conducive to existentially valuable learning.

A Vanishing Phase. Traditionally, the phase just described was the time of courtship. This term no longer has currency, and the type of relationship to which it referred is definitely on the decline. Courtship consisted of a period of mutual acquaintance in conditions of increasing privacy and intimacy but excluding total genital gratification. This stage between the emotional burst of falling in love and the clinching of a lasting bond used to be regarded as particularly significant for the future of the relationship. The requirement of sexual abstention was strongly emphasized by social and religious norms and was, on the whole, endorsed by the principals—largely, one may assume, because of the biological consequences to which they would expose themselves in the absence of effective means of birth prevention. As a result of the control now achieved on the biological plane, social norms have lost their strictness, leaving the decision as to whether or not to engage in total sexual intimacy to the principals. The latter, no longer supported by a unified culture, tend understandably to yield to their natural inclination—actually tending to consider sexual abstention a sado-masochistic attitude.

In principle, this newly won freedom from biological consequences and social ostracism represents progress, for it allows people to act reflectively and autonomously in accordance with their philosophy of life, their conscience. In fact, however, things are not altogether so positive. For a person's philosophy of life is seldom sufficiently formed at the time (increasingly early) at which a stand is being taken; nor has his conscience had much opportunity to exert itself in significant matters, hence, to mature. Considering the powerful thrust of the sexual impulse, it is therefore a question whether a young person's preference for one course of action over another can truly be called a decision (with the operation of reason and volition implied by this term); in other words, it is questionable whether the choice can truly be called free and, hence, valid.

Love as Emotion and as Sentiment. Before moving on to the concluding phase of the love story, we must acquaint ourselves with a distinction that pertains to the focal point of this book: the illumination of man's specifically human features. As I mentioned earlier, social behavior in humans is considerably more diversified than in animals. Within its affective sector, numerous qualitative differences are also observable. One difference that is seldom sufficiently investigated is that between emotion and sentiment.

Emotion, the more powerful and elementary of the two, expresses itself fundamentally through body language—physiological cues of variable intensity—and other verbal or nonverbal phenomena. An emotion can burst into existence and strive for satisfaction with primeval force, and it can turn into its opposite as quickly and irrationally as it came about. Examples of this type of affective involvement are sexual desire and gratification, jealousy, fear, anger, disgust—any feeling that is intense and rather impulsive or, at least, unreflected. Examples of sentiment are warm affection, tenderness, gratitude, respect, admiration, devotion—all of which have a broader experiential basis. Sentiment—unlike emotion, which is apt to be triggered by particular perceptual phenomena—has to do with broader areas of the self-structure. Sentiment is also more durable, more shock resistant than its emotional counterpart. It is on the level of sentiment, then, that affectivity is characteristically human.

Both forms of affectivity can, of course, amalgamate to lend not only intensity and strength but depth and durability to feelings or feeling complexes. Both are present in the mature, full-fledged expression of romantic love. Emotion predominates during the first phase, but "being in love" is the experiential soil from which sentiment and fulfillment germinate.

FULFILLMENT: THE END OF THE JOURNEY. If mutual attraction outlives its earlier phases and if these phases developed beneficially, the relationship gravitates toward a stabilization of the emotional involvement in an enjoyably comfortable, secure, and productive arrangement. Being in love has a built-in tendency toward consummation and consolidation: we all want to keep and insure what we hold most dear. This is the time that the tendency materializes. It usually takes the form of a publicly proclaimed bond sanctioned by legal dispositions and religious ceremonies, according to the beliefs and values of the principals. At the time that it is established, this bond is viewed and desired as lasting (though I understand that the vow "until death do us part" is beginning to be replaced by "as long as our love lasts").

This third phase marks the completion of the romantic venture; at the same time, it is a beginning. Part of this beginning is the gradual evaporation of that intoxicating spirit that pervaded the relationship before it was sealed into a lasting bond. Indeed, romantic love thrives on anticipation, on a measure of unfulfillment, and a longing for consummation. Where every form of separation—physical, social, and personal—is abolished in favor of the fullest intimacy possible, a change in the quality of the relationship is unavoidable. One cannot long for what one possesses, although one can deeply cherish it.

A prosaic and minor illustration of this change of feeling can be found in the difference between appetite and satiation. Appetite, especially for one's favorite food, is a uniquely enjoyable sensation that literally hungers for satiation. But satiation unavoidably means the end of the appetite. Something of the sort is characteristic of this third phase: to achieve the growth and gratification of fulfillment, the excitement of the earlier phases must give way.

Enlightened and mature lovers are aware of the inevitability of such a development. In most cases, however, this change in the quality of the relationship is perceived as a loss instead of the condition for an enrichment of the bond. One of the major pitfalls of marriage in its early years is precisely this ignorance about the development and ultimate destination of romantic involvement.

From Face-to-Face to Side-by-Side. The new situation provides a climate for a fuller actualization of both male and female, as not only partners in a love relationship but also persons with a many-faceted destiny within the human community. Energies once concentrated upon each other now became available for achievement in other spheres, in part jointly, in part separately: making a living, establishing a life-style, raising children, achieving occupational competence, participating in community service. This change in focus can be visualized, according to C. S. Lewis (1960), as a shift from a face-to-face to a side-by-side position and can be represented graphically by two profiles looking in the same outward direction rather than facing each other and, in the process, blocking each other's perspective.

But this change in orientation doesn't come about without sometimes acute growing pains. Usually the shift starts with and is most visible in the providing party (usually the male), though a corresponding, albeit different, shift may take place in the female, especially in relation to parenthood. The spouse is moved out of the center of the other's sphere of attention. She (or he) tends to feel that she is being moved out of the picture and understandably reacts in accordance with this painful perception. Actually, the shift is from the *center of preoccupation* to the *center of existence*. He or she now fills the sphere of the other's life instead of being only its pivot: each one has become part of the other's life. Since "the eye does not see itself," married people may tend to take each other for granted.

To Know Yet to Love. Despite all earlier learning and despite having lived within the confines of a lasting bond, partners are likely to discover that they still harbor considerable illusions both about each other and about the union they so eagerly desired. They may also discover some negative traits in their own characters. However, if they are defensive, they will tend to misinterpret these discoveries, perceiving their own inadequacies as shortcomings in their partners. These distortions will prevent them from discovering the roots of the trouble. According to Putney and Putney (1964), the characteristic problem of romantic involvement is the tendency for either or both partner(s) to project upon each other qualities that they themselves would like to possess or undesirable attributes of their own that they do not want to acknowledge. Being ignorant of the real dynamics involved, they will ascribe the normal crises of the first years of marriage to changes within the other. They feel entitled to meet these assumed changes with corresponding changes. The latter, being real, elicit further change, and a chain reaction develops. Mutual alienation sets in, and the marriage breaks up. Partners set about to repeat the venture often with little if any gain in understanding the intrapersonal and interpersonal dynamics at work. Conversely, if partners are open-minded, they may discover a few sobering but valuable things about themselves.

A diffuse feeling of emotional letdown is not unusual after the transplantation of the relationship into a new soil, nor does it necessarily reflect unfavorably upon the person who experiences the letdown. Where happiness is concerned, man's horizon is geared to infinity. It takes years before he learns to bring that horizon in line with his own finite nature. Thomas Traherne long ago formulated the prescription for harmonizing man's fondest dreams with his existential reality: "Infinite love cannot be expressed in finite room. Yet it must be infinitely expressed in the smallest moment. . . . Only so is it in both ways infinite" (Eiseley, 1970, pp. 46–47).

More soberly formulated and more explicit than Traherne's formula is Fromm's concept of "the practice of love" (1956). That concept is admittedly far from euphoric. The cover of *The Art of Loving* announces "The world famous psychoanalyst's daring prescription for love." It is daring, however, not in any sensational sense but in the sense that it describes the practice of love (understood as a life-style rather than an episode) in terms such that it cannot but appear as a task—supremely rewarding but still a task. Here are the timeless but not old-fashioned qualities Fromm lists as essential for love to be a lastingly fulfilling experience: discipline, concentration, patience, supreme concern, the overcoming of one's narcissism, humility, faith, and courage. For people who know each other in the stark reality of their limitations and unfinished personalities, not much less than Fromm's formula will achieve the state of knowing and loving. It is probably safe to say that when love can be kept alive within the confines of a stable bond, such a bond offers a better basis for the actualization of a broad spectrum of human potentialities and satisfactions than other styles of life.

A New Formula for Marriage

Marriage as a relationship and an institution is currently in a state of crisis. The crisis may be transient, a mere reflection of the acute turmoil of our era. More likely, however, marriage is due to undergo significant and lasting change (Rogers, 1972). Many factors—economic, sociological, psychological, legal, and medical—contribute to the crisis. But perhaps the most significant, and the only one falling within the compass of this work, concerns the vastly changed relations between the sexes.

In Western cultures, at least since the end of the Middle Ages, marriage has been based mainly upon romantic attraction, not upon the dynastic, caste-determined, or other socio-economic concerns that still prevail in many non-Western cultures. In recent years, however, this romantic basis has been questioned; for example, Casler (1969), whose notion that romantic love is a pathological condition has been previously mentioned, and Putney and Putney (1964), who declare it the worst possible basis for marriage.

In my estimation, these conclusions are based upon an incomplete view of the romantic process, especially the phase of infatuation characteristic of its onset. The aroused feelings generated by this first incandescent phase by themselves indeed constitute a shaky basis for a satisfying and lasting bond. Intense romantic involvement not balanced by maturity is exposed to side effects that are apt to dissolve the bond before it has consolidated. But if romantic love is allowed to ripen and evolve to the point where the partners' initial "cosmetic" image of each other is replaced by more sober, duly tested perceptions, I hold that romantic attraction is then a promising and highly gratifying basis for marriage.

Beyond the question of whether traditional romantic love is a suitable basis for marriage is the question of whether it can develop in the emotional climate generated by the new conditions governing the relations between sexes. Until recently, romantic love, like sex, seemed to have a nearly universal affective dynamic, something often described as an alternation between agony and ecstasy. Suddenly, however, things have changed so spectacularly that one wonders whether we are witnessing the dissolution of this type of love. Feelings and yearnings once assumed to be engraved on man's being seem to undergo a confusing, disconcerting change in not only the eyes of the observer but, not infrequently, also in those of the parties involved. As the date of marriage approaches, both parties are apt to confide that, while they feel certain the other is the very one for them, they don't experience any of the things that "ought" to be felt at this point.

FROM SEGREGATION TO HOMOGENIZATION. Perhaps the change of mood—from exalted to comfortable; from wildly idealized and passionate longing to an enjoyable, fairly down-to-earth and relatively even relationship—can be accounted for by the conditions within which young people can now meet and get to know each other. In the past, a rigorous, culturally imposed segregation of the sexes separated the lovers by a multitude of social barriers. Privacy was at an extremely high premium, creating a social-emotional climate that generated powerful tension and breeding a state of longing and desire so intense that it distorted and obscured the parties' perceptions of each other.

Compare this state of affairs with current practices, which allow the sexes to be integrated to the point of homogenization—unisex dress, hairstyles, roles, rights, occupations, and professions. While one kind of emotional episode is apparently on the wane in the relations between the sexes, a new and significant emotional bond seems destined to take its place. It is a bond that develops progressively under conditions—mainly educational or occupational—that allow men and women to spend considerable time together as equals. As a result, they come to know each other's interests and values in terms of action, not merely talk.

This new relationship significantly resembles the affective tie described in Chapter 8 under the name of friendship. Like friendship, it is autonomously engaged in, free from ulterior motives (for example, the social pressure to achieve married status, sexual privilege, or economic security), and respectful of the other's individuality and legitimate attitudes. It is loyal, "transparent," and psychologically focused upon intimate and shared communication and experiences that are marked by genuine sexual attraction yet free from possessiveness and obsessive passion.

A relationship of this kind holds promise of better and longer wear, based as it is upon greater mutual acquaintance, more equality, and better and fuller communication than the traditional conjugal bond. The partners' interests and attention are socially more open-ended, less exclusively focused on each other, and less susceptible to side effects. In an affective framework like this, the highs are something less than ecstatic, but the lows are considerably less than agonizing. In sum, it is a relationship that, cemented by sex, may result in a formula for marriage that qualifies for the ancient's characterization of erotic friendship: the last gift of the gods.

A Concluding Observation

"At no time in history has so large a proportion of humanity rated love so highly, thought about it so much, or displayed such an insatiable appetite for word about it" (Hunt, 1959, p. 341). This chapter and the preceding aimed to illuminate the power, wonder, and delight of that cardinal virtue that is love. From all the evidence here adduced and discussed, the reader may be inclined to believe that an abundance of love can be observed everywhere and that, by comparison, his own share of this precious commodity is, perhaps, meager.

When discussion is focused upon a particular phenomenon—especially one with a strong affective accent—one is apt to gain a magnified impression of its nature or incidence. Actually, when any phenomenon—other than a novelty—moves into the spotlight, it is often because all is not well with it. Things are apt to move into the focus of attention because their quality or quantity (or both) is insufficient or on the decline.

Love is doing very well academically, as evidenced by the growing amount of literature on the subject. But existentially it seems to be in short supply and in a state of crisis. My students confirm this impression, supporting it with added evidence. The causes of this regrettable but hopefully transient phenomenon seem to be related to a prevailing state of confusion brought about by the "explosion" of opportunity, independence, self-sufficiency, freedom, and the affective indifference that they may generate.

Something of the essence of the contemporary love crisis and of its possible remedy seems to be contained in the following poem. The first part, the widely known lines by Fritz Perls, contains much that is true and practical—though severely limited. It offers a *modus vivendi* for individuals living *among* other individuals, not *with* them. In other words, it does not offer a model for a relationship, for it leaves out the warmth, the care and concern that form the essence of human commerce.* The second part, by Tubbs, beautifully supplements the first by stressing the need for awareness and mindfulness of the other, and for active reaching out for mutuality.

BEYOND PERLS†

I do my thing, and you do your thing.
I am not in this world to live up to your expectations,
And you are not in this world to live up to mine.
You are you and I am I;
If by chance we find each other, it's beautiful.
If not, it can't be helped.††

FRITZ PERLS

If I just do my thing and you do yours,
We stand in danger of losing each other
And ourselves.

I am not in this world to live up to your expectations;
But I am in this world to confirm you
As a unique human being.
And to be confirmed by you.

---

* I wish to emphasize my conviction, however, that the author, Fritz Perls, had only constructive purposes in mind when writing these lines. I assume indeed that his aim was to denounce the aggressive dependency, symbiotic attachment, possessiveness, and similar forms of immature affectivity that, for many, continue to pose as expressions of love.

† Walter Tubbs, "Beyond Perls," *Journal of Humanistic Psychology*, 12 (Fall 1972), 5.

†† Fritz Perls, "Gestalt Prayer." Copyright © Real People Press 1969. All rights reserved. Reprinted with permission.

We are fully ourselves only in relation to each other;
The I detached from a Thou
Disintegrates.

I do not find you by chance;
I find you by an active life
Of reaching out.

Rather than passively letting things happen to me,
I can act intentionally to make them happen.

I must begin with myself, true;
But I must not end with myself:
The truth begins with two.

10 The Will
to Beauty

Man's sense of beauty, like his capacity for speech, is universal. Every culture throughout history exhibits a multitude of nonutilitarian objects, spectacles, and events whose presence can be accounted for only by the delight they generate in their makers and beholders. While the sense of the beautiful is ubiquitous, the objects capable of eliciting and stimulating it are culturally and individually as diverse as the languages and idioms in which mankind's linguistic potential expresses itself.

This state of affairs is colorfully illustrated by the following anecdote, whose origin must have been lost in the telling. Sometime in years past, before the media had given everybody a nodding acquaintance with everything, a distinguished young Japanese was visiting New York. After a day of sightseeing, his American hosts took him to Carnegie Hall. They arrived well ahead of time and watched the musicians taking their seats and tuning their instruments. The program featured a sampling of the very best of Occidental music. At the conclusion of the concert, the guest was asked which of the selections he had enjoyed most. The answer came without hesitation: the piece played first. Since the first number on the program was by Mozart, his hosts commented appreciatively. But the Japanese guest, sensing a slight kink in the communication, clarified his reply, saying that he was referring to the very first piece, that which preceded the Mozart. The free, unpatterned play of sounds, the random, disorderly "creativity" of the musicians' tuning was more enjoyable to him than any of the other distinguished offerings.

In the Eye of the Beholder

Esthetic experience is too often thought of as a luxury, something for the wealthy, the leisure class, and the initiated. Not so, claims Sir Herbert Read, who, as a philosopher of art, staunchly supports the thesis that esthetic experience is a universal, specifically human phenomenon. As he crisply quipped, "Beauty wasn't invented in ancient Athens or anywhere else" (1963, p. 13).

The mistaken notion that it was, or might have been, no doubt stems from the widely prevailing confusion between beauty and art. Conditions of affluence and leisure indeed tend to spur artistic creation, especially in those individuals who are professionally engaged in the arts. And such conditions are also apt to sharpen or broaden the average citizen's capacity for art appreciation. But esthetic experience, the enjoyment of beauty, is not dependent upon the presence of works of art. It is an intrinsic element of man's sensitivity to his environment. It may be elicited by anything, natural or man-made, that strikes the subject as pleasing or delightful.

Art, on the other hand, is a cultural activity whose products may or may not be experienced as beautiful by a particular individual or even an entire culture or subculture. Especially during periods of cultural transition, during which style may undergo radical change, appreciation of contemporary art may fail almost completely. Indeed, many artists and art critics would claim that art does not necessarily aim at expressing beauty. They would contend that art is a valid means of inventively expressing something significant, that artistic creation may be a statement of the ugly, the tragic, the awful, and evil, as well as the beautiful.

We are here concerned with experience of beauty, however, which is far more encompassing than art and essentially independent of culturally sanctioned esthetic categories and norms. In the case of the young Japanese, for example, the reply was couched in subjective, phenomenological terms of enjoyment, not in the "objective" terms of artistic canons according to which Mozart would certainly score far above the tuning of instruments. Granted, the young man's enjoyment was more than probably affected by cultural influences, but this does not invalidate the genuineness of his reply nor the enjoyment referred to. All human experience is at least perceptually affected by cultural factors.

Experiencing Beauty

Barring severe neurological or endocrinal deficiency, it is safe to say that everyone experiences beauty countless times. For beauty (or more precisely, the occasion for esthetic experience) is ubiquitous and polymorphous. Anyone who has seen—*and* noticed—a healthy baby, a happy couple, the face of an aged person with the "right" wrinkles in the "right" places, has encountered beauty; anyone who has watched a lively pup or, after a spring rain, a robin digging for worms or dust dancing in a shaft of sunlight filtering through foliage or any one of a million individually variable things, has experienced beauty, although he may have failed to make the most of it.

Anthropologist Edmund Carpenter, in his collection of crisp and colorful observations, *They Became What They Beheld* (1970), reports a sample of the answers some British children gave to the question "What are the twelve loveliest things you know?" One boy's list went:

> The cold of ice cream.
> The scrunch of leaves.
> The feel of clean cloze.
> Water running into a bath.
> Cold wind on a hot day.
> Climbing up a hill looking down.
> Hot water bottle in bed.
> Honey in your mouth.
> Smell in a drug store.
> Babies smiling.
> The feeling inside when you sing.
> Baby kittens.

A little girl's answers were:

> Our dog's eyes.
> Street lights on the river.
> Wet stones.
> The smell of rain.
> An organ playing.
> Red roofs in trees.
> Smoke rising.
> Rain on your cheeks.
> The smell of cut grass.
> Red velvet.
> The smell of picnic teas.
> The moon in clouds.*

The freshness, the startling variety, and the existential quality of the children's answers tend to confirm the works of Murphy (1963), Campbell (1949), and Drews (1968), each of whom found that children have a built-in sense of beauty that develops as esthetic judgment and taste if they are given the opportunity to express what is seen. Incidentally, one might argue that the above lists describe delight rather than beauty. But delight is the product of the experience of beauty—as it likewise is of love and play.

While the child's sense of beauty is almost solely emotional, the adult's response is more integrated, involving both feeling and thinking. As Hattwick points out (1949, pp. 292–94), it is "more than skin deep." In fact, since adults are usually preoccupied with utilitarian concerns, their esthetic sensitivity may be so tightly integrated that it fails to register the kaleidoscopic bits of potential beauty that flow across their perceptual

* *They Became What They Beheld*, written by Edmund Carpenter, photographed by Ken Heyman (New York: E. P. Dutton, 1970).

field almost uninterruptedly, for beauty is everywhere for anyone who can recognize it. In John Cage's idiom: "Everywhere we do is music. Everywhere is the best seat" (Carpenter, 1970). The fact that the child's esthetic awareness is not usually in sharp focus does not mean, however, that he is unaffected by objects and scenes that commonly elicit experiences of beauty. Such experiences are characteristic of all phases of life, as Clay argues convincingly in *The Origin of the Sense of Beauty* (1917), and are apt to be a vitally important influence.

Incidentally, one reason the edge of responsiveness to the beauty that marks everyday experience is blunted in many adults is the unfortunate fact that in certain cultures, especially subcultures, such polymorphous esthetic sensitivity is regarded as a lack of maturity and/or masculinity. This, of course, leads to a deplorable narrowing of the range of esthetic phenomena the adult attends to and even to a repression of the feelings of delight that arise from the more subtle and, therefore, all the more socially disapproved sources of beauty.

Universal and Intrinsically Human

To say that the sense of beauty is universal and intrinsically human does not mean, of course, that it is innate, any more than language is. What is innate is the capacity for esthetic experience and the apparently irrepressible tendency to actualize that capacity, through either contemplation or creation of things experienced as beautiful. Man's affinity for deriving gratification from a certain play of shapes, colors, and sounds is manifest through time and space.

IS THERE A NEED FOR BEAUTY? People may love to talk about beautiful things, objects, plays, and places they have seen. But few except those who speak in a professional capacity—philosophers, artists, architects, and now also psychologists—engage in discourses about beauty per se. In fact, the average person seems to be rather bashful about his esthetic emotions and his craving for beauty.

We know about the urge to beauty first from direct personal experience—from the arresting quality of certain perceptions, from their reverberation through memory and the longing for their return. We know about it from the realization that the outstanding moments of our existence were marked by an aura of beauty, a delight of the senses or of something that reaches beyond the senses. We know it further from empirical sources—historical and contemporary, immediate and remote—all of which reveal people's striving to bring at least an element of beauty to their surroundings and, especially, to associate it with the significant areas and events of their lives.

Of course, the need for beauty is not a survival need. Failure to attend to it regularly does not result in noticeable ill effects. A number of other needs must be met before people can consciously turn to the esthetic areas of their need spectrum. Nevertheless, beauty qualifies as a need, even in the strict dictionary sense of the word *need* as "the lack of something which, if present, would tend to further the welfare of the organism or of the species, or to facilitate its usual behavior" (English and English, 1964, p. 339).

In fact, where beauty is concerned, this definition may be regarded as an understatement. Considering the universality of the striving for beauty, it seems closer to an urge, particularly since "urge" implies "impelled" but not "conscious." However, in the current, fluid state of psychological semantics, it is of little consequence whether beauty is referred to as either a need or an urge, as long as it is recognized as specifically human.

In the following brief discussion of various channels through which humanity expresses its esthetic dimension, we will see that each is uniquely human and that all are aimed at beauty as it delights either the senses or, in more purely symbolic ways, the self.

PICTURES, STATUES, MUSIC, AND DANCE.   Only man paints and draws pictures, carves statues, composes songs, makes music, and dances—all of it for the pleasure of eyes or ears, of body or mind and independent of, but compatible with, utilitarian purposes. Testimony to these urges is worldwide and can be traced to prehistoric times in paleolithic cave drawings, rudimentary carvings, and the decoration of such utilitarian objects as the handles of knives and swords, vessels, and receptacles.

One might argue that the drawings discovered on the walls of prehistoric caves and rocks—like a variety of sculptured likenesses of animals and human figures found by archeologists in tombs and sacrificial places—were actually fashioned for purposes of worship and ritual. This interpretation is quite likely correct and simply indicates the prevalence of metaphysical concerns over esthetic needs, not the absence of the latter. Indeed, while the primary purpose of those artifacts was probably ritualistic or talismanic, the care and selectivity with which they were shaped and, especially, decorated clearly reveals a striving toward beauty.

Similarly, the urge to achieve pleasing effects with sound and motion, culminating perhaps in the intricate symphonic works and ballet of our day, seems to go equally far back in time. This inference is based upon the observation that the few remaining preliterate tribes—or the tradition of other, assimilated cultures—engage in chant and vocalizing, in rhythmic handclapping, and foot-thumping rituals, as well as the construction and use of rudimentary instruments to impart and accentuate rhythmic sound patterns. Anand, who has given considerable thought to matters of beauty, surmises that man is obeying some rhythmic impulse from within: "Since man emerged on this earth, he has been compelled by some rhythmic forces within him to do something, to move, to express himself. This force may, perhaps, have been the sheer exuberance which made primitive men thump the ground in the one, two, three beat before killing their prey or after gathering the harvest, or which makes children play about with mud and clay or with crayons" (1963, p. 4).

BUILDING FOR BEAUTY AND PROTECTION.   Perhaps the earliest, most enduring, and perhaps most impressive testimony of man's urge to beauty is expressed in the dwellings and other buildings he has erected since the dawn of time.

> As man—the savage—emerges from the natural cave to build one of his own, origins of the history of architecture are lost in perspective. As he civilized himself he adorned these artificial caves as he set them upon the ground out under the sun. Soon after came buildings from the mind of man himself. He created space in which to live; not only protected from the elements but protected from his fellow man as well. But that was not enough—to live content, now civilized, he *meant* to make these cave buildings beautiful. Then architecture was born (Wright, 1962, p. 11).

Architectural building reveals a search not only for effectiveness but for style; that is, for patterns that are either pleasing, inspiring, or otherwise esthetically satisfying. "Style" is used here in the sense of "variable and changing patterns" of construction and decor. Without this qualification, it could certainly be said that numerous animals—birds, ants, bees, rabbits, beavers—build exquisite "style" into their shelters. But their patterns, intricate and functionally effective though they are and beautiful though they may appear to the human eye, are strictly stereotyped in that they are species-predictable and uniform through time and space. Thus, the living and working quarters of ants and roaches, which paleontologists discovered in volcanic rock formations (preserved since prehistoric ages), reveal the very same patterns that these structures assume today. In contrast, human dwellings—from early man's most primitive structures to Buckminster Fuller's geodesic domes—typically reveal patterns that change with time.

PERSONAL APPAREL AND ADORNMENT.   This is an area in which the universality of the pursuit of esthetic values is particularly marked and varied. Granted, not all vestmental endeavors and personal adornments are aimed purely at beauty. Clothing, aside from its protective functions, plays a significant role as an indicator of public status, power, or function; for example, ritualistic, military, and academic apparel. It also conveys certain values, intentions, purposes, or attributes of the wearer—conventional or unconventional, modest, seductive, attention getting, prestige seeking, counterculture oriented, and so on. Nevertheless, what clothing reveals more than anything else (if it is freely chosen) is an attempt to beautify the wearer.

The intensity of need or drive is commonly regarded as a function of the intensity of the obstacles that the organism is willing to tackle in order to gain satisfaction for that need. If this criterion is valid, the urge to beauty reveals itself as particularly strong. At all times, apparently, and everywhere, people have been willing to suffer torments in order to be thought beautiful or, at least, to improve their looks. Throughout time and cultures, there are instances of fashion and other cultural norms of physical appearance whose pursuit causes intense discomfort and deprivation to the aspirants and is even occasionally liable to impair their health. While the male of the species has not been entirely immune to cultural demands and concerns of this nature (for example, the perforation of ears and nose that was customary in certain cultures of the South Pacific and, even closer to us, high, stiff shirt collars), it is the female who has commonly been subjected to demands for personal esthetics.

In the past, and perhaps even now, the focus of cultural norms governing personal appearance was decidely the female, and the demands of these norms have ranged from the unreasonable to the cruel. The ancient Chinese custom of binding the feet of the female from childhood on, to lend her a presumedly graceful gait, is probably the worst. A close second to this cruel practice used to be customary in Cambodia. The necks of young women of high standing were stretched through the gradual superposition of unremovable metal rings around the neck—the final effect of which evoked the idea of a long-stemmed flower issuing from the shoulders. A similar practice, plus the stretching of the lower lip of the female, was the custom among certain African tribes, also.

More familiar to Western peoples is the age-old emphasis on the slender waist. This canon was probably aimed at accentuating the fullness of the female bust and hips and still prevails in contemporary beauty contests, despite the physically liberating turn that recent fashion has taken. Ever since the Middle Ages, fashionable women of the Western world have submitted to the ordeals of corsets and girdles, starvation diets and dangerous drugs, to achieve the shape required to be beautiful or, short of that, to appear beautifully dressed. Again, it might be argued that such dietary and vestmental acrobatics are aimed at gaining social status or approval as well as at pleasing the eye. But the two are not incompatible, nor does it invalidate the power of the urge to beauty to find it used as a means to secure the satisfaction of certain elementary social needs.

FOOD AND DRINK. Only man cooks his food and salts, sweetens, pickles, heats, or chills it. He does all this with an investment of time, effort, care, and skill sufficient to classify these culinary stunts as an art. Where scarcity does not interfere with a normal concern for food, changing it into an obsession, eating serves not merely to nourish but also to please the palate. And where material civilization permits, refinement in the presentation of the food becomes an aim, also. With the exception of the United States (where food and eating are often viewed as matters of health) very few advanced cultures consider food primarily from the point of health and nourishment. In those cultures, the *choice of food* is governed by the pursuit of delight—though the *fact of eating* is, of course, commanded by hunger or at least by appetite.

Somewhere at the periphery of the pursuit of beauty is the cross-culturally observed pursuit of pleasure through excitants and intoxicants: alcohol, tobacco, hemp, hashish, "magic" mushrooms, and so forth. Most of these produce a potentially harmful feeling of visceral well-being, and some, especially LSD, are known to cause hallucinatory experiences of inexpressible beauty that the user is anxious to relive.

FICTION AND FACT. So compelling or spellbinding is beauty that tales, legends, and other forms of literature in which human imagination can give itself free reign frequently depict the good guys (and gals) as physically beautiful to heighten the quality of their character and virtue. The deeply rooted human tendency to associate physical beauty with moral goodness is observable even in daily life. There is not only considerable anecdotal and everyday evidence that physical beauty influences our evaluation of people; research also reveals this tendency. For example, Berscheid and Walster (1972) report that "unattractive [nursery school] boys were more likely to be described by their classmates as aggressive and antisocial than were attractive boys. Children said that the unattractive boys were more likely to fight a lot, hit other students, and yell at the teacher" (p. 44).

The researchers were unable to conclude from their observations that the unattractive children actually did misbehave more than others. Instead, their reports suggest numerous a priori judgments on the part of both adults and children.

On their work with grade-school children, Berscheid and Walster further report that "contrary to the popular belief that 'beauty and brains don't mix,' there is evidence that physical attractiveness may even influence which students make the honor roll" (p. 45). This conclusion was reached on the basis of a study involving four hundred fifth-grade teachers who were asked to examine children's report cards. Attached to each card was a photograph of a child. "We predicted that the child's appearance would influence the teacher's evaluation of the child's intellectual potential, despite the fact that the report cards were identical in content. It did" (p. 45).

Berscheid and Walster found that college students "thought good-looking persons were generally more sensitive, kind, interesting, strong, poised, modest, sociable, outgoing, and exciting than less attractive persons" (p. 46).

The researchers also studied interview data taken from women now in their late forties and early fifties. Their analysis revealed that the "physical attractiveness of each woman in her early twenties bears a faint but significant relationship to some of the life experience she reports over two decades later. . . . The more attractive the woman had been in college, the less satisfied, the less happy, and the less well-adjusted she was twenty-five years later" (p. 74). Beauty, like everything else, can have its problematic aspects.

Esthetic Behavior and the Bowerbird

With respect to the esthetic dimension of man's behavioral repertoire, we must examine—as we have done with his symbolic and linguistic dimension—the objection formulated by certain psychologists and ethologists that this behavior is not uniquely human. The affirmation that only man aims to incorporate beauty into his buildings and to decorate them with pleasing, nonutilitarian features and objects, is challenged by those psychologists and ethologists who find man only quantitatively (not qualitatively) different from other animals. Their case, in this instance, is tenuously perched upon the observation of a curious feature in the behavior of one animal species, the bowerbird of Australia and New Guinea.

At first sight, the case is as perplexing as it is fascinating. This is especially so when one learns about it from one with a gift for telling a story, drawn, however, from well-documented sources.

> Archbold's bowerbird, for example . . . clears a small stage in his high mountain forest and carefully carpets it with fern. Then he decorates it with snail shells, dead beetles, lumps of charcoal, and other attractive bric-a-brac. He waits, perched well above his sidewalk display. If a female comes by, he drops to the middle of his stage, crouches, makes begging sounds, crawls toward her. Should she be unimpressed, she will move on to another Archbold's bowerbird. The rejected one will rearrange his ornaments and resume his wait like a patient Arab. (Ardrey, 1966, p. 74).

> At the other and more evolved extreme is the gardener bowerbird, frequently referred to as a maypole-builder. He leans sticks against a sapling in the shape of a teepee, adding more and more until the structure may be taller than a man. The most advanced species, the crestless gardener, will create internal chambers in his tower, then top it with a broad roof against the forest's heavy rains. In the cleared area around the tower he plants moss for his dancing stage. He will decorate his little lawn with shells, berries, and piles of cut flowers (p. 75).

Ardrey then proceeds to describe what he calls "the cultural champions of the nonhuman animate world" (p. 75), the satin bowerbirds, which not only build a house but paint the interior black by chewing charcoal, mixing it with saliva, and applying it with a spongelike wad of bark that serves as a brush.

When Ardrey calls the bowerbird "a cultural genius," he is speaking with the legitimate rhetorical license of the novelist but without the sophistication of the authoritative critic. For the latter we call upon Adler, who uses as his criterion for differentiating human behavior from all other Hebb's concept of "species-predictability" (1958) of a given form of behavior—or, as Lorenz terms it, the "ubiquitousness of its distribution" among *all* members of a species *without exception* (1952, p. 77). Adler concludes his examination of the case by stating that ". . . the 'interior decoration' of the bower-birds, like the 'operatic warbling' of other species of birds, is species-predictable and instinctive . . . [therefore] the activities in question, though they may look like interior decoration or like the making of music, are not at all comparable to the human performances they resemble, anymore than the instinctive dance-language of the honey bees is comparable to human speech" (1967, p. 117).

Because of the fundamental nature of the issue, because it comes up again and again in regard to the quantitative or qualitative difference of man, it seems worthwhile to reproduce here the essence of Adler's argumentation:

> With respect to any statement about some performance that man and man alone exhibits—and which some men may, in fact, engage in and others not—an apparently similar performance by another species of animal does not constitute an infirmative negative instance if the latter is instinctive or species-predictable, while the human performance is acquired or learned and voluntarily or intentionally exercised, as evidenced by its nonubiquitous distribution and by its wide range of variability within the human species (1967, p. 117; Adler's italics).

Need I reiterate that the issue is here emphasized not to boastfully assert the superiority of man but only to emphasize his specificity. The issue pertains to the necessity to study man as a being *sui generis* who cannot be understood in terms of the functioning of animals and/or machines, and to the social and other consequences of this specificity.

A Mode of Communication

Beauty, like love—also, perhaps, like ritualistic play—offers a path to knowledge of a kind that cannot be adequately gained or imparted in intellectual ways. It is intuitively recognized as an effective vehicle for the expression of certain personal, especially affective, messages. "Say it with flowers" is not merely a florist's line. Love may speak more convincingly through this medium than through words, unless the words are chosen with a keen concern for beauty (hence the literate lover's bent for writing poems).

The following poem is an example of the unique capacity of the esthetic medium for communicating the indescribable quality of certain experiences. It is particularly illustrative because it reveals the universality of this means of communication. Although it was written by a person far removed from us in time, space, status, and culture, these differences do not preclude meaningful affective sharing. Indeed, its author succeeds in lending an extraordinarily vivid presence to the poignancy of his emotion.

> The sound of her silk skirt has stopped.
> On the marble pavement dust grows.
> Her empty room is cold and still.
> Fallen leaves are piled against the doors.
> Longing for that lovely lady
> How can I bring my aching heart to rest?
>
> (Emperor Wu-ti, 200 B.C.)*

The event that the poet describes can be stated in one sentence: he mourns his deceased wife. But it is the *quality and depth* of his feeling that is communicated by his selection of spare, still, desolate images. Almost as beautifully phrased as the emperor's plaint is MacLeish's comment on it: "Four images, one of sound, two of sight, one of feeling, each like a note plucked on a stringed instrument. Then a question like the chord the four would make together. And all at once we *know*. We know this grief."† Indeed, we know it not in intellectual terms but by way of its affective contagion, its expression of a quality of understanding that eludes explanation.

Music lovers will insist that music "speaks" to them and speaks in different tongues expressing many and distinctly different things that cannot be put into words. Articulation would destroy the quality of the message. For music speaks not of particular experiences but of the *essence* of certain experiences. In Richard Wagner's words, "What music expresses is . . . not . . . the passion, love, or longing of such-and-such an individual on such-and-such an occasion, but passion, love, or longing in itself, and this it presents in that unlimited variety of motivations, which is the exclusive and particular characteristic of music, foreign and inexpressible in any other language" (Langer, 1963, pp. 221–22). Langer concludes that "Music is . . . *formulation and representation* of emotions, moods, mental tensions, and resolutions . . . a source of insight" (pp. 221–22), in other words, a cognitive medium as well as a source of delight. Similarly, when asked the meaning of her dancing, Isadora Duncan replied, "If I could tell you what it means, there would be no point in dancing it" (Carpenter, 1970).

---

* Arthur Waley, *Translations from the Chinese* (New York: Alfred A. Knopf, 1955).

† Archibald MacLeish, "Why Do We Teach Poetry?" *Atlantic Monthly*, March 1956, p. 52.

METAPHYSICAL INSIGHT. Just as beauty is the choice means for the affective communication of emotion, so it tends to offer privileged access to metaphysical understanding. It is no coincidence that, especially in the past, the great art of all cultures was expressed in the construction and decoration of temples, cathedrals, and even village churches. The convergent effect of the experience of beauty and the idea of perfection tends to elicit the notion of ultimate transcendence, of the sublime and the divine. In fact, the experienced connection between the esthetic and the divine is so intimate that certain churches come very near to substituting the one for the other. Similarly, quite a few individuals of esthetic disposition claim to encounter the divine in nature. The beauty, drama, and awesome grandeur of nature, perhaps more than that of anything man-made, serves to introduce many individuals to a truth that defies verbal description and systematic teaching: "Nature never taught me that there exists a God of glory and of infinite majesty. I had to learn that in other ways. But nature gave the word *glory* a meaning for me. I still do not know where else I could have found one. I do not see how the 'fear' of God could ever have meant to me anything but the lowest prudential efforts to be safe, if I had never seen certain ominous ravines and unapproachable crags" (Lewis, 1960, p. 37).

An Alternative to "True-False" and "Multiple Choice"?

In conclusion, we may consider MacLeish's anecdote on the importance of poetry. "In ancient China the place of poetry in men's lives was assumed as a matter of course; indeed, the polity was based on it. . . . For thousands of years the examinations for the Chinese civil service were examinations in poetry, and there is no record that the results were more disappointing to the throne than examinations of a different character might have been" (1956, p. 52).

Such a practice may strike technological man as absurd or, at best, amusing. Obviously, in our world no amount of poetic talent would help fix the elevator, the computer, or even the typewriter. But as far as civil service roles are concerned, it might be argued that ancient Cathay's exams were perhaps as valid as ours. The capacity to express significant content in beautiful form—that is, cogently and elegantly, with due regard for necessary detail, selection, balance, accentuation, or mitigation—requires qualities approximating those that employers are apt to look for in any place at any time. The ability to create beauty "on assignment" requires the interplay of intelligence and sensitivity, discipline and imagination, character and the capacity to harmonize conflicting demands. The question is, however, where would we find the examiners for such exams in a culture that tends to consider beauty a mere frill?

IV Freedom, Responsibility

The question of freedom is basic to the humanistic concept of man. Does man have a variable margin of freedom, of genuine choice in the face of alternative courses of action? Or is he entirely subjected to biological and social pressures and pulls, a toy tossed about by impersonal forces? This, perhaps, is the central question. Since there is no responsibility where there is no freedom, neither can there be ethics without freedom.

Related to the question of freedom and responsibility is the undeniable evidence of man's inhumanity to his fellow man and of the bursts of destructiveness and cruelty that have marred his record from its earliest beginnings. While humanistic psychology recognizes and celebrates man as the eminently capable, competent, incomparably endowed, and transcending animal, it is neither blind nor indifferent to his tragically somber side. Is man in his deepest recesses evil? Or has he so far failed to outfit his mind's eye with a lens wide enough to encompass his fellow man's predicament and his own? Is he indeed the unfinished animal, saddled with the difficult but exhilarating task of achieving his own completion? The fate of civilization may depend on the answer to, and subsequent action on, this question.

11 Human Freedom: Real or Illusory?

From the moment that the child stands upright, wobbly and top-heavy on his two little legs, he wants to go his own way. Especially during his so-called negative phase, the healthy child displays countless, often amusing, signs of a budding urge for freedom (in the elementary sense of release from external physical and symbolic constraints). One of the first words a child learns is *no,* and he will use it with gleeful self-assertion even in situations that call for neither "Yes" nor "No."

In the healthy adult, the urge for freedom aims for more than mere independence from parents, offspring, or mate. Nor does it stop at a desire for independence from physical and economic forces or the demands of his fellowmen. Frequently, even before he has achieved these elementary freedoms, man wants to be free to think, to value, to love as he wants, and to make his own choices and decisions even in matters that are of no consequence to his survival or physical well-being. Indeed, he typically insists on the freedom to make his own mistakes. Beyond the freedom *from,* he wants the freedom *to.* Failure to move beyond the former forfeits mature, responsible functioning and, as Fromm masterfully demonstrated in *Escape From Freedom* (1941), is apt to entail severe consequences for the individual and society.

The quest for freedom starts with the need for independence—an elementary and not necessarily constructive form of freedom. Ideally, this need for independence matures into a more evolved form, designated as autonomy or self-rule. Autonomy differs from independence in that the need for increasing liberty develops in combination with a growing awareness of the requirements for structure in a life that is personally and socially effective. The healthy individual, free from crippling dependency, tends toward this state of increased self-determination, that is, toward wanting to regulate and run his own life despite the effort and hardship inherent in such. This tendency represents a mature parallel to the child's urge to stand on his own feet and walk by himself rather than be carried by others who could move him faster, surer, and without effort and risk on his part. So strong is this need that the young, upon reaching adolescence, typically reject the symbolic restraints—the do's and don'ts—that governed their childhood. Even when those rules are indispensable for effective living, it seems that the individual must discover them on his own before he realizes their usefulness.

As his awareness expands, the individual gains an insight into the inherent lawfulness of existence, especially of coexistence with his fellowmen. For instance, he gradually becomes aware of the power of habits— the behavioral ease, economy, and reliability of good habits, of the social and personal liabilities of bad habits. As a result, he tends—operationally, if not reflectively—to introduce certain regularities into his behavior. These regularities lend a certain order or structure to his existence, but correlatively they reduce freedom—at least the freedom to act capriciously, unpredictably, and arbitrarily. As the individual matures further, he realizes that rules and regulations actually allow considerable room within which he can achieve autonomy and a satisfying life. Thus, with relatively few exceptions, most people succeed in gradually organizing a relatively autonomous existence within the bounds of both self-evolved and existing legal and social structures—without forsaking their right to orderly modification of those structures when necessary.

Paradoxically, then, man's need for freedom culminates in the need to devise and comply with restrictions in order to maximize that freedom.

The Victorian Notion of Free Will

It used to be believed and taught that if you wanted something enough, you could achieve it, and this applied to almost anything that belongs to the human repertoire but especially matters of morals, attitudes, and character. Thus, it was believed that by dint of sheer willpower you could become either sensitive or tough, relaxed or exciting, self-confident, loving, happy, religious, successful, and so on. Similarly, stern educators and reformers insisted that anyone hampered by deeply ingrained, undesirable habits could bring these to a screeching halt by a heroic act of will. Because of its emphasis upon effort, control, and persistence, May (1969) calls this the Victorian concept of free will—an absolute, exalted, and unrealistic notion of man's volitional capacities.

To deny the validity of the Victorian notion of free will is not to deny, of course, that most people are able to set goals for themselves and follow through with them, or at least make significant progress towards them. There is abundant evidence, certainly, that some individuals are capable of achieving spectacular results, often against incredible odds. However, man's volitional capacity does have limits, as recent developments in a variety of areas (psychology, psychotherapy, sociology, and biochemistry) have revealed. Thus, addiction to hard drugs clearly cannot be overcome by voluntary control, even though the will to overcome is doubtless an important variable in the process. Psychopathological conditions also may severely affect man's volitional capacities (Arieti, 1961, 1972; Farber, 1966).

In the more specifically human realm, openness, undefensiveness, or congruence cannot be achieved by fiat because these modes of functioning are to a greater or lesser extent dependent upon such social-environmental variables as the absence of threat to the self. Other limitations of man's volition are defined in the work of psychiatrist Leslie Farber who, in *The Ways of the Will* demonstrates that there are modes and attributes that are resistant to self-coercive development. The subject can acquire the style and external characteristics of these things but not their mode of being. "I can will knowledge, but not wisdom; going to bed, but not sleeping; eating, but not hunger; meekness, but not humility; self-determination . . . but not courage; lust, but not love; religiosity, but not faith" (1966, p. 15).

Consistent with this is Maslow's observation (1968) that such personality attributes as creativity, spontaneity, excitability, humor, originality, and similar *expressive* modes of being are not nearly as achievable through sustained effort and practice as the development of attributes that require mainly *repressive* control; for example, perseverance, industriousness, endurance. All this casts doubt, of course, upon the validity of such time-honored expressions as "Where there's a will there's a way." Such notions are not based upon observation and reasoning, but are a priori expressions of value orientation. The Victorian concept of free will is, like ideological notions generally, unexistential, an abstraction at the service of a misleadingly high-minded affirmation of man.

It hardly seems necessary to point out, too, that in the context of this discussion, *freedom* does not mean freedom of action—for example, the physical freedom to move about unrestrained; the political freedom to vote, hold public office, speak out, assemble, etc.; the economic freedom to engage in commercial or financial transactions. All these refer to prerogatives, to physical, social, civil, or other freedoms which are not achievements but come automatically as part of legitimate membership in a particular society.

Conditions for Freedom

For a free action to be possible, several conditions must be met. Autonomous behavior does not follow, of course, from the presence of these conditions—it wouldn't be free if it did. Necessary conditions are not sufficient conditions.

Agency. First, there must be an agent. This requirement may seem redundant; indeed, where there is no agent there can be no action. The important thing, however, about this seemingly tautological statement is the *nature* of the agent. Any agency—animate or inanimate, human or nonhuman—has a certain nature, certain powers, certain limitations. Thus, it belongs to the nature of a piece of granite to be hard, dense, and (if large) also heavy. No properties of this sort belong to, say, a planarium worm—whose particular nature is such that, cut in half, it grows into two planaria. In turn, the power to divide and replicate is not in the nature of a dog. Clearly, the nature of the agent is a source of both powers and limitations; planaria can split but cannot bark, dogs can bark but cannot split. As for man, his nature is all that is described in this book and much more, though it can be stated also in terms of limitations. It follows from all this that if one wants to make sense in talking about man, one must consider him as an agent *with the nature of man.*

Taken by themselves, these considerations are obvious and serve only to introduce my point. Less obvious is the fact that because of the nature of the human agent, such *specifically* human behavior as choosing can occur *only in response to values*—the term *value* here being taken in the broadest sense of anything that can be the object of desire. Even his non-specifically human functions—eating, drinking, sexual activity—occur in remarkably selective ways. This selectivity is, of course, far more pronounced when it concerns such behavior as believing, learning, loving or, for that matter, their opposites.

Because of his particular nature as the value-searching animal, man can choose only what he perceives, in one respect or another, as good. Thus, he cannot deliberately hurt what he loves, nor can he destroy solely for the sake of destruction. True, he can cause pain and suffering to those he loves, but only for purposes that he sees, in one respect or another, as serving a good for others or himself; for example, correction, just punishment, retaliation, even vengeance—which he is then apt to call "teaching a lesson." In so doing, he is, of course, still pursuing values—either rationally or irrationally. (Need I add that man is capable of causing particularly great pain and damage to his "loved ones"; i.e. relatives and friends who ought to be and usually are a person's loved ones, but may no longer be such.) He can even choose to endure great discomfort and pain, and to expose himself to loss of life—but always for the sake of a good which, rightly or wrongly, he deems proportionate. The relevance of this first condition to the freedom/unfreedom issue will become clearer after an examination of the next condition.

Alternatives. To speak meaningfully of choice, there must also be alternatives. Where only one course of action is open, there is, of course, the alternative of nonaction. But this is often a purely theoretical case, for the alternatives must be, generally speaking, acceptable. Thus, the POW's "alternative" to treason may be torture and death—hardly an alternative.

According to Miller (1961), the larger the number of alternatives, the greater the freedom. This, however, must be properly understood. To enhance freedom, the alternatives must be, or must be perceived to be, significantly different. The numerous brands of soap or cereal displayed on the supermarket shelves hardly increase the buyer's freedom. For differences are rarely a matter of substance, cost, or quality but merely of advertising. On the other hand, if the differences are really worth considering, the individual is able to take into account more significant personal variables and thus augment his chances for a satisfying choice. Only in this limited sense can it be said that multiple alternatives afford greater freedom. Actually, one single alternative, *if acceptable*, suffices for a person to act freely. Increasing the alternatives enhances freedom only in the sense that it offers broader latitude or that more people are apt to be served.

Knowledge or Information. It should not be overlooked that the value of alternatives is predicated entirely upon the subject's knowledge of their nature. He must be able to visualize or calculate the results likely to follow from his choice. Where adequate knowledge is lacking, there is no true choice. Given a "choice" between season tickets for series "A" and series "B" without any information as to whether one may have to do with concerts and the other with sports and without any information as to which is which, the subject may be offered a fine thing in any case, but not a choice. Similarly, the opportunity to choose from a slate of candidates without adequate knowledge of their backgrounds, records, or platforms offers no more than the chance to mark a ballot. Under such conditions, multiplying the alternatives ad infinitum would not increase one's freedom.

Proper Means of Implementation. A fourth condition for meaningful freedom is an environment that provides means, structures, or institutions without which one could not exercise his prerogatives. For example, most employees are required to be at work by eight or nine A.M. and are allowed to leave by five or six P.M. However, if a job seeker's residence is a considerable distance from his employment and if no transportation is available, he is for all practical purposes not free to choose to work for that employer. Robinson Crusoe was free to go home, since neither external coercion nor internal compulsion prevented him from leaving his island. But he lacked the means to carry out his choice. The same applies to members of severely underprivileged cultures or subcultures; they may be free to learn all kinds of skills and trades, but the environment may fail to provide the means for such freedom to become a reality.

Adequate Psychological Functioning. The degree of freedom of any choice is further dependent upon the quality of the subject's psychological functioning—his experiential unity, personal integration, or "congruence," as Rogers (1959) calls it. *Congruence* refers to a state of relative accord existing at any particular moment between the individual's perceptions and his experience; more simply, between what he *actually* feels and what he *thinks* he feels. Discrepancies between experience and perception are due to deletion and/or distortion (repression) of certain threatening elements of experience that the subject "wants" to ignore. Since repression amounts to a form of ignorance and since ignorance always restricts freedom, repression limits the individual's ability to choose meaningfully. (The removal of repression and substitution of insight is the reason, incidentally, that therapy is called a process of liberation: it allows pertinent data to rise in awareness and consequently enables the subject to choose with greater knowledge, hence greater freedom.)

The Question

The question, then, is, Does man have the capacity to make the relatively self-determined moves commonly called choices and what are the grounds for concluding that he does? But why not simply ask whether man has the capacity for self-determination?

If one were to put the question in this neat and lean way, one would have to make sure that those to whom it was addressed were aware of the inescapable fact that no choice is purely self-determined; that allowance must be made for the universal fact that all man's actions occur within "a situation," as the existentialists call it, referring to the infinitely complex fabric of biological and social variables within which free action occurs. Thus, when antitraditionalists like Sartre (1956), who can hardly be suspected of Victorianism, make the startling affirmation that man is *absolutely* free, one must remember that they first make full allowance for the play of biological, social, and physical determinants, the totality of which Sartre subsumes under the concept of "in-itself" (*en-soi*). This leaves absolute freedom operative in the specifically human sphere which he calls the "for-itself" (*pour-soi*). For those who are acquainted with Heidegger rather than Sartre, I might add that the "in-itself" corresponds to Heidegger's concepts of *Umwelt* (environmental determinants) and *Mitwelt* (biological determinants); the *pour-soi* to his concept of *Eigenwelt*, that is, the world of the personal, the symbolic. Because of these distinctions, both Sartre and Heidegger can affirm that man is able to exert his freedom even amidst the most repressive and dire conditions.

The Answers

The answers fall essentially into two antithetical categories, the free and the nonfree, as has always been the case, for the controversy did not begin with some "discovery" by modern science. Thoughtful people of all times have noticed the play of external and/or personal determinants of behavior, and numerous attempts have been made to resolve the issue in terms of one or the other of these determinants. But it can be resolved in neither purely mentalistic nor purely physicalistic terms, as I hope to indicate in a moment. Progress in the resolution of the question was hampered for a long time by the opponents' ideologies: moralistic-theological in the case of the traditional atheistic or religious humanist; and materialistic-iconoclastic in the case of behaviorists and assorted social scientists whose concept of man was rooted in nineteenth-century mechanistic philosophy.

Humanistic psychology and other humanistically oriented disciplines are, of course, fully cognizant of the part played by genetic and sociological determinants in man's behavior. Choice can exist only within the latitude afforded by these determinants. Heredity and environment are warp and woof of the fabric of man's existence; choice is the design he introduces into the fabric of these givens.

One might wonder if such an issue, persisting throughout the generations, must be considered insoluble. Not at all. In fact, to anyone familiar with both the phenomenological and the (nonmechanistic) empirical epistemologies, it seems like a vanishing issue. Conversely, he who views it from a mechanistic point of view continues to see an issue here because he looks for an explanation in terms of such antecedent causes as govern the interaction of, say, billiard balls. Because psychology is still largely viewed in mechanistic terms, therefore, the issue must be dealt with.

THE BEHAVIORIST POSITION. B. F. Skinner, the contemporary leader of neo-Watsonian radical behaviorism, holds that freedom—that is, man's capacity for autonomous behavior—is pure illusion, an error in interpretation whose roots plunge deep into prescientific ages when man was ignorant of the causes of natural phenomena. Just as primitive man invented gods to account for "doing" the thundering, the raining, or the growing, so he invented agencies like the "will" to account for his "willing." Similarly, Skinner contends, such concepts as "person," "self," "personality," and the like are expressions of man's prescientific urge to attribute an agency to his various environmental responses. In keeping with such primitive modes of thought, man sought to reify these presumed agencies, to make them re-al or objectlike, as if they were expressions of a *homunculus* (a little man) operating from somewhere within the organism. Thus, according to Skinner, what is termed "autonomous man" is but an ancient mislabeling and reification of man's ignorance about the conditioning effects of his social environment.

In Skinner's view, behavior is solely a function of "the contingencies of the environment." Whenever a particular behavior is positively reinforced, its rewarding character increases the probability that the individual will repeat that particular action. Thus do patterns of behavior—habits, styles, cultures—develop. The humanistic psychologist admits that there is much truth in this but contends that this is not the only way that the human process unfolds. Some of the most significant actions do not occur solely in response to environmental contingencies but originate from a complex exchange of "internal" and "external" variables. To this, Skinner replies that the human being does not control anything of significance; that he is, instead, controlled by environmental forces which have operated throughout history, at cross-purposes and randomly.

He predicts, too, that unless man assumes control, substituting rational regulations for the wildly irrational and destructive forces still in command, this disorderly process must lead to the demise of mankind. Skinner, who paradoxically devoted a lifetime of effort to the development of insight and of mechanisms for an alternative, rational environment and, consequently, for a rationally and socially responsible style of life, must be recognized as a man of great, if mistaken, humanitarian purpose. He cannot, however, be considered a humanist since he denies the reality, indeed, the very possibility, of self-determination, of consciousness, and of selfhood—notions that are at the core of the humanistic concept of man.

The basis of Skinner's extremely far-reaching doctrine lies in his experimental work with animals—mainly rats and pigeons—with which his approach is remarkably effective. With humans, his theory of positive reinforcement has been applied in systematic fashion only to young children, hospitalized mental patients, and in behavioral therapy dealing with the removal of such minor forms of undesirable, deficient, or harmful behaviors as phobias or compulsions. Such scant evidence is hardly a sufficient basis for valid generalizations about human life as it is typically spent: as a complex process unfolding not in the laboratory but in the outside world and covering a span of time that reaches, on the average, some seven decades.

One must keep in mind throughout this discussion that Skinner recognizes only quantitative differences between man and other species: to him, what is true for the rat is true, in principle, for man. Neither man nor beast has a self-structure, according to Skinner; hence, neither is capable of being guided from within. Both are determined exclusively by the positively reinforcing contingencies of the environment. Through systematic "manipulation of these contingencies" in such a way as to make them rewarding and to call forth the desired responses, the behavioral engineer can condition mice and men to behave in the desired direction.

This much is true—as far as it goes: Man can be controlled by outside forces. We constantly witness such successful manipulations by the media, politics, education, and our immediate environment. We ourselves practice such control upon those with whom we interact, sometimes deliberately, sometimes involuntarily. However, the issue here is not control but freedom. That man's behavior can be controlled does not mean that it cannot also be free. The fact that I can be induced to drink tea when thirsty and without an alternative does not mean that I cannot choose to drink what I like better—say, coffee—if given a choice. What the humanist disagrees with is not Skinner's affirmation that man can be controlled by the contingencies of reinforcement but his denial of the very *possibility* of autonomous human action when the conditions for such action are present.

THE HUMANIST PERSPECTIVE.   This discussion will not be cast in terms that Skinner scornfully labels "the literature of autonomy." It will not exalt the greatness and glory of man's freedom, nor will it stress the necessity of recognizing man's autonomy *for the sake of* safeguarding his feeling of responsibility (for which freedom is, of course, a requisite) or maintaining his dignity, his preeminently rightful place in the universe. Such purposes are admittedly respectable in their own right, but in the present context they are not strictly to the point. The conclusion that man is capable of acting freely need not serve any ulterior purposes; *that conclusion follows from the evidence about man.*

A Comparison

Certain portions of the behavioristic and humanistic positions, then, are similar. According to Skinner, *positive* reinforcement will cause the subject to react in the predicted direction. According to the humanist, the subject will choose what he perceives as a good. Since positive reinforcement is by definition perceived as a good (and assuming no alternatives other than that given by the experimenter) these portions of the two theories run parallel, except for their basic assumptions: choice/no choice (that is, self-determination versus determination from without). This can be diagrammed as follows:

Faced with two behavioral courses of action,

is *determined* by
the subject   the alternative deemed most rewarding.
will *choose*

The divergences of the two positions are summed up below.

	Behaviorism	**Humanism**
Focus of the explanation:	the external determinants	the internal determinants
Critical variable:	the contingencies of the situation	the subject, his active nature
Concept of man:	passive, merely reactive	active, selective
Concept of behavior:	mechanistic	phenomenological

Proceeding from the humanistic premise, I will develop briefly the following three propositions: 1) perception is an active process: 2) man acts on his perceptions; 3) man perceives himself as free.

PERCEPTION IS AN ACTIVE PROCESS.   Let us begin by stating the case in terms of the kind of evidence—experimental—that our opponent recognizes as valid. Most experimental work showing the active nature of human perceptions comes from gestalt psychology, self-theory, and organismic psychology. Characteristically, the findings demonstrate a difference between what the subject is *given* and what he (perceptually) *receives*. Widely known among the results of gestalt and other research in perception is the tendency of the human organism to perceive configurationally, that is, in organized wholes and patterns. For instance, the seven stars that form the Big Dipper are, physically and ontologically, wholly unrelated but are perceived phenomenally as forming an organized whole, a constellation. This dynamic property of perception underlies the well-known, basic tenet that "the whole is more than the sum of its parts." And it is this dynamic property that led Michotte (1963) to conclude that perception is infinitely richer than the stimuli.

PERCEPTIONS, NOT STIMULI.   The following example, taken from Snygg and Combs's well-known introduction to phenomenological psychology is typical of the common experience that behavior is guided not by objective reality but by perception—even when perception is (objectively) erroneous:

> Several years ago one of the authors was driving a car at dusk along a western road. A globular mass about two feet in diameter suddenly appeared directly in the path of the car. A passenger in the front seat screamed and grasped the wheel, attempting to steer the car around the object. The driver tightened his grip and drove directly into it.

> In each case the behavior of the individual was determined by his own phenomenal field. The passenger, an Easterner, saw the object in the highway as a boulder and fought desperately to steer the car around it. The driver, a native of the vicinity, saw it as tumbleweed and devoted his efforts to keeping his passenger from overturning the car (1949, p. 14).

Professor Skinner insists upon his tenet that man "has the illusion of acting freely." Which in the above example functions as the illusion, the rock or the tumbleweed? Either way, once perceived and acted upon, the illusion has the force of reality.

MAN PERCEIVES HIMSELF AS FREE.   That man perceives himself as essentially self-determining is a universal fact. Instances to the contrary are felt as strange or abnormal, and persistent feelings of this sort are clinically regarded as symptomatic of severe disturbance. Assuming that in many instances the subject's feeling of autonomous agency is in fact erroneous —that it is, indeed, as the behaviorists contend, a mislabeling of his ignorance—the fact remains that man perceives his actions as self-determined. In fact, the feeling (illusion) of self-determination is a significant part—in certain cases the most significant part—of the experiential input of the move.

As we know from computer science, where input is concerned, error functions as data. Errors, like facts, affect output. Consequently, to the extent that an action is perceived as free, to that extent it is free. Thus, an individual who is, from all available evidence, an ordinary citizen may find himself in a situation where he can save another man's life, but only at the risk of his own. Let us assume there are no witnesses to reward or blame him for his decision. Let us assume further that he ponders the situation, if only for a few seconds. In this fleeting moment of indecision, he may realize that his upbringing presses him to follow one course of action but 1) that his life—that is, everything—is at stake, and 2) that nobody may ever know about the situation and that he himself may not be around to experience the satisfaction of having acted according to his values, and so on. Then he decides to take the risk. During that moment of deliberation he exercised his freedom, in May's phrase, by "throwing the weight of his choice, however slight that weight may be, on the side of one alternative . . ." (1966, p. 175).

The behaviorist might reply that the man in the above example had been conditioned to respond altruistically. This stand, however, is as ideological in nature as the traditional belief in the absolute freedom of the will. It is, of course, impossible to *prove* that a flesh-and-blood person— not a laboratory subject—could be conditioned to sacrifice his life *in secret* for the sake of another. Aside from the fact that such sequences cannot be proven, there is no evidence that the human being, faced in a real-life situation with a matter of life and death, will deny the powerful urge to live because of prior and possibly quite remote and indirect conditioning. (I except from this the individual who has been, for example, culturally conditioned to commit hara-kiri or systematically trained for kamikaze.)

An Alternate Approach

The preceding demonstration of the role of human agency in determining human behavior was formulated in phenomenological or experiential terms. But it is worthwhile, too, to examine the issue in more traditionally academic terms. The terminology in which the issue has been traditionally discussed—for example, determinism, indeterminism, freedom—is still very much in use and stands in urgent need of both clarification and disentanglement. Some of the concepts (freedom and determinism) used to be regarded as direct antitheses, even though in the human sphere they actually are mutually dependent. Others (freedom and indeterminism), traditionally considered synonymous, have proven antithetical upon closer analysis.

Given the confused terminology, the question of whether or not there is such a thing as freedom could not be answered, and many have concluded that freedom is a shaky, ideologically trumped-up notion that cannot withstand rational scrutiny. A brief and rectified definition of each of these terms will lend insight into the futility of much past argumentation and, hopefully, clarify the issue.

Determinism.   To say that an event or process is "determined" means that it does not occur randomly but has one or more known determinants. Applied to man, determinism basically means that human behavior is not a random process, that it has a number of determinants—many of them known, some perhaps unknown. In the humanistic framework, one of these determinants—in many cases, the most important—is man himself. Determinism, then, does not necessarily mean that man is unfree and entirely subjected to forces beyond his ken or control. It simply refers to the operation of known determinants. Unless the nature of these determinants is totally naturalistic—that is, independent of and unaffected by human agency—determinism, as recently redefined, does not necessarily imply a negation of freedom.

Freedom, Autonomy, Liberty.   These concepts have been and continue to be validly used as synonyms. Each refers to a variable measure of man's capacity for partaking in the process of his behavior and, more particularly, his decision-making behavior. Freedom, then, does not mean absolute command over all variables involved in acts of choice. Nor, as I have noted, does it represent the antithesis of determinism. Indeed, freedom presupposes determinism.

Indeterminism.   This refers to a state of affairs in which the causal forces operate in a totally random, uncontrolled manner. Indeterminism is the direct opposite of both determinism and freedom since it stands for total lack of order, coherence, and predictability.

Free Will.   This notion, now largely fallen into disuse, traditionally referred to the absolute or near-absolute freedom of certain acts. It was, however, the opposite of determinism (as it was traditionally defined).

Unfreedom.   This newcomer replaces the notion of determinism as it was formerly used, that is, as the radical opposite of freedom. Unfreedom, then, refers to an absolute lack of freedom, genuine choice, or other human capacity for voluntary action. The concept applies to man as viewed by B. F. Skinner.

Hard and Soft Determinism. If freedom and determinism are not necessarily antithetical but (in the view of most contemporary authors) complementary, new labels are necessary to differentiate determinism in the naturalistic sense from determinism comprising both naturalistic and human determinants. *Hard determinism* designates the former and *soft determinism* the latter.

Freedom: Inconceivable Without Determinism

In his tightly reasoned "Determinism: Prerequisite for a Meaningful Freedom," Stevens (1967) incisively demonstrates that freedom is inconceivable without determinism. To those familiar with the traditional freedom/determinism polarity, such a statement must appear puzzling, at the very least. Perhaps an example may help to convey the gist of this interesting position.

Suppose that, to flex the muscles of my freedom, I decide to do something very uncongenial to my inclinations: make it a habit to get up at 5:00 A.M. The first morning my impulse is to bury the alarm clock and go back to sleep, which at that particular moment seems to me the only sensible thing to do. But stirred by the challenge I have set myself, I force myself to get up, however miserable the feeling. The next morning the situation is not much different, but I maintain my resolve despite the cost. By the fifth or sixth day, however, the sound of the alarm no longer offends me, nor does the thought of getting up appear cruel and absurd. I am able to get up without feeling miserable or even disgruntled. After two to three weeks, I beat the alarm, awakening "spontaneously" before it has a chance to rouse me. From now on, I wake automatically around five o'clock; the habit has set in; I have become "determined" by it.

Is this remarkable change the result of a decision, or is it an adaptation in the nervous system? It is obviously both. Neither of these forces alone could cause me to awaken regularly, early in the morning, and get up without effort—a form of behavior entirely inconsistent with my history and inclinations. If determinism did not join forces with free choice, human life would be totally inconsistent, unpredictable, and incoherent. Character, personality, life-style—all would be impossible, since all instances of behavior would be uncoordinated, once-in-a-lifetime types of events.

Determinism as a requisite for freedom also accounts in significant measure for the overall predictability that characterizes the choices and decisions of the well-integrated person when he deals with matters that require reason and principle. It therefore follows that, contrary to a widespread notion, the prediction of a certain course of behavior is in no way an indicator of its unfreedom. (Nor is it, of course, necessarily an indication of freedom.) Predictability may be based upon a variety of psychological phenomena—upon rationality or upon habit (rationally or irrationally rooted), upon rigidity, or upon other more or less pathological conditions.

The determinants peculiar to the individual and those inherent in the physical conditions of human existence cannot but cooperate in the act of behavior. How often do we say, after all, "I am determined to do this" when we are *voluntarily* bent on accomplishing something?

12 The Ethical Animal

Humanistic psychology, dealing with man as an existential whole, not a collection of parts and functions, and aiming to place him in center field, is particularly concerned with the ethical dimension of its subject matter. Within the repertory of specifically human behavior, ethics are indeed omnipresent and preeminent. Without a concern for right and wrong, man's unique symbolic capacity becomes a unique liability: Man the Thinker becomes Man the Manipulator (Shostrum, 1967); the technological whiz turns into a genius of destruction; the lawmaker into tyrant; play and love lead to exploitation; and contemplation to scheming. Whether tacit or implicit, recognized or dismissed, ethical values are so inherent a part of our existence that ethical awareness, if not actions, is inescapable.

One of the major reasons established psychology must now yield to new humanistic approaches is because it has left out those aspects of ourselves that we feel stirring most deeply within us. Among these is our awareness of the rightness or wrongness of certain actions and the gnawing internal reverberation that results if we fail to act according to this awareness. This is an admittedly burdensome awareness that is prized, however, by the fully functioning person. Established psychology, instead of illuminating and developing this built-in (and generally reliable) source of guidance for interpersonal behavior, has reduced ethics to propriety: an awareness of and sensitivity to sociologically determined rules and norms that leave only a watered-down notion of man's lawmaking and law-abiding capacities. These capacities, while valuable human assets, are only instrumental and organizational. Ethics, however, aims beyond organization to hominization—the actualization of the higher reaches of man's potential that presuppose freedom and imply a vision of the good life.

Oughts, Shoulds, and Musts

In all societies, people are motivated, at least in part, by an awareness of obligation. They may not always heed that awareness in behavior, but few will deny that they experience various prescriptive promptings from within. Some of these promptings are felt as compelling, though not coercive: "I ought to declare myself responsible"; "I ought to speak in his defense." Others appear more or less optional: "I shouldn't let them wait"; "I should send her condolences." Still others are coercive, entailing specified external sanctions when not heeded: "Drunk drivers (must) go to jail."

In everyday life these categories of injunctions—the ethical, the social, and the legal—do not always appear to be clearly separated from one another. Moreover, certain injunctions fall into more than one category—for example, the injunction against drug abuse, which offends both moral and legal codes of behavior. Of these three categories the ethical is the most fundamental, the other two being in various degrees conditional upon the former. This is clear in the case of the law, which is ineffective without the cooperation of the citizen's conscience. Even social obligations, though only a function of custom and passing fashion, may, under certain conditions, acquire an ethical flavor. For there are the duties of love, compassion, and sympathy as well as those of justice.

The weight and incidence of the ethical component in human interaction vary greatly, depending upon whether the social structure is a society or a community—a *Gesellschaft* or a *Gemeinschaft*, to use Tonnies's (1912) fundamental distinction between optional (for example, clubs) and necessary (for example, the family) forms of group life. Authorities unanimously recognize that a necessary social structure (*Gemeinschaft*) could not maintain itself, much less prosper, without a minimum of consciously or preconsciously enacted *oughts*. Nor could it, at this juncture in human evolution, manage without a good deal of *musts*—paradoxical though this may seem for a free society. As for the good life—something well beyond the survival level—it also requires quite a few of those ball bearings of interpersonal commerce, the *shoulds*.

Only the radical nihilist (a rare breed even in theory) takes exception to these views. But even he is likely to zigzag through his world with the help of arbitrary rules that are either self-chosen or imposed by his reference group and often followed with blind docility.

Is It Ethical?

The basic ethical issue of our time is probably not a failure to recognize or even to act upon ethical injunctions. Notwithstanding the contemporary chorus bemoaning the decline of morals, there is no hard evidence to indicate that actual or perceived unethical conduct is greater now than at any other time throughout history. The forms of conduct may be strikingly different and, in certain cases, their consequences may be immeasurably greater now. But it is hard to argue that there is less ethical *awareness*. With the spread of education or, at least, of schooling and information, the conditions for ethical awareness are actually expanding. The recent involvement of the young in public issues dramatizes this tendency. Since the current wave of social *consciousness* concerns itself with matters of justice, it is, theoretically at least, also a wave of social *conscience,* that is, of ethics.

The basic problem, then, does not seem to lie with ignorance or indifference. Rather it consists of a pervasive confusion about ethics, their nature, meaning, and reality; that is, their binding character. The famous historical cop-out, "What is truth?" is now applied to right and wrong in academic discourse or in everyday language, in thought or in action, implicitly or explicitly. Granted, ethical controversy is not new. There have always been individuals, even schools of thought, proclaiming that right and wrong are purely matters of convention and convenience. In the past, however, such positions were relatively isolated and never gained a broad following. People's beliefs in the reality of behavioral oughts remained deeply anchored in faith, in conscience, in reason, or in a combination of these, since none necessarily excludes the others.

Now, however, the disruptively rapid change that characterizes our world and a bewildering stream of information have created a climate of thought in which even those who mean to take ethics seriously feel increasingly uncertain of what is right and wrong—or whether the question even remains pertinent. Such incertitude has, of course, a debilitating effect upon commitment. One social psychologist summarized the paralyzing effect of this state of affairs with this facetious rule: "Confuse your opponent and you have him supine."

INTRINSIC OR MAN-MADE.   The prevailing confusion and scepticism reaches well beyond the practical *how* and *what*. On the fundamental, theoretical level, one finds authors asking whether there is something specifically ethical in the human make-up or whether ethical values and precepts are purely man-made. In other words, is there a *sense* of right and wrong that develops *from within* (although also dependent on environmental conditions); or are the notions of right and wrong entirely rooted in the cultural soil, out of which they developed as a function of chance and expediency?

Like the questions, the answers are essentially antithetical. Each of these polar positions is represented by both scientists and philosophers. The humanistic sector of psychology, however diverse its composition, seems unanimous in its stance that ethics are inherent in man's nature. These psychologists recognize, of course, that the development of the ethical sense—like the development of language or toolmaking—is dependent upon environmental conditions. Established psychology, on the other hand, clusters around the cultural pole of the issue. Ethical values and injunctions are conventional in origin—that is, man-made to meet the needs of interpersonal commerce under different historical or geographic conditions—and instilled in the young as part of their largely unconscious assimilation of the cultural patrimonium. This is an appealingly simple theoretical position that, as we shall see, fails to withstand scrutiny.

ETHICAL RELATIVISM. The confusion, doubt, and reduction of ethics to sociology can be summarized in one word: ethical relativism. To say that a thing is "relative," however, does not actually say much unless one qualifies the statement. All things are in some way or another relative because they are contingent upon or conditioned, modified, or affected by one or more things. Even an elementary question—Does a tree falling in a forest, unheard by anyone, make a noise?—is relative. For there is no noise where there is no one to hear it.

Relative is apt to signify one thing in one context and its exact opposite in another—for instance, its antithetical contexts in the social sciences and theoretical physics. Fortunately, the two fields are not likely to collide, and their contrasting use of the term is only a minor semantic problem. The elasticity of *relativity*, however, causes confusion in the domain of values, especially ethical values, where it is commonly used to designate two related yet incompatible positions of key significance.

One of these positions, representative of the humanistic view, is that ethical notions and values are intrinsic to man's linguistic ability, on both the preliterate and the literate levels. Correlatively, since this position regards ethical sensitivity as part of the basic human equipment, it also regards the fundamental injunctions of ethics as universal.

The opposite relativistic view is that ethical notions are entirely determined by the cultural environment, that their origin as well as their various manifestations lie entirely and exclusively in historical contingencies.

To reduce the confusion generated by the semantic elasticity of the term, the distinction between *relativity* and *relativism* observed by a number of authors will be used here. *Relativity* refers to the culturally determined variability of rules that are absolute in principle but relative in manifestation; for example, to everyone his due—an absolute rule that may be implemented in a variety of ways. *Relativism*, on the other hand, indicates the radically reductionistic concept that explains ethical behavior, in both principle and fact, *exclusively* by environmental forces.

The same semantic rules will be applied to the words *absolute* and *absolutism*, although these words do not play a key role in contemporary ethical discourse. The former indicates the property of rules that are invariant in principle but require specification in practice. *Absolutistic*, on the other hand, is used to refer to systems that are rigidly invariant in both principle and practice; systems that imply a literal application of absolute dictates and are decidedly on the decline in the modern world.

The Naturalization of Ethics

A massive shift in the center of gravity of man's thinking about himself has developed over the last two centuries or so. The shift has removed man from his position as a specific being who, despite all anatomical and physiological commonality with other primates, is nevertheless significantly distinct from the rest of nature. In the vocabulary of theories and systems, the process is most aptly characterized as the naturalization of man. The effects of this change are most noticeable in the deeply altered moral outlook of our times.

The term *naturalization* may surprise those not well acquainted with the vocabulary of the history of thought. How can something as obviously natural as man be naturalized? Doesn't the human being represent nature at its fullest? Indeed he does. This is precisely the point that humanistic psychology aims to emphasize in its stand against the reduction of man to nature in its minimal expression, which is the ultimate end of naturalization.

Naturalism is a philosophical position that limits nature to the physico-chemical order and its sociological derivatives; its methods, correlatively, are geared solely to the study of that order. As an organism, man is, of course, part of physical-chemical reality. But this concept of nature is too restricted to encompass man, who, as the symbolic animal, is capable of introducing judgment, purpose, and choice in the behavioral equation and of pursuing values other than those imposed by external biological or social pressures. Because of this, man is not as completely the sport of chance and necessity as the rest of nature. Since his capacity to transcend nature, thus conceived, cannot be adequately studied by physicalistic methods, *naturalism leaves out precisely that which is most distinctly human.*

Some may wonder whether an opposition to naturalism as a framework for the study of psychology implies a supernatural view of man. Although humanistic psychology focuses on the fullest expression of the human phenomenon and does not exclude anything pertinent to the human venture, its compass does not extend beyond the confines of the human order. It does include the study of religious behavior and experience—both of which have historically been among the most characteristic expressions of human specificity. But these are natural, not supernatural, phenomena. Humanistic psychology is open even to the preternatural—that is, to observations and reports not explainable by currently known theories and laws. However, extraordinary phenomena assuredly are not the *focus* of humanistic psychology. And the supernatural is distinctly outside the province of this psychology.

Furthermore, naturalization cannot be equated with secularization, which is the separation of ethics from religious authority. Indeed, not all traditional ethical systems are religiously based. Naturalization represents something far more fundamental than secularization. It inevitably down-grades a specifically human phenomenon to a more elementary level.

CONVERGENT INFLUENCES. The changes brought about by the shift in ethical outlook are revolutionary. Yet the manner in which the shift occurred was not in any way revolutionary, no frontal attack was ever made upon established ethics or on ethics as such, at least not in any ostensible or systematic way. An attack of this sort would elicit militant opposition from many quarters. For ethical concern and belief run deep into man's being. What took place over the last two centuries and came into the open during the last few decades is something far more complex than a revolution, something with a ramified root structure that developed well before the surface growth could be identified as pertinent to ethics.

Pulling together some of the many tributaries involved in the stream of events leading to a sharply divided ethical outlook seems particularly appropriate in an introductory work. The forces involved in the natural-ization of ethics also account for the naturalization of modern psychology as a whole and provide a highly relevant backdrop for humanistic psy-chology.

FROM PHILOSOPHY TO SCIENCE. In terms of fields of study, the change may be viewed as a shift from philosophy (in the predominantly meta-physical sense) to science (in the predominantly empirical sense in which the term is now used). Traditionally, ethics belonged exclusively to the domains of philosophy and religion. The systems evolved within these frameworks were based on either natural law—whose dictates are derived from the exercise of reason applied to the study of human nature—or divine law, whose commands are derived from revelation. Underlying both approaches was the sense that right and wrong are part of the basic human "equipment" and therefore universal, that is, common to mankind through time and space.

Today, however, the study of ethics and the criteria for right and wrong are increasingly centered in the new and essentially empirical disciplines, the social sciences. The change did not occur because philos-ophy and religion had somehow been "proven" wrong. Theories about the nature of things—a fortiori positions of faith—cannot be proven. Neither philosophy nor religion has lost its relevance or ceased its contri-bution to the subject. But as a result of the decline in the credence once granted these disciplines, both have undeniably lost the monopoly of their authority in matters of ethics. However, it must not be forgotten that the credibility of a proposition or a doctrine—as distinct from its truth—is largely a function of the *Zeitgeist,* or historical climate of ideas (Polanyi, 1946). Until quite recently, that climate had been distinctly unfavorable to metaphysical and speculative modes of thought—largely as a result of the very same process that accounts for the naturalization of ethics.

This shift in fields of study was paralleled, of course, by a similar methodological movement—from speculation to observation, from deduction to induction, from reasoning to recording—in keeping with the methodological model, the language and techniques that the new disciplines (the social sciences) had borrowed from the prestigious physical sciences. The superficial resemblance thus developed between the established physical sciences and their budding social counterparts largely accounts for the extraordinary credibility that the social sciences came to enjoy. The similarity suggested that the conclusions of the new sciences had the verifiability and effectiveness of the established hard sciences (or, at least, of their applications, since the *theories* of the physical sciences are as subject to error as any other form of knowledge).

Probably more than anything else, this similarity accounts for the impact of the new social sciences upon the ancient ethical doctrines and for their overall success in recent decades. The bases of this success, however, are now coming under severe scrutiny from both outside and within the social sciences (Andreski's *Social Sciences as Sorcery* [1972] is one example).

LOCKE'S EMPIRICISM. The earliest roots of the current orientation to ethics reach back as far as the Renaissance. The revival of Protagoras's principle that human experience, not metaphysics, is the measure of all things came to dominate Western thinking. This created an intellectual climate conducive to far-reaching changes. Conspicuous among these was the emergence of the philosophical doctrine known as British empiricism. This radically new view of the origin of knowledge resulted in not only a new epistemology but the groundwork for a new outlook on man and, consequently, ethics.

According to John Locke, the key figure of British empiricism, all knowledge, capacities, tendencies, and values are acquired by experience; that is, they are formally and informally learned through the interaction of man's consciousness with his environment. Nothing is innately given, not even such elementary notions as causality, time, space, quantity, quality, or any other categories whereby we think. At birth, man is nothing but a clean slate, a *tabula rasa*, on which the environment ceaselessly inscribes its story and its dictates. The only intrinsic human equipment is a set of biological-instinctual mechanisms. Since nothing is innate, a sense of right and wrong does not develop from the inside out along with judgment and maturity; like all else, ethical awareness and sensibility are instilled in the process of learning the concrete rules and regulations that make up the particular ethical system into which the individual is born and in which he is raised.

Though the empiricist philosophy of Locke is not the most direct cause of the change in ethical thinking, its radical denial of such innate givens as a sense of, or attunement to, certain values is doubtless the most fundamental step in the naturalization and reduction of ethics to a product of the social environment.

UTILITARIAN AND HEDONISTIC PHILOSOPHIES.   More directly influential than Locke were the utilitarian (egoistic) philosophies of Hobbes and Bentham. According to Hobbes's *Leviathan*, the ultimate standard for judging right and wrong is the interest, gratification, and well-being of either the self or its immediate extensions, the family, caste, or related in-groups. The overarching ethical principle of these eighteenth-century systems was that each man is the ultimate judge of his own case.

Originally, this viewpoint appeared defensible on a number of counts. But when it spread beyond the confines of academia and pervaded the economic and political frameworks of such collective structures as the nation, the ruling class, and other groups, its pernicious effects were awesomely dramatized. Large-scale implementations of these utilitarian principles were, for instance, slave trade and slavery and the exploitation of the working classes by the industrial policies of economic liberalism and the genocidal polices of national socialism—all of which were regarded by their proponents as consonant with the ethical outlook originated by Hobbes and Bentham. These principles are recognizable today in the self-assured arbitrariness with which certain individuals and groups view right and wrong.

DARWIN AND THE SOCIAL SCIENCES.   The most spectacular and widely recognized event in the thrust toward a naturalization of man and, therefore, ethics is doubtless the Darwinian revolution. The new perspective on man's origin and evolution not only affected the natural sciences but gave a biological slant to the humanities. Its effect on ethics was to challenge all universal and nativist elements of existing philosophical and religious systems and prompt new explanations in terms of biological and social environmental forces.

Paralleling and strengthening the Darwinian influence upon man's thinking about himself was the conspicuously positivistic, environmentalistic orientation of the social sciences, which emerged around the same time under the influence of Comte. The twentieth century saw its mushrooming growth as a scientific perspective. The impact of these new disciplines, especially of early cultural anthropology, upon the changeover from a universal to a relative ethical model was more significant than any other historical forces.

Just as Darwin journeyed to the Galapagos in search of data on undomesticated fauna, so the early anthropologists trekked to exotic islands to study primitive (more precisely, pre- or nonliterate) cultures. Perplexed by the strangeness of the mores, beliefs, and values observed among these tribal populations—and perhaps a bit intoxicated at being the first to observe them—the early fieldworkers concluded that people's notions of good and evil, right and wrong, and so on, were determined solely and entirely by the particular cultural setting. On the basis of such hastily gathered and coarsely processed data, Sumner, in his *Folkways* (1940) (for decades, the classic in American sociology), emphatically declared that "the mores can make anything right" (p. 521). This extreme stand was supported—though voiced with much more sophistication and smoothness—by such leading anthropologists as Benedict, who remarked on the "widely differing but equally valid" patterns of life (1936, p. 257).

In light of these startling anthropological imports, the universalism and absolutism of traditional Western thinking about the nature of man and of ethics came to appear embarrassingly parochial, anachronistic, and, in places, dead wrong. Gradually, however, it appeared that the generalizations of the anthropologists were vastly premature. Indeed, in drawing their conclusions, many authors had failed to make the distinction between observation and interpretation. With the development of *pattern analysis*, it became apparent that numerous behavioral phenomena, first regarded as entirely accidental in their origin and arbitrary in their content or substance, were actually remarkably consistent with a rationally cogent system of thought and bore a previously undetected resemblance to the fundamentals of traditional ethical systems (Goldschmidt, 1960).

MECHANISTIC PSYCHOLOGY. Among the social sciences, that most responsible for the view that ethics are man-made and negotiable rather than intrinsically human and binding is probably psychology. Developed out of the climate sketched above, it introduced a concept of man that has pervaded contemporary thinking until very recently. Ever since its inception as an independent discipline, psychology has adopted an elementaristic and physicalistic orientation. This orientation, moreover, implied a reductionistic and environmentalistic philosophy that regarded man as a product, the outcome of the combined forces of heredity and environment. The individual, far from being capable of significant initiative or control, is viewed as passive and malleable, a bundle of elementary drives whose concrete expressions are shaped by external agency. Thus, according to the behaviorists, there is no such thing as human "nature"—in the sense of a cluster of inherent needs and tendencies—beyond the drives that man shares with other organisms. Beyond those elementary impulses, the human organism is infinitely plastic: just as a dog can be made to salivate at the perception of stimuli lacking any natural connection with salivation, so man can be fashioned to adopt any set of values and any code of conduct dictated by the social environment.

As for the traditional psychoanalytic sector, though its thinking proceeded along pathways strikingly different from those of behaviorism, it arrived at the same reductionistic view of man as an organism animated by blind instinctual forces and regulated by environmental (that is, social) demands and pressures coordinated by a "shadowy ego" (May, Angel, and Ellenberger, 1958, p. 46). The effect of psychoanalysis upon the ethical outlook was the abolition of the traditional concept of conscience as an inherent center of ethical regulation and its replacement by the sociologically determined superego. This diminished view of man certainly was not adopted maliciously. "It was part and parcel of our whole culture. Industrial civilization for the past hundred years or more has operated on the faith that happiness came by means of mechanical progress. We mechanized the human being, and we more and more tended to lose the significance of the person himself" (May, 1957, p. 174).

REDUCING ETHICS TO FEELINGS. Among the most recent, most academic and, therefore, perhaps least recognized of the forces involved in the ethical revolution is logical positivism or, more precisely, one of its ramifications, known as analytic philosophy—a linguistically oriented discipline specifically concerned with the analysis of statements. This philosophy recognizes only two kinds of statements: the cognitive and verifiable (the observations and conclusions of empirical science) and the subjective-emotional utterances (approval, admiration, horror, and so forth). The task of the philosopher is to analyze and clarify verbal discourse in terms of these two categories and to work with the cognitive statements, since only those are regarded as having meaning, the others being merely expressive of feeling.

Since judgments of right and wrong are unverifiable by sense observation, they are regarded by this branch of logical positivism as mere expressions of pleasure or displeasure. Ayers (1936), one of the most vocal representatives of this point of view, reduces the meaning of such a statement as "Stealing is wrong" to an expression of personal disapproval or painful protest similar to "You are stepping on my foot!" Stevenson goes even further, actually combining ethical reductionism with arbitrary authoritarianism. In *Ethics and Language* (1944) he offers the following radically subjective but prescriptive model for the analysis of ethical statements:

"(1) 'This is wrong' means *I disapprove of this; do so as well.*
(2) 'He ought to do this' means *I disapprove of his leaving this undone; do so as well.*
(3) 'This is good' means *I approve of this; do so as well"* (p. 21; Stevenson's italics).

Such an outlook amounts, of course, to a liquidation of the realm of ethical thinking or, as Bertrand Russell quipped, ethics becomes "the fine art of recommending to others what they should do in order to get along with oneself" (Adler, 1970, p. 127).

PROCESS THINKING. Another likely influence is far subtler and episte-mological in nature. It has to do with certain changes in the concept of knowledge and especially with contemporary man's attitude toward these changes. Traditionally, reality was conceptualized in terms of constants: essences, substances, or otherwise rigidly fixed entities. Similarly, estab-lished knowledge was regarded as certain: findings contrary to the pre-vailing outlook were considered errors or chance variations from a hidden but basically stable order.

Contemporary thought, on the other hand, is conceptualized in terms of process, time, and ongoing flux. Consequently, change and variety in the images of both human and physical reality are no longer regarded as transient phenomena to be brought in line through further study. Neither are they considered deviations, even though they may cause problems in man's adaptation to this changing order. Instead, change and variation are expected as part of man's evolving grasp of the universe, and their discovery tends to be uncritically hailed as evidence of the progress of knowledge.

Perspectives on a Common Ethic

With the computer-regulated cybernetic contraction of the world through communication and transportation, the need for a common ethic becomes far more necessary than that for a universal calendar. Therefore, one of the most urgent long-range tasks for modern man is ethical uni-fication—not just standardization or codification. The latter would be merely a legal, not a moral, process. This task, however, is also one of the most challenging, considering the entrenched and often contrary na-ture of people's moral beliefs and commitments, their prejudices and fears and, paradoxically, the fact that they tend to regard a closed mind on the subject as part of their ethical duty.

To the question of the possibility of a gradual ethical unification, the humanistic psychologist's answer is a well-considered yes: *in principle,* a common ethic is possible. Not that the humanist is romantically com-mitted to mystical beliefs in the "goodness" of man. But he can visualize the feasibility and, indeed, the ultimate necessity—barring global "acci-dents"—of this unification.

Humans, as members of the same species, share the same basic needs and values. Primordial among these is survival—admittedly a biological, not an ethical, value, but a condition for ethics as for everything else. Globally intertwined as mankind now is, survival is a value that cannot be maintained without concern for more evolved values in the social and ethical categories. Furthermore, the slow but steady process of unification with surface differentiation is in line with the evolutionary character of man, both as a species and an individual: from less alike to more alike;

from less aware to more aware; from less communication to more communication. These are just a few of many dimensions that are conducive to concern for mutual well-being. Such concern may be prompted initially by selfish rather than altruistic motives, but the effect is nevertheless in the direction of ethical progress.

This confidence in the possibility of human progress is not based on mere opinion. Existential evidence of the parallelism between experience and maturity, on the one hand, and moral insight (if not always moral conduct), on the other, should be available to any thoughtful observer of self and others. Scholarly evidence, too, is close at hand in a time when all living things are viewed in an evolutionary light. The following samples from diverse fields testify to a centrifugal trend in the development of ethics from instinctual to rational, from vague to focused, from tribal to global.

According to Piaget (1932), the development of a child's sense of justice involves three (major) stages, occurring roughly between ages seven to twelve. At first, *the child views justice as entirely a matter of adult authority.* So long as the authority figure acts consistently, whatever he dictates is just—though the child is already capable of recognizing certain instances of injustice; for example, when the adult breaks his own rules, punishes indiscriminately, etc. At the next stage, *equality replaces authority as the criterion of justice* and outweighs every other consideration; punishment and privilege must be the same for all ("if he can do it, I can"). At the third stage, ages eleven to twelve, *equality begins to be tempered by circumstances;* differential treatment may be allowed for good reasons—for example, protecting a younger child, favoring a handicapped child, and so on. There is throughout this process, Piaget believes, a rational development in which reason, as it is "gradually refined and purified," tends toward a norm, a form of equilibrium. "For reciprocity imposes itself on practical reason as logical principles impose themselves morally on theoretical reason" (1932, p. 316).

A tentative resolution of the predicament may be Edel's suggestion (1955) that morality need originate from neither dogmatic authority nor emotional caprice but from judgment. There is a place here, as in other matters, for the authority of competence. It is for the individual to ponder that authority and act consistently yet not mechanically.

The work of cultural historians and other observers of the human process contains numerous references that tend to support this evolutionary perspective. "The primitive ideal of honor . . . is superseded in more advanced phases of civilization by the ideal of justice, or rather, this ideal attaches itself to it and, however miserably put into practice, henceforth becomes the recognized and desiderated norm of human society" (Huizinga, 1949, p. 100). Similarly, semanticist Korzybski (whose concept of time-binding is discussed in Chapter 3) recognizes an unmistakably forward-moving, ethical trend in the process of maturation: "On this inherently human level of interdependence, time-binding leads inevitably to feelings of responsibility, duty toward others and the future, and therefore to some type of ethics, morals, and similar social and/or sociocultural reactions" (1950, xiii).

Anthropologist Walter Goldschmidt identifies a trend toward unification of ethical systems. In *Ways of Mankind* (1954), which, paradoxically, was written in the heyday of cultural relativism, he states that "in the course of human cultural development there has been a gradual though faltering progression toward enlarging the area brought within a single ethical system. The logical (and undoubtedly necessary) end of such an evolutionary process is the establishment of a world community and the permanent elimination of borders that limit the application of basic ethical codes" (p. 107). As an example of a universal principle, he cites "the one known in our law as the 'general-welfare principle'—that a person may not take any action considered inimical to the general welfare of the community" (p. 107). Goldschmidt, however, is very realistic about the magnitude of the effort that will be required: "It takes a strong man to recognize the validity of alternative ethical assumptions, and yet live—as he must—strictly by his own ethical principles" (p. 108). It need scarcely be pointed out that the question of human progress in its essential human dimension is and has always been a matter of controversy. (For more extensive treatment of the subject, the reader might profitably consult Edel's *Ethical Judgment,* from which I have drawn many of the insights contained in this chapter.)

TOO OPTIMISTIC A STANCE? Many will consider the establishment of a common ethics without, in the process, manipulating or violating human prerogative as an impossibility. This position, however, reveals a basic misunderstanding about the notion of ethics. For it confuses ethics—that is, *oughts from within*—with laws, or some manner of systematic conditioning or control, all of which are *musts from without*. But the essence of ethical behavior is that it is free from coercion and free from legal sanction—though not free from internal conflict. In brief, it is a function of the person. Granted, an appreciable measure of socially constructive behavior can be achieved through systematic conditioning. But a measure sufficient to assure and promote the cause of hominization appears inconceivable without some measure of ethical involvement, and such involvement cannot be achieved by coercion or conditioning.

To be sure, certain external guidelines that express the cultural consensus regarding the concrete expression of the inherent sense of right and wrong are useful, even necessary. But they usually can be formulated only in principle, since most of the situations to which they apply cannot be defined in standard fashion. Ethical behavior is much less a function of a certain system than it is of a certain kind of person, characterized by a high level of awareness combined with a keen sensitivity to and abiding concern for things human. Such persons are alert to the potential harm in certain courses of action and are eager to protect themselves from that peculiarly lasting inner pain that is guilt and that arises from lack of reasonable commitment to the fellowman, whoever he may be.

In spite of the built-in tendency toward social and ethical growth here affirmed as an attribute of mankind, it is granted that those who deny the possibility of ethical progress may be proven right. Indeed, doubt and confusion may lead to attitudes of ethical indifference, scepticism, and even cynicism. When sufficiently widespread, such attitudes may cripple mankind's potential for specifically human, as distinguished from technological, progress. At the present juncture, this danger is in fact very real. The notion of specifically human progress—which means, essentially, ethical progress—is quite unpopular, at least among intellectuals. "The word *progress* is now extremely unfashionable. Anyone who is bold enough to assert that it has occurred, or even that the word has a definite meaning, is likely to be dismissed as merely naive and unsophisticated. . . . It is, in my opinion, merely a confession of intellectual inadequacy if the Western intellectual finds himself forced to confess that he cannot see any way in which this belief can be rationally justified" (Waddington, 1960, pp. 14–15). Attitudes of this kind may be self-fulfilling prophecies; individual beliefs about the outcome of a process in which one participates tend to confirm the prediction.

Promoting the Ethical Process

The conditions for the acceleration of ethical development are not clearly known, for the very reason that the psychological study of ethical behavior—unlike its philosophical-theoretical counterpart—has received scant attention so far. Certain basic propositions can be offered for consideration, however, and two of these will be discussed briefly by way of concluding this chapter. Since both have to do with education—the first in a direct, the second in an indirect way—a few introductory thoughts on education seem appropriate.

Since Jefferson first proclaimed the values of education, its abundant dispensation has not led to a commensurate increase in our personal competence as either citizens or persons. Nevertheless, Jefferson's thesis has never been proven wrong for the very reason that it has never, as yet, been fully put into practice. Although we have more schools now than ever, they offer essentially instruction, not education. The former is a process of imprinting or inculcation (from *in-struere*, "building in"); the latter, at its very best, is a process of releasing, of leading out (from *educere*, "guiding out").

Instruction is indispensable, and the skills and knowledge that must be acquired for life in a technological society constantly increase. But where the implementation of internal resources—thought, imagination, substantial initiative, comprehensive understanding—is concerned, it seems that the general population is not much better off now than in ages with less schooling. In fact, as Lewis observes in *The Discarded Image* (1970), in the past most people realized that they were not educated; hence they had to make the most of what personal resources they could muster. Today, believing ourselves educated, we may make too little effort to compensate for the gaps and false directions in our personal development.

My first proposition regarding promotion of the ethical process has to do with teaching. Korzybski states the case very sensibly when he writes: "It is often said that ethics is a thing which is impossible to *teach*. Just the opposite is true—it is impossible not to teach ethics, for the teaching of it is subtly carried on in all our teaching, whether consciously or not . . ." (1950, p. 322). This proposition seems promising. Upon reflection, however, it becomes apparent that messages transmitted in so subtle a fashion can be negative as well as affirmative.

It is safe to assume that few teachers explicitly deny or advocate disregarding the value of ethics. The reassurance that emanates from this is, however, tenuous. Indeed, ethics encompasses the unethical as well: only a being who exists in the ethical dimension is liable for unethical behavior. Since, according to Korzybski, such teaching is "subtly carried on" and may be unconscious as well as conscious, it follows that it is chiefly a matter of conditioning rather than informing. The student does not recognize the indoctrination, and consequently, cannot defend himself against it. Thus he may preconsciously learn that ethics is a generally irrelevant matter of rhetoric and lip service or that it is real and essential, depending on the conditioning he undergoes. If we assume, as we probably may, that both positions are actually conveyed in the classroom, the student ultimately will be either confused or uncommitted.

To counteract the likelihood of this ambiguity and unintentional indoctrination of one kind or another, a more extensive and articulate ethical education for teachers seems mandatory. Because ethical concern cannot be taught the way ethical theories and principles can be, however, formal teaching would have to be supplemented by a process of witnessed self-expression and self-exploration. Such a process could probably be carried on satisfactorily within the context of appropriately focused group sessions. Through mutual exchange and clarification, members of such groups could be helped to discover the discrepancy that frequently exists between one's professed or assumed stance and one's actual or operational values and convictions.

The second proposition relative to the promotion of ethical concern is related to the first and has to do with the culture. Indeed, ethics cannot develop in isolation from the total cultural context. The current trend toward world culture involves at least the visible cultural structures of technology, instruction, architecture, dress, food, habits, and, to an extent, politics and language. This *uniformization* is not yet a *unification,* which would involve the intangibles, the nation's spiritual values. But uniformity may be seen as setting the stage for unification and, therefore, as offering unprecedented opportunity. The ethical synthesis that may eventually arise from a uniform cultural pattern may well prove to be an extremely complex venture. But with the world scene set as it now is, it seems a possible and, for a change, a peaceful task.

So vast a project—not an event but a process—can hardly be achieved within a single generation. It is the crucial phase of the evolutionary unfolding that Teilhard de Chardin calls "hominization" (1959, p. 164). But while no single generation can achieve this goal, each takes an indispensable step in the march whose impulse and direction is built-in but whose unfolding is no more guaranteed than the organism to reach maturity—however inherently it is geared toward that state. Nor will this process be mediated by a single stroke. Primordial, however, among the many necessary means is the classical prescription: education.

THE NEED FOR A PSYCHOLOGY OF MAN. The overwhelming prevalence of instruction over education in our schools is the subject of an important paper by Rogers (1964) entitled "Graduate Psychological Training: A Passionate Statement."[*] With a forcefulness that contrasts with his usual restraint, Rogers denounces the technical indoctrination that currently represents graduate training in psychology as "an unintelligent, inefficient, and wasteful job of preparing psychologists, to the detriment of our discipline and society" (p. 1).

Rogers's courageous statement leads directly into my concluding point, which is also the *raison d'etre* of this entire book: *the need for the development of a psychology of the whole man.* The reductionist, "nothing but" image of man that has been presented in systematic fashion to millions of young people—and in nonsystematic but no less pervasive fashion to the population at large—not only fails to promote the unfolding of the ethical process but distinctly impedes it. For it is an image devoid of that which is most crucially human about human beings: freedom and ethical accountability. A lively awareness of these twin dimensions of the human make-up is a condition for breeding an ongoing concern about the possible rightness or wrongness of the choices and courses of action with which man is continually faced. Without a recognition of these core elements—freedom and accountability—man's impressive array of symbolic, conceptual, and technological capacities is apt to serve his demise more effectively than his fulfillment.

[*] The American Psychological Association refused to publish this paper in its official journal, *The American Psychologist,* but it can be obtained from the Western Behaviorial Sciences Institute, La Jolla, California.

As long as people are presented with an image of man in which freedom is an illusion (Skinner, 1970) and ethics a convention or a mere feeling (Ayers, 1936; Stevenson, 1944)—not a matter of necessity but of option, taste, and expediency—ethical progress is likely to proceed at the pace of geological time and may even decline. Conversely, if a psychology evolves that reveals the human being in the fullness of his nature and allows the individual to figure out for himself the attitudes and conduct without which the good life cannot possibly be achieved, human progress will be in sight.

Once it is realized that the "fittest," those who survive, may well be the most ethically committed, mankind is likely to make unprecedented progress.

13 Some Dubious Capacities

Humanistic psychology is deliberately eupsychian (Maslow, 1965); that is, it focuses upon man at his best, his richest and most promising. It adopts this focus because the aim of this psychology, at the present stage of its development, is to correct the pathologized and truncated image of man that has prevailed in modern psychology's presentations. Along with an attempt at rehabilitating that image, humanistic psychology aims to provide contemporary man with a sense of excitement about being a member of his superbly endowed species.

Adopting a eupsychian approach, however, makes it all the more necessary to avoid offering an exalted image of the human animal. Indeed, the assets that assure his superiority in the creative, self-transcendent order are the very same that have long earned him the epithet *homo homini lupus,* the creature who is a wolf to his fellow creatures. In the face of his extremely checkered historical record, it will not do to romanticize mankind; his superiority is far from being actualized or uniformly edifying. Towering high in the conceptual, the technological, even the esthetic areas, his achievements are perilously lagging in the social and moral spheres. Man is indeed far from having actualized the higher reaches of his potential repertoire, isolated instances of human excellence notwithstanding.

It cannot even be said that man's performance is in every respect superior to that of animals. Think of the eagle's eyesight, the antelope's swiftness, the homing pigeon's uncanny sense of orientation, the dog's sense of smell, and the capacity for early self-maintenance of which all animals, small and large, prove capable. In all these respects, man, unaided by technology, is definitely second-best. No other species however, has the multiform capacity, the versatility, and creative genius that enables man to compensate for and overcome his limitations and deficiencies. He has the potential to create himself as a person within the limitations imposed upon him by cultural and biological givens.

Such extraordinary potential, however, is not without liabilities. Man's nature is comparable, in some respects, to something like atomic energy: inherently neither good nor evil but endowed to an awe-inspiring extent with the potential to both harm and enhance. Unlike atomic energy, man has consciousness, the capacity to evaluate, initiate, and control his action. It is a type of consciousness that, combined with his symbolic ability, allows him to conceptualize the consequences of at least some of his actions. He has an empathic ability that allows him to infer the direction of his fellow creatures' reactions, to symbolically transcend some of the historical-cultural determinants of his existence; hence he is significantly accountable for his behavior. Therefore, at least some of his actions qualify as either good or evil. However, it is not always within the capacity of the observer to decide which is which. Even the courts make pronouncements only on the legal, not the ethical, nature of the actions brought before them.

The Deceptive Animal

Man, living in a phenomenal world, knows and relates to his world through interpretation. He has no choice but to interpret and, naturally, he does so in terms of his experience, his needs and, understandably, his wishes and fears. Or as someone put it, with slight but justifiable overstatement: *Man sees things not as they are but as he is.* This state of affairs implies some serious liabilities. For it places the individual in a world that is as complex, changing, and unique as he himself. It is within the context of this uniqueness that he perceives and evaluates everything, including his own actions. Thus, certain actions viewed from one man's frame of reference may appear neutral, even constructive. But from another's frame of reference, they may be experienced as extremely hurtful and destructive.

Another basic fact about man is that his behavior is propelled by the "actualizing tendency" (Goldstein, 1939); that is, by the tendency to maintain and enhance himself. However, this tendency, like the individual himself, operates within a subjective phenomenal framework. The subject can enhance himself only in ways that *appear* enhancing to him. In his efforts to do so, he is guided by his self-concept or self-image. Because this self-image is not always accurate, however, it is apt to misguide him. Thus the human being is intrinsically liable to err. Worse, he is apt to be deliberately deceptive—to trick himself or others either consciously or unconsciously and in a variety of ways.

LYING AND CHEATING. The most primitive, the earliest, and possibly the most common deceptive behavior is directed at others for the sake of either symbolic (escaping punishment) or utilitarian (obtaining favors, benefits, or goods) personal benefit. When distortion or substitution of the truth is done consciously, we call it lying. Sartre classifies lying as a form of transcendence—an elegant designation indeed but, strictly speaking, accurate: lying deliberately goes beyond or against the facts, supplants them by fiction, and is one form of man's capacity for symbolic manipulation.

The practice of deception is itself deceptive. In significant though not usually spectacular ways, it turns against the agent. It testifies to the deceptive individual's immaturity that he is not able to foresee, however dimly, that his behavior will entail adverse consequences. The use of deceptive or dishonest means shortchanges the individual in several ways. First, it prevents him from acquiring habits of effortful activity. (This effort need not, of course, be manual or muscular; rather, it is usually strictly symbolic, either mental or emotional.) He thus fails to acquire the habit of expending the effort that is the legitimate price of the symbolic or tangible things he wants to obtain. And beyond the acquisition of good habits, he cheats himself out of the rewards that flow from successfully making an effort commensurate with his objective.

By far the worst side effects of deceptive practices is that they rob the individual of the strengthening and comforting rewards of the ethical life. The exploiter and cheater is unable to trust, love, and respect others, for he comes to view them according to the only model with which he is familiar, himself. Thus he condemns himself to living among people he can only distrust and despise.

Significantly, certain forms of verbal behavior that have all the makings of the lie nevertheless escape the blame attached to the lie proper. They are condoned, even encouraged, by many cultures. Thus, Western society tolerates "white lies" told out of courtesy or charity. In certain cases, when legitimate and vital interests—one's own or one's fellowman's—are at stake, withholding the truth is believed to be one's moral duty. Such approved, even honored, distortion or substitution of the truth shows once more that for the symbolic animal the intention often counts more than the action itself.

Often mislabeled as lying is what could be called "sifting the truth"—a practice that is legitimate for the rational animal, endowed with the capacity for judgment and for empathy. The mature individual knows that injudicious expression of the whole truth may cause more harm than good. Something can be said in favor of selective rather than indiscriminate expression of all we could say or of all others would have us say. But this practice lacks legitimacy if one is unclear in his own mind about the soundness of his motives and the criteria operative in such selective expression. But just because someone has the curiosity, the interest, or the impertinence to ask certain questions does not place a person under the obligation to express all he knows and feels. This holds true even in court—provided, of course, that one invokes the Fifth Amendment.

Circumspection in voicing one's knowledge or opinion testifies to man's capacities for judgment and foresight. It can prevent the erosion of human relations that the expression of raw truth is apt to cause. However, it would seem that excessive caution, however well intended, creates a climate of interpersonal insecurity that may be, in the last analysis, more trying or impairing than the occasional bluntness of the naked truth. This conclusion would seem particularly valid in regard to close relationships whose nature requires near transparency between or among parties.

NEUROSIS AS DECEPTION. A more complex and subtle form of man's unique capacity for deception is neurosis. Like lying, neurosis is a function of man's symbolic and transcendent capacities, but the individual himself is the victim. Neurosis can be characterized as a tricking of the self by the self for the purpose of saving face. It is a peculiar case of (predominantly) unconscious duplicity aimed at fraudulently gaining or maintaining the esteem of persons who are more or less significant to the individual and whose favorable impression he needs in order to maintain a spurious self-esteem. More technically phrased, neurosis is an organized state of incongruence; that is, the discrepancy between the individual's experience and his perception of that experience, a state of disaccord between what he feels and what he thinks he feels. Neurosis develops gradually as a response to threat to the ego. The threat does not have to be real; it need only be perceived as such and it is easily perceived by insecure or anxious individuals overeager to protect or defend a weak ego. Hence the term *defensiveness* to designate the behavior of neurotic persons.

Of course, no one chooses to be neurotic. The process itself is deceptive. It begins, innocently enough, with single instances of varying and relatively unconscious, self-serving distortion or denial of experience. When maneuvers of this sort are successful—that is, when they appear to overcome the immediate threat—they are increasingly resorted to. Not that single instances of experiential distortion are bound to lead to neurosis. Indeed, twisting or doctoring an unbecoming truth about oneself is a natural—though potentially hazardous—manifestation of a healthy tendency of the human organism: the tendency to seek or to maintain self-enhancement. But frequent use becomes habituating; it tends to crystallize into a substitute self-structure that soon tricks even the subject himself. The initially isolated instances begin to interlock and something like a coat of mail begins to build itself around the individual. Armored garments, however, wear uncomfortably; one loses his flexibility, his grace, his appeal, and his freedom. Despite the discomfort, the individual who feels threatened seeks the deceptive safety of his armor. But due to the operation of his reflective awareness, he will often realize that in some diffuse and unspecified manner he is increasingly vulnerable. Hence the neurotic person is typically an overtly or covertly anxious person.

The term *experimental neurosis* is sometimes applied to laboratory animals that manifest a rather sudden and dramatic change of behavior. This use of the term is, however, metaphorical and frequently misleading, for it designates an acute form of behavior disorganization either accidentally or deliberately induced in the laboratory animal. When a disturbance of this kind occurs, it is usually as a result of such experiments as conditioning for discrimination. A situation is set up where the animal learns to discriminate between, for instance, two geometric forms, one circular, one oval, alternately projected on a screen. Upon presentation of one of these forms, he is conditioned to press a lever and is rewarded with food. If he presses the lever when the wrong form is presented, he receives an electrical shock. When the correct response is duly established, the experimenter gradually modifies one form until it closely resembles the other. The animal then becomes unable to discriminate successfully and can neither obtain the reward nor avoid punishment. He reaches a peak of frustration and displays the acute behavioral disorganization that accompanies such a state.

In man, however, neurosis is a different matter. It is a disturbance that centers around the ego or self and is, therefore, exclusively human. The ego aims at protecting a self-image that is threatened or perceived as threatened; hence it is an entirely symbolic process. The reaction of the hungry dog to what appears to him as arbitrary deprivation of food or application of punishment is a survival-related phenomenon, not a symbolic process. Second, neurosis occurs gradually, usually over months or even years, whereas experimental neurosis can be induced in a matter of weeks, even days.

As Szasz (1961) demonstrates, neurosis is not a disturbance in any clinical sense of the word. It is a form of psychosocial pathology, a way of coping with situations that are too hard on the ego. The result of neurosis is alienation. Although neurotic behaviors do not necessarily alienate us from a great number of individuals in our daily life, they prevent us from encountering many situations and many aspects of our own personality and in this way alienate us from ourselves.

The Irreversible Deed

All animate beings apparently have a deep-seated urge for self-preservation. But only man is capable of countering this urge radically: he is the only animal to commit suicide. For only he knows reflectively that he is alive, that he exists in time, and, hence, that he has a future—admittedly of unknown kind or duration, but a future that is in his own hands and that he may either espouse or abolish.

Suicide, the refusal of life and its possibilities, is condemned in most cultures, especially in the West. However, not all forms of self-inflicted death are marked by the social and moral stigma usually attached to the act in our society. In Japan, for instance, the institution of hara-kiri used to be the only honorable death for persons who had disgraced themselves. Similarly, heroism is socially exalted in all cultures, even though it does not necessarily involve death but only the willingness to expose oneself to death. In the case of heroism, death is usually only self-chosen, not self-inflicted (though the difference may be slight; Japanese kamikaze pilots used their airplanes as the instruments of their death).

Until recently, the Trobriand Islanders of the South Pacific practiced an institutionalized suicide that consisted of jumping to death from a high tree and was performed in retaliation for having been gravely wronged by another party (Malinowski, 1954). It was believed that committing this act caused one's ghost to haunt the offending party for the rest of his life. Although there is no ceremony and the suicide victim often lacks conscious recognition of his true motivation, many suicides in Western culture are committed out of frustrated anger and the urge to punish a real or imagined offender. Fatal actions of this sort constitute a tragic comment on the destructive potential of the ego. They can also be interpreted, however, as an expression of man's passion for justice or, at least, for retribution.

THE MYTH OF THE LEMMINGS.   Until very recently, most comparative psychology texts featured the lemming as an animal that engages in mass suicide. In fact, periodic lemming migration has been popularly accepted as suicide for so long that the myth will probably survive for many more years: "Every few years, according to legend, great numbers of lemmings march to the sea and drown themselves. However, scientists no longer believe this. The animals do move away from their mountain home because of crowding caused by increase in the number of lemmings. But few ever get as far as the sea. Most of them die of starvation or are killed by other animals" (*World Book Encyclopedia,* 1971, p. 171).

The behavior of the lemmings (a mass exodus with a fatal outcome), strange though it appears on first sight, must be understood as an essentially biological phenomenon related to the survival instinct. It is not unlike other migratory behavior motivated by life-preserving tendencies. When a behavior is species-wide and occurs at regular intervals, it is, genetically or hormonally, that is, biologically determined. That it is triggered by environmental conditions, as is the case with the lemmings, is incidental.

By contrast, human suicide is unpredictable, variable, and seldom occurs collectively. Granted, it usually has sociological determinants and, in certain cases, biological factors play a part. Nevertheless, it remains an essentially personal decision. The fact that the incidence of suicide for a certain national or sociological population can be predicted with relative accuracy does not detract from the unpredictability of the individual act.

The "suicide" of the lemming is one more example of the reductionistic thinking that pervades the traditional textbook on comparative psychology—a leveling compulsion that goes so far as to deny man the (usually) inglorious distinction of being the only animal capable of performing the awesome and irreversible act that is suicide.

Homo Homini Lupus

The symbolic animal, free from bondage to concrete stimuli and to the immediate moment, is apt to experience and pursue something like a sense of boundlessness that tends to express itself in every area of significance to him. This sense may find expression in love and concern or in power and domination. Thus, man is capable of bending his genius to the purpose of hurting as well as serving his fellowman. Significantly, however, he seldom conceives of his destructive behavior as an end in itself. The cruel misdeeds portrayed in Dagobert Runes's *Despotism: A Pictorial History of Tyranny* (1963) are in every instance interpreted by their perpetrators as an exercise in reason, justice, or rightful privilege. No doubt some of these actions must have been prompted by motives genuinely perceived by the agent as meritorious. The proper indoctrination generally succeeds in institutionalizing mass murder. In this regard, Hannah Arendt (1959) proposes that the individual may be so steeped in ethnocentric enculturation that his conscience in regard to certain issues is irretrievably inverted.

THE KILLER "INSTINCT." Whatever the motive, there is reason to assume that man's homicidal tendencies are rooted in his distant past. Mankind has a long history of institutionalized killing for purposes other than retribution. For instance, as far as historians can tell, human sacrifice was once a part of almost all cultures. The motivation in all forms of institutionalized murder is not deliberate cruelty but high purpose: the propitiation or appeasement of the deity; the warding off of evil spirits; the purging of wrongdoers; the elimination of persons perceived as potentially dangerous; and so forth. In other words, such practices as cannibalism, mutilation, and headhunting, are symbolic actions—expressions of the same intelligence that has created man's highest achievements.

According to such ethologists as Schaller (1964), Lorenz (1966), and van Lawick-Goodall (1971), there is no evidence that any but the human species kills its own kind (except for the "ritualistic" killing related to the mating habits of certain insects). Animals may accidentally kill members of their own species by failing to moderate the intensity of their attack or defense in the heat of fighting over prey or mate. But such accidents are extremely rare; the weaker of the fighters usually has the "wisdom" to retreat before he is too badly mauled.

THE ULTIMATE PERVERSION. Certain uncommon forms of behavior are called "perversions" solely on the basis of cultural standards. Thus, certain societies would consider potlatch (a custom of certain Northwestern American and Canadian Indians that involves the destruction of personal property in a competitive display of wealth) a perversion. There is, however, one category of perversion that is not a matter of culture or cult: the deliberate infliction of pain on one's fellowman for the sake of inflicting pain and the pleasure derived from it. A close second is the unjustified—or insufficiently justified—causation of physical pain to animals. Such behavior represents unqualified perversion because the awareness that certain acts cause pain to animate beings is an immediate and universal given for anyone except young children and mentally handicapped persons.

The most ignominious item in this token inventory of the darker reaches of man's potential would seem to be cruelty practiced solely for pleasure and without as much as a rationalization to self or others.

Such outrageous acts are seldom performed for their own sake. Nevertheless, it is a tragic fact that such is sometimes the case, and worse, that it *seems* to be on the increase. Coleman (1964) reports a disquieting change in the motivation of what he calls the "new" criminal. While material gain used to be the predominant motive, crime is increasingly prompted by the search for excitement: "The 'new' criminal is in many ways a different type of personality. Although interested in money, his crimes are perpetrated primarily for ego status and 'kicks' . . . often he gets his 'kicks' by senseless acts of violence. . . . The final consequence (often homicide) is not really anticipated. However, the brutal violence that he inflicts on some helpless victim 'makes him feel good' " (p. 378).

Because of the extensive legislation that protects the citizen against physical abuse, most contemporary cases of cruelty are mental and emotional rather than physical. Child abuse, however, continues to occur with distressing frequency (in this connection, see Bakan's *The Slaughter of the Innocents*).

Sadism. So clear-cut a perversion is cruelty that it is classified in civilized society as pathological. One designation for this form of pathology is sadism. Strictly speaking, sadism is the association of sexual satisfaction with the infliction of physical pain on others. Broadly speaking, however, it is not necessarily connected with either overtly sexual behavior or physical pain. Always, however, it implies gratification from inflicting pain upon others through any number of hurtful practices, ranging from severe verbal punishment, humiliation, abuse, and other forms of symbolic wounding to physical exploitation and torture.

Fortunately rare are such gruesome instances of pure sadism as that described by Meyer Levin in *Compulsion* and perpetrated by two wealthy Chicago youths, Leopold and Loeb, upon the latter's younger cousin. The more recent "moors murders" in England set public sentiment ablaze. Feeling ran so high that the trial had to be conducted in secret for fear of citizen reprisal, and the murderers were kept in solitary confinement to protect them from other imprisoned criminals. The criminals' tape recording of the screams of terror and pain of at least one of their victims, a girl of ten, made the case especially heinous. (Pamela Johnson, the novelist wife of C. P. Snow, was invited to record her observations of the trial and published them under the title, *Some Personal Reflections on the Moors Murders*.)

The Unfinished Animal

More than anything, perhaps, the kinds of behaviors just reviewed reveal that man is, in Teilhard de Chardin's view (1965), the unfinished animal—shortsighted, often blind, altogether incompletely emancipated from irrational impulse. In figuring "how to make the most of it" (a workaday synonym for the operation of the actualizing tendency), man often acts like a child who fancies he is "getting away with something" when secretly toying with knives, scissors, matches, and other "no-no's" or gloats at the thought that he beat them all at the game by hiding in the discarded refrigerator.

As the symbolic animal, man is stunningly superior. Without the regulating power of a sense of good and evil, however, symbolic ability may lead to the degradation and ultimate demise of man. "We, mankind, contain the possibilities of the earth's future, and can realise more and more of them on the condition that we increase our knowledge and our love" (Julian Huxley, in Teilhard de Chardin, 1965, p. 28).

V Man Transcending

Part Five examines man as the being who, at his soundest and best, is the searching, questing animal; the only one who has foreknowledge of his finitude or death; the one who has the capacity and the tendency to conceive of ultimate ends and values; and who, in the pursuit of these values, is capable of near-limitless transcendence.

Peculiar to the quest that presses man onward is its independence from practical, visible-tangible, or immediate reward—a characteristic that points to the overriding power of an urge from within rather than a call from without. Particularly striking is man's ability to derive life-enhancing value from both the awesome certainty of his death and the uncertainty of its time—an ability that may well represent the height of his self-transcending potential.

Whether spurred by the realization of his finitude or by a built-in nostalgia for completion, fulfillment, and perfection (however mistakenly he may perceive or pursue these goals), man reveals an ineradicable concern for ultimates. Along with this concern is his readiness to gamble on existential stakes and scales —pain, loss, and doubt notwithstanding—propelled by an intimation that dawn is ever about to break over his horizon.

14 The Questing Beast

The human animal is a born explorer. Ask any parent about his youngster's compulsion for questions. So marked and revealing is the child's level of perceptual and motor curiosity that it is regarded in psychological testing as a primary indicator of overall potential. Goble (1970 p. 49) cites Thorndyke's study of a group of children with extremely high I.Q.'s (over 180). Every child in the group manifested an almost insatiable curiosity that needed no encouragement but appeared to be a powerful hunger, drive, or need. Harlow (1950), in his studies of rhesus monkeys, goes even further. His experiments showed that monkeys would put a great deal of effort into the solution of puzzles even when no reward was forthcoming. (One may wonder, of course, whether the kind of effort expended by Harlow's subjects is operative in the adult's quest for cognitive penetration and mastery or whether it is a form of playful exertion, akin to Lorenz's (1966) concept of "militant enthusiasm.")

Only Man Asks Questions

Cognitive urges, then, seem to run deep throughout the animal kingdom. But contrary to the animal's curiosity, man's search is not focused on survival purposes, except of course under conditions of deprivation; however, even adverse circumstances are not always a deterrent to man's desire for knowledge, as evidenced by the behavior of known explorers and other individuals propelled by a powerful urge to know. Nor are man's explorations necessarily aimed at profit or limited to the tangible world. For man is the animal who is concerned with questions and issues that often have little to do with his personal comfort or fortune and whose answers may be hard to get, hard to bear, or both. But they are questions that man is apt to perceive as vital. What lies beyond the horizon? Where is the source of the Nile? Can Everest be climbed, the moon be reached? How do I compare with others—from charm to intelligence to genitals? Is there a Santa Claus?

The difference here referred to is not a matter of verbal capacity. Curiosity need not express itself in words. It can take operational forms. Thus, opening boxes, listening to people, looking through windows, in closets, in bags, sampling, taking apart, reassembling, seeing what happens when photographic plates are left in the presence of pitchblende, or when a key is moved along a kite string during a storm—all are manifestations of the questing urge that do not necessarily involve verbalizations.

Man's questing and questioning covers several levels. He usually first wants to know what things are in the sense of what they are *for*. This elementary, active cognition is common to both man and subhuman animals. Many animals, like man, know either from instinct or from learning the cue value of numerous things. They know in the sense of being capable of identifying things, places, persons, events, or situations. But even that knowledge is limited to the relation of these things to the animals themselves. They do not know the meaning of anything independent of "what's in it for them." Neither do they understand what they know in terms of *causes*—as distinct from immediate *antecedents*—or implications and long-term consequences. By contrast, man's understanding of implication and logical relation comes so naturally that he is not even aware of the depth of his latent knowledge unless it is challenged, prodded, or brought to light in one way or another.

Man's spontaneous, untutored capacity for inference, for generalization, and for drawing conclusions brings to mind Socrates' demonstration with the untutored slaveboy in the *Meno*:

Soc. (pointing to the drawing of a square) Tell me, boy, do you know that a figure like this is a square?

Boy I do.

Soc. And do you know that a square figure has these four lines equal?

Boy Certainly.

Soc. And these lines which I have drawn through the middle of the square are also equal?

Boy Yes.

Soc. A square may be of any size?

Boy Certainly.

Soc. And if one side of the figure be of two feet, and the other side be of two feet, how much will the whole be? Let me explain: if in one direction the space was of two feet, and in the other direction of one foot, the whole would be two feet taken once?

Boy Yes.

Soc. But since this side is also of two feet, there are twice two feet?

Boy There are.

Soc. Then the square is of twice two feet?

Boy	Yes.
Soc.	And how many are twice two feet? Count and tell me.
Boy	Four, Socrates.
Soc.	And might not there be another square twice as large as this, and having like this the lines equal?
Boy	Yes.
Soc.	And of how many feet will that be?
Boy	Of eight feet.
Soc.	And now try and tell me the length of the line which forms the side of that double square: this is two feet—what will that be?
Boy	Clearly, Socrates, it will be double.

Well this side of the satisfaction of his immediate concerns or physical well-being, then, man tends to concern himself with issues. When fully engaged in his quest, he is apt to be scornful of all but his most elementary needs and in some cases of even his life. This is where his nature as the symbolic animal stands out clearly. What he is after is symbolic: answers to questions—even just getting his questions right!

Beyond Knowledge to Understanding

In casual speech, the terms *knowledge* and *understanding* may be used interchangeably. Strictly speaking, however, they stand for significantly different levels of cognition. We all *know* the meaning of words like *telephone* and *telegraph*, maybe even *neurosis* and *psychosis*. But few of us understand what telephone, telegraph, or neurosis really consist of. Such radio slogans as "From A.M. to P.M. it's FM" are pretty generally understood to mean "Good music all day long" (which is, of course, what matters, practically; but the point here is illustration, not operation). Most familiar symbols and objects are known in terms of their cue or action value, which is the minimal level of cognition.

One might ask incidentally whether the tendency for people to stop at this elementary level of knowledge about their environment does not point to indolence rather than curiosity. Few if any of man's behaviors are guided and regulated (solely) by any one principle. Along with the urge to explore, man also manifests a deep and extraordinarily flexible adaptability—which is fortunate since he could not reach any degree of effective living if he were to explore the constitution, genesis, or history of every common object and symbol. Therefore, the adult's questing urge usually doesn't get into gear until his attention is caught by either the newness of a thing, its perplexing character, or anything else that stirs him out of the semi-lethargy that tends to accompany the state of adaptation.

Man's urge to understand and his verbal or operational questions are precisely what have earned him the epithet "rational." Notice how admirably the verb *to understand* expresses the idea it is designed to convey: to *under*-stand, to get underneath things with the mind's eye and see what is "really" beneath the surface. Man typically wants to know not only the news but the news behind the news, not only the show but the goings-on behind the sets, not only the motions but the motivation. Beyond a knowledge of cues, man aims to understand the constitution, the nature of things. Beyond surface characteristics and antecedents, he wonders about history and origin. Human beings typically want to know about causes and reasons, not only effects; about ends as well as means; about regularities in nature, which they call physical laws; about order in human transactions, which they institutionalize as civil and penal law; about order in thought and language, which provides syntax and logic; about rights and obligations, or ethics; about the just and proper way to organize community life or politics; about harmony, balance, and pleasing effects, or esthetics. Most of all, perhaps, the unending search aims at the discovery of pattern within diversity (Murphy, 1958) and of the whole to which all the fragments belong.

BEYOND UNDER-STANDING TO COM-PREHENSION. Not content with the kind of understanding that results from opening things up, taking them apart, looking into or underneath them, man strives for a type of understanding that comes from drawing things together and grasping their totality (comprehending)—so far as he can see that totality at any particular point in his existence. In other words, beyond analysis he aims at a synthesis; beyond explanation he longs for meaning.

To illustrate the ascent from the plateau of understanding keyed to evidence and explanation to the plateau of comprehension where meaning is reached, take the case of the late anthropologist, Louis Leakey. After forty years of searching northern Tanganyika's Olduvai Gorge, Leakey discovered, in 1964, the remains of a skull that antedated earlier evidence of the origin of man by at least one million years (now updated to about 2.5 million years). Recovering from the intoxicating confirmation of his lifelong hunch, Leakey thoughtfully asked, "Now what is the meaning of all this?" For facts are only the beginnings. When new facts are gained, new meaning must be derived. And often the mystery seems to increase as the discovery progresses.

BEYOND THE RATIONAL TO THE TRANSRATIONAL. Beyond knowing and understanding the *how* and *what*, man wants to gain an insight into the *why* of things (Cantril, 1950). He has an urge to place knowledge in ever broader contexts until particulars fall into place and a new Gestalt emerges. He reaches for a vision that is neither confined by the bounds of rationality nor obscured by irrationality but that expands into the transrational—a Gestalt that, having achieved a certain experiential ripeness, tends to crystallize into something of a total vision. This unified vision or world view is often designated by the term *Weltanschauung,* perhaps because the German *Anschauung,* more than the English *view* conveys something of the alive yet serene wonderment that accompanies the contemplation of this total yet never-final vision.

The Stunted Quest: Trained Incapacity

This ongoing quest is typical of the fully functioning man. The individual may be conditioned to stop his quest, however, well this side of his capacity and urge. The effect of such conditioning is known as *trained incapacity,* or artificially stunted development of one or more psychological potentialities. The phenomenon may be called "trained" because it does not necessarily result from anyone's malicious planning but from the systematic operation of thought-stunting forces within a certain cultural, subcultural, or even familial sphere.

Conditions apt to kill the urge for thoughtful inquiry and pacify it with a mere label are found, for instance, where strictly authoritarian domestic or political regimes prevail, and where, consequently, autonomous thought may lead one into trouble; or in technologically advanced cultures where many things cannot be understood only by the exercise of judgment unsupported by specialized information. Likewise, specialized education without a liberal foundation tends to result in a loss of autonomous judgment and critical thought, leaving the individual inclined to capitulate in the face of "research findings." These peculiar mind-stunting effects also may result from an upbringing "by the book" that deprives the child of a human model of inquiry and problem solving.

The lifelong study of autistic children by Bruno Bettelheim (1967) suggests that an arbitrary interruption of the neonatal infant's searching and exploring activities (mouth for the nipple; hands for the holding of a bottle) is an important contributing factor in the weakening of ego strength in the formative first months of life. Checked and inhibited from natural survival-motivated participation in his environment, the infant's interest in organizing its world diminishes until the resultant self-structure is only an empty shell.

Toward a Philosophy of Life

When the individual's cognitive potential develops under culturally and educationally favorable circumstances, it tends to culminate in a comprehensive vantage point from which matters of judgment and action may be reliably if not infallibly guided. This is a philosophy of life: a system of usually informal (and even unformulated) principles, firm yet flexible, for the conduct of practical, existential affairs; a point of view that allows the individual not only to gain an insight into the totality of things but to find his place within it; a point of view that lends stability to his outlook and behavior and helps him in meeting the vicissitudes of his life with relative effectiveness and satisfaction. It is a philosophy, then, of life as an experiential synthesis—tentative and always open to review—that provides structure and coherence to the flux of experience.

Finally, a self-acquired and tested philosophy of life is ultimately related to the individual's mental health. For it has the capacity to project meaning into confusion, frustration, and anxiety, and to maintain stability throughout change. The framework and perspective that it provides go a long way toward avoiding the shaky, fragmented mentality of him who knows the price of everything and the value of nothing, or has everything to live with and nothing to live for.

15 Foreknowledge of Death

Of the two things in life reputed to be inescapable—death and taxes—only one actually is. The very young, the poor, and the cunning go toll-free. But death is for all. And, barring severe mental impairment, so is foreknowledge of it. Like the other characteristics discussed in this analysis of what is human about human beings, this knowledge is specifically and exclusively human. There is no empirical or inferential evidence of such awareness in animals: "Man . . . is alone in realizing that he is subject to illness, alone in knowing that he must die. The rest of nature goes on its expanding course in absolute tranquility. Although plants and animals are the sport of chance, they rely on the passing hour as they would on eternity" (Bergson, 1935, p. 129). Certain animals, dogs in particular, are known to manifest something remarkably close to the human expression of grief at the separation of their mate or of a person to whom they are particularly attached. However, the point here is not emotion but knowledge or, more precisely, existential insight.

Man's capacity for realizing the inevitability of his death stems from his capacities for symbolizing, for reflecting and questioning from his time perspective. He acquires this knowledge not necessarily by introspection, however, but as part of the process of cultural assimilation. Riley, reporting on Blauner's (1966) research, notes: "In no known culture is the individual left to face death completely uninitiated. He is provided with beliefs about 'the dead' and about his own probable fate after death. Similarly, all these cultures include norms governing the imperatives imposed by death: a corpse must be looked after; the deceased must be placed in a new status; his vacated roles must be filled and his property disposed of; the solidarity of his group must be reaffirmed; and his bereaved must be reestablished and comforted" (1968, p. 20).

The Study of Death

Where so fundamental a matter is concerned, it is astounding that until quite recently the subject of death—as a fact of life—was totally absent from academic psychology, taboo even in clinical circles. Not only did it not fit in the framework of a psychology that followed a strictly nonexperiential and quantitative model but it was somehow taboo even where it did fit—as it would have in a psychoanalytical framework. To propose death as a topic for seminars, colloquia, or other formal or informal discussions would have been interpreted by yesteryear's trigger-happy diagnostician (now fortunately on the decline) as a symptom of a depressive, possibly suicidal personality. The situation was not very much different even in medical circles, as we learn from the eloquent writings of Kubler-Ross (1969).

The observation that Freud dealt with the subject in the late nineteenth century is not quite to the point. He dealt with the death instinct as a force that led behavior away from the pleasure principle toward constriction and even actual death; an unconsciously operating force and hence not a deliberate confrontation of the fact of death. Even "Mourning and Melancholia" (1968) did not pertain to man's foreknowledge of death, but to grief reactions in victims of bereavement.

Rather suddenly, although not inexplicably, as we shall see, death has become an academically fashionable topic. In the last few years, the subject has appeared in a wide variety of contexts—mainly in professional journals, but also in the national weeklies; thousands of readers responded to a very personal survey of attitudes toward death in *Psychology Today* (Shneidman, 1970). The present pace at which books and articles, colloquia, and symposia are featuring the subject points to a radical about-face. The steep rise of interest is particularly significant in view of the fact that even in 1965 the bibliography of Western social science literature on death was still quite limited (Kalish, 1965).

The gathering momentum has spawned two journals: *Omega,* concerned with time perspective, death, and bereavement; and *Archives of the Foundation of Thanatology*—their key words aptly esoteric and therefore suitable for a still-wary general public. The American Association of Public Opinion Research has also joined the process of "declassifying" death, while feelings and attitudes associated with the topic are increasingly studied by means of research techniques that vary from projective tests and physiological response measures to direct interviews. The outcome of this research not only may lead to an understanding of the dynamics related to foreknowledge of death, but may help people to confront the thought of death, to integrate it harmoniously with their existence, and, in so doing, to enhance their appreciation of life.

CAN DEATH BE MADE ACCEPTABLE? In this, as in all other areas of knowledge, "art precedes science," and anecdote leads to datum. We may not as yet have much systematic knowledge on the psychological meaning of death as the key event in everyone's future, but world literature provides a wealth of observations and insights from which one might formulate worthwhile research hypotheses. The general direction of these intuitive statements is that the person who has lived a full life is not particularly fearful of dying.

The research data obtained so far confirms this general direction (Diggory and Rothman, 1961; Parsons, 1963). Parsons found two attitudes toward death: one a positive, active orientation; the other a negative attitude of denial. In connection with what Parsons calls the "active stance" is the positive correlation between his subjects' educational attainments and age (analyzed jointly) and their attitudes toward death: "The higher the education, the less negative the respondent's image of death . . . and the more active his adaptation to death. This may suggest that as the general level of education in the Western world rises, a new orientation toward death may be in the making" (Riley, 1968, p. 24).

The Unmentionable Conclusion

Historically, Western culture generally has taken a decidedly life-oriented stance. In this respect it differs markedly from the ancient Far Eastern and North African cultures whose perspective was focused upon death, or, rather, the after-death (for example, the pyramids of ancient Egypt,* designed as highly visible dwelling places for dead kings or other public figures). In connection with the pyramids, one may wonder whether the showy memorials that abound in Forest Lawn Cemetery in Los Angeles are not a contemporary counterpart of the Egyptian notables' funerary structures. From an external point of view, the question is well taken, but from a psychological point of view, the parallel does not hold. First, the pyramids were constructed during the lifetime and by order of the future occupant himself. Memorials, on the other hand, are usually commissioned by surviving relatives or friends of the deceased. The motives that prompt these memorials stem from a variety of psychological concerns—respect, love, piety, regret—to symbolic attempts at making amends or relieving guilt feelings. Such feelings may be combined with or altogether replaced by the sociological forces of conventionality, prestige, one-upmanship, and similarly lugubrious ways of "keeping up with the Joneses"—concerns that may expose the surviving parties to particularly unpleasant psycho-commercial maneuvers (Mitford, 1963). More significantly, while pyramids symbolized a concern about life and death, there is little evidence to

---

* "In Egypt alone about eighty of these imposing edifices have been found—not all of them nearly as imposing as the well-known pyramid of Cheops—but archeologists claim that structures of this type were also built in the Sudan, Ethiopia, western Asia, Greece, Italy, India, Thailand, Mexico, and on some Pacific Islands" (*Encyclopædia Britannica*, 1972).

support, and a good deal of it that casts doubt on, the presence of any such concerns on the part of the thoroughly secularized celebrities entombed in the glamorous monuments of the "memorial parks" referred to in Mitford's caustic work. Those who believe in the reality of life after death usually conceive of it as a purely spiritual existence in which both bodily needs and ego needs have ceased to make sense.

Returning for a moment to the life/death orientation of the ancients, it is interesting to note that ancient Greece, especially during the fourth century, B.C., combined an intensely life-oriented culture with a philosophy in which death was a central theme of speculation. At this time Plato developed his theories of the interlocking relationship of knowledge and the immortality of the soul—a juxtaposition of ideas destined to play a dramatic role in the history of Christendom. Typical of the Stoics, Socrates among them, was the belief that the ruling concern of the philosopher should be a lifelong preparation for death.

As for the philosophical orientation of the West in regard to death, it is of course deeply rooted in Christianity's emphasis on the after-life. Within that context, death appears as a source of either comfort or anxiety and often a curious blend of the two. For while Christianity does not associate death with annihilation but with eternal life, that life is conceived of as one of either eternal reward or punishment, a potentially powerful and, at least in principle, constructive regulator of behavior. The religious attitude toward death, then, is a form of disregard rather than denial. This disregard of death as the ultimate rite of passage is, of course, perfectly consistent with the core of faith, for it concerns death as only the decomposition of the body, the interruption of worldly business, the separation from earthly possessions. As for separation from friends and relatives, it is regarded as only temporary and phenomenal, that is, only according to sense perception. That the awareness of such views is becoming existential rather than doctrinal is evidenced, for instance, in the growing incidence of "white" funerals in Catholicism.* Death as an event is disregarded in favor of its meaning, its mediating function.

The secular denial of death, engineered very largely by vested interests of an essentially commercial nature catering to man as consumer, is very different. The once prevalent, wholesomely life-oriented attitude becomes a near-phobic disregard and concealment of life's inevitable conclusion. This systematically, if indirectly programmed, attitude fortunately seems destined to decline as the topic of death is gradually brought into the open.

WHERE THE BELL NEVER TOLLS. Some of the things that isolate modern man from direct contact with death are independent of his volition. With the increased incidence of violent death and with the spread of health and

---

* The vestments of the officiating clergy are white—symbolic of the celebration of life—instead of the traditional black—symbolic of mourning.

hospitalization insurance, fewer and fewer persons die at home, surrounded by relatives (Fulton, 1965). Whenever it does happen, the corpse is usually immediately transferred to the funeral home. Similarly, the bell never tolls in the New World—partly for lack of bells, partly because it wouldn't reach the contemporary ear for both physical and psychological reasons. The din of modern life leaves no room for the archaic idiom of the bells, whose tolling would not be recognized from their pealing. Modern society has, of course, other and more effective means of informing the community than bells. The point I am trying to make, however, is concerned not with the dissemination of the event but with the realization of its personal significance by the surviving community. To elicit the appropriate mood and, with the mood, something of the meaning of the event, the judicious use of sound would seem far more effective than a newspaper notice.

Where the funerals of public figures are concerned, we do have visual means that compensate for the emotional neutrality and remoteness of the printed notice. Short of actual attendance, hardly anything can match the power of television for creating an extraordinary sense of group identification and participation in an event. As Riley (1968) observes, the burial of great men produces an integrative (if transient) effect on a nation or on the world. It affirms values held by the fellow citizens of the deceased and often by humanity at large, and it tends to stir civic feelings, etc. The same can be said, I think, of the burial of "ordinary" men when the circumstances of their death—say, in obvious or extraordinary service to their fellowmen—conveys the interdependence of all men and their relatedness in an individual yet ultimately common fate. Such participation seems a most effective way for the survivors to accomplish what Freud calls their "grief work."

Mourning: A Morbid Custom?

In a number of cultures, mourning is still something of an institutionalized rite, usually marked by prescribed dress and behavior. The custom is apparently designed, at least in part, to protect the privacy of the bereaved and grant them the freedom to give uninhibited expression to their emotions. The seclusion afforded by the mourning period allows the mourner to recover psychologically or to linger in the cherished memory of the departed, trying to prolong his or her presence by attending to the intense experiential reverberation of past moments, undisturbed by outside events. Freud confirms the beneficial effects of the culturally sanctioned privacy of bereavement: "We found . . . that, in mourning, time is needed for . . . reality-testing to be carried out in detail. When this work has been accomplished the ego will have succeeded in freeing the libido from its lost object" (1968, p. 252).

The emphasis on privacy, however, should not be understood to mean that bereaved persons necessarily should be left alone to indulge in the distillation of sadness, regret, or perhaps guilt. On the contrary: "Adults *need* help in living through the phase of intense grief; but I question whether they can appeal for help at all, explicitly, in a society such as contemporary Britain, where the majority wish to ignore grief and treat mourning as morbid" (Gorer, 1965, p. 131). In our society, also, as Riley confirms, the bereaved are expected to do their "grief work" quickly. In connection with the mourning ritual, Steiner notes that "the phenomenon of group participation in mourning pervades all cultures throughout history—whether this be part of a ritual reaffirmation of beliefs concerning eschatology, the cosmos, or interpersonal relatedness. . . . The process of working through one's relationship to the deceased and adapting to loss takes place within the group context which is culturally institutionalized. . . ." (1970, p. 80). The feeling that his loss is shared by others makes the pain of separation more bearable for the bereaved.

Cosmeticized Death

The extremes to which American society will go in its efforts to deny and disguise death are pungently portrayed in Mitford's *The American Way of Death*, a detailed exposé of the cosmetic approach to the grave. She describes "a new mythology, essential to the twentieth-century American funeral rite . . . to justify the peculiar customs surrounding the disposal of our dead" (1963, p. 17). Aside from exorbitant funeral costs, "dressing up" death seems perfectly harmless. But what about the psychological effects? Repression is not generally considered beneficial, and such elaborate avoidance of an inescapable fact of life must affect the manner of our existence.

In this connection one may legitimately speculate whether the specifically American glorification of youth is part of this process of repression and denial of the transience of life. Women especially are the object of an "etiquette" of youthfulness. Being over thirty is an embarrassment for many—hence the common joke about a woman's ten best years lying between twenty-nine and thirty. Hence also the fate of such advertisements—of admittedly dubious taste—as the invitation to "curl up and dye" issued by a beauty salon.

The New Repression

The relation between death and love has been a favorite theme in the arts, especially in literature and the theater but also in painting and music. Not only romantic love, but parental, brotherly and filial love, friendship, and, in particular, *agape* can be linked with death as crucial dimensions of existence.

What I propose to deal with, however, is not love but sex and, specifically, the remarkable attitudinal parallel between sex and death. At least in Western culture, both were once the great unmentionables. As late as 1890, William James, briefly touching on the subject of sex in his *Principles of Psychology,* felt it necessary to comment that "these details are a little unpleasant to discuss" (1950 p. 439). Now, however, sex is so profusely discussed that Henry Miller—no prude on the subject—expressed the hope on the occasion of his seventy-fourth birthday that "the youth of today may find a better cause to fight for than the sex-revolution" (Miller, 1966).

Interestingly, as sex emerged from its Victorian hideaway, death took its place underground. Considering the ancient relationship between the two, the liberation of the one and the increased suppression of the other do not seem unrelated. Both events seem to gravitate around an urge for limitless power: one by removing all barriers to gratification; the other by abolishing the very notion of ultimate limitation. In *Death and Mourning,* Geoffrey Gorer, the British anthropologist, writes: "There seem to be a number of parallels between the fantasies which titillate our curiosity about the mystery of sex, and those which titillate our curiosity about the mystery of death. In both types of fantasy, the emotions which are typically concommitant of the acts—love or grief—are paid little or no attention, while the sensations are enhanced as much as a customary poverty of language permits" (1965, p. 173).

Gorer recognizes, of course, that in terms of numerical data, death—especially violent death—is very much a part of the daily informational and fictional input of modern life. His concern is with the anxious concealment of death as a natural event: "While natural death became more and more smothered in prudery, violent death has played an ever-growing part in the fantasies offered to mass audiences—detective stories, thrillers, Westerns, war stories, spy stories, science fiction, and eventually horror comics" (p. 174). The effect of all this on the modern psyche has been to boost the sensation while removing the emotion.

An Existentialist Shocker

One of the few theses shared by most existentialists is the notion that people exist on a level of awareness so low that, for all practical purposes, they sleepwalk through life. Accordingly, certain existentialists, the French at the helm, have a yen for coining fresh, bold, sometimes crude expressions clearly aimed at shocking people into awareness (for example, Sartre's invidious dictum: "Hell is people"). Existentialist thought, despite its irritating, often quite unnecessary obscurity and occasional contradictions, has the unique value of focusing on relevant, life-related issues.

One of existentialism's more startling pronouncements is the contention that it is through death that life acquires meaning. Heidegger, one of the foremost proponents of this thesis, took as his point of departure Kierkegaard's view of man as being-in-a-finite-world and the sense of anguish and forlornness that oppresses him as he realizes the limits of his existence. Heidegger (1927), however, proposed to take the sting out of death by lifting it from the depths of the unconscious into awareness. There, by lucid questioning, the individual could transcend the everyday world of the impassive "anyone" and assert his essence and personal destiny through "resolute decision." Similarly, in Camus's *The Myth of Sisyphus* (1955), man transcends the anguish of death by determined confrontation of his finiteness. Such theories assume that in proving himself capable of such a confrontation, man converts his ultimate defeat into the symbol of his ultimate achievement.

Such oversimplifications are rarely convincing; indeed, they seem more academic than existential and are tinged with an extremism that is aversive to the common sense of many who do not represent the (to Heidegger) nonquesting "anybodies." Fortunately, there are more moderate and enlightening versions of the same theme. Among them is the voice of Viktor Frankl, the author of *Man's Search for Meaning* (1962). In several of his other books and articles, he conveys the substance of the existential attitude toward death in eminently meaningful and constructive ways.

Let us look briefly into the meaning of the paradoxical thesis that it is death that gives meaning to life by first eliminating what it does not mean. Contrary to Judeo-Christian thought, death is not necessarily viewed as the passage from a transient form of existence to an eternal life of either bliss or woe. Second, the idea that it is death that lends meaning to life should not be understood as anything heroic or otherwise exalted. Death is not valued as a means to something *beyond* the act of dying (although this would not necessarily detract from its existential value). The focus is upon the function of death within the context of life. The following testimony of a young kamikaze pilot writing to his parents would be dismissed by the typical existentialist as inauthentic, the fruit of doctrinaire conditioning: "Please congratulate me. I have been given a splendid opportunity to die. . . . I shall fall like a blossom from a radiant cherry tree. . . . How I shall appreciate this chance to die like a man! . . . Thank you, my parents, for the twenty-three years that you have cared for me and inspired me. I hope that my present deed will in some small way repay what you have done for me. . . ." (Feifel, 1959, p. 63).

To the existential mind in particular and the Western mind in general, the exalted tone of such an attitude casts doubt on its felt value. More often, we are persuaded that such attitudes are the result of the ultimate in psychological programming. But if the proposition that it is death that gives meaning to life refers to neither metaphysical nor heroic forms of the redemption of death, to what does it refer?

A VITALIZING EFFECT. The existential intent, far from transferring the focus of life outside of life, is to place it squarely on the here and now. "Our concern with death is not the sign of a cult of indifference to life or a denial of it. Rather, in gaining an awareness of death, we sharpen and intensify our awareness of life" (Feifel, 1959, p. 123). Man cannot fully understand himself nor achieve the good life without integrating an awareness of this momentous fact into the process of living. The existential engagement with death, the recognition that it is inseparable from life, is not a morbid attitude, not a sign of depression, but an intensely life-affirming stance. The possession and enjoyment of life become more precious, enhanced by an awareness of its fleeting nature.

This "poignance of the transient" is aptly conveyed by Wertenbaker in reference to Giraudoux's *Amphitryon 38*. In the play, Jupiter, the immortal god, takes on the disguise of Amphitryon's mortal flesh in order to make love to Amphitryon's mortal wife. Recounting his amorous experience to Mercury, Jupiter says that Amphitryon's wife uses expressions that are unknown to him and that widen the abyss between the immortal god and the mortal woman: "She will say—'When I was a child'—or 'When I'm old'—or 'Never in all my life'—This stabs me, Mercury." Then Jupiter says of the gods: "But we miss something, Mercury—the poignance of the transient—the intimation of mortality—that sweet sadness of grasping at something you cannot hold." And Wertenbaker adds: "I realize now that mortals miss it, too, when they do not think seriously about death" (1957, p. 70).

To convey the heightened awareness cast by the shadow of death upon one's experience of the ordinary, few testimonies surpass Ciardi's poem:

The Gift*

In 1945, when the keepers cried *kaput*,
Joseph Stein, poet, came out of Dachau
like half a resurrection, his other
eighty pounds still in their invisible grave.

Slowly then the mouth opened and first
     a broth, and then a medication, and then
     a diet, and all in time and the knitting mercies
     the showing bones were buried back in flesh,

and the miracle was finished. Joseph Stein,
man and poet, rose, walked, and could even
beget, and did, and died later of other causes
only partly traceable to his first death.

He noted—with some surprise at first—
     that strangers could not tell he had died once.

  * John Ciardi, "The Gift," *39 Poems* (New Brunswick, N.J.: Rutgers University Press, 1959).

He returned to his post in the library, drank his beer,
     published three poems in a French magazine,

and was very kind to the son who was at last his.
In the spent of one night he wrote three propositions:
That Hell is the denial of the ordinary. That nothing lasts.
That clean white paper waiting under a pen

     is the gift beyond history and hurt and heaven.

Only he who subtly weaves death into the canvas of life knows the wonder of ordinary, daily existence.

A Collective Neurosis

Feifel (1959) notes that attempts to expel or ignore the notion of death are a deception committed by man on himself. Modern society's conspiracy to repress the notion of death is regarded by a number of authors as one factor in our current, endemic psychological malaise. If we define mental health in terms of contact with reality, it follows that consistent operational denial of the one thing that is certain in life must exert a psychologically debilitating influence upon the individual and, finally, upon society at large. Yet this is precisely the dominant orientation of our psychology, our education, and our culture, none of which fosters—hardly even tolerates—an interest in existential issues.

Throughout its history modern psychology has concentrated on either methods or myths. Behaviorism's pseudorigorous emphasis upon quantification had no room for the person as a center of existential concerns. As for (traditional) psychoanalysis, its focus was upon highly speculative dynamics and symbolisms, combining the deeply mysterious and the trivial in a vast body of near-esoteric thought. Fortunately, psychoanalysis now veers toward an existentially oriented ego psychology focused upon the person rather than dynamics. Education in turn, through its heavily vocational and idea-shunning orientation, contributes in no small measure to an exclusively means-oriented world view. As for the consumer-centeredness of our culture, it fills our free time to overflowing with the pursuit of constantly changing promises of the gratification of immediate and usually sensate needs, leaving us no opportunity to pause along the way and take stock of what we are achieving or where we are going. Not everyone, of course, falls victim to this massive, culturally engineered repression. But those who lack awareness of life's alternative also lack a sense of its preciousness and are likely to treat life as just another replaceable commodity.

Also related to the fact that contemporary Americans seem unable to achieve satisfaction under basically normal conditions is a general inability to get "high" without resorting to alcohol, drugs, or violent sensations. This hedonic deficiency also seems related to a lack of awareness of the preciousness of life. The value and real or perceived availability of a given commodity are closely related (the law of supply and demand). The value of something as boundless as sand in the desert is so low that, for all practical purposes, it ceases to be an economic good. This devaluation seems to extend even to life itself in a society that systematically dodges the notion of its transience. Existence then assumes an endlessness that becomes a "drag."

But life cannot be kept exciting. Just maintaining approximately the same level of excitement would require, due to the effect of adaptation, a continuous increase in pleasurable stimulation. And since man's potential for stimulation is itself limited and it is bound to decline gradually, this is an inconceivable situation. True, for a small minority life appears, at least from the outside, like a succession of good times. But this is not the point. Unless there is some awareness of the alternative to it, even life is, existentially speaking, lost upon its fortunate owner. The individual who is entirely absorbed with the *content* of existence—things, people, events—has little awareness of its *process,* the journey in which he is both pilot and passenger. Such a person seldom, if ever, grants himself a chance to behold the panorama of his life: its highs and lows; the paths he has cut through the thickets; the directions he has taken, should have taken, can still take. He does not experience the existential joy and gratitude for having had the privilege of life for a span of time sufficient to build whatever it is he may have built.

Man Is His Choices

The fact of his death constantly forces the existentially living being to choose and order his priorities. By his choices, more than anything else, the individual fashions and reveals himself: "I am my choices," wrote Sartre (1956). If life lasted forever, significant choices would be rare since we could do everything at some point in our unending existence. There would be no necessity, not even a justification, for evaluation and choice; identity and uniqueness would fade as they do in Huxley's *Brave New World.* But worse, there would be no way to evaluate the sum total of one's choices—that is, life itself. Awareness of life would be impossible for lack of anything from which to differentiate it.

Foreknowledge of and normal concern about death is a dimension of the human condition that can powerfully enhance our way of living, forcing us to evaluate, to choose—judiciously and existentially—and thus to engage in the supreme creation—making a good life for ourselves.

16 Ultimate Concern: The Religious Animal

Dr. Karl Menninger, asked once by a journalist whether he believed in God, counseled with himself for a second and replied, "Yes. But I don't know whether what you have in mind is what I have in mind." This aptly qualified reply probably represents the attitude of most educated people today. Indeed, despite the fact that the 1968 International Gallup Poll reveals that "religion is alive and kicking" in America (Marty et al., 1968)—98 percent of the sample admitting to a belief in God—there is a keen awareness of the growing ambiguity of the question, even among religious leaders.*

Impersonal statistical surveys are not entirely devoid of meaning, but their sleight-of-hand quality commands great caution in the interpretation. Indeed, the individuals polled were probably answering from a bewildering variety of motives and contexts. One thing may safely be assumed: belief in God does not necessarily imply adherence to a formal, ritualized, and doctrinal system. The only thing the respondents possibly have in common may be something for which Tillich aptly coined the expression *ultimate concern* (1952, p. 47), which he recognizes as the essence of religious thinking. From a psychological point of view, then, these poll data—however low their information value from a strictly religious point of view—nevertheless say something significant about contemporary man.

---

* That the proportion of "religious belief" is relatively stable, at least in contemporary U.S., follows from a comparison of the 1952 and 1965 Gallup polls showing a mere two-point change (99 percent versus 97), averaged out to one point by the 1968 poll.

A Universal Phenomenon

In terms of ultimate concern, it seems that man has an inherently metaphysical bent. Every man, according to Allport, "whether he is religiously inclined or not, has his own ultimate presuppositions. He finds he cannot live his life without them, and for him they are true . . . whether they be called ideologies, philosophies, notions, or merely hunches about life" (1955, p. 95). Such presuppositions exert creative pressure upon his awareness with questions as to "what all this is about" and "what is it all leading to"—regardless of whether he is theistically or atheistically inclined. Furthermore, as psychology and especially cultural anthropology have shown, these pressures are apt to result in some kind of ritualistically colored behavior—of a kind that may lie well this side of religion as commonly understood.

Religion is experientially and behaviorally universal. In each of these respects it may take on a variety of forms—depending upon historical and geographical conditions—extending from primitive magical thinking and superstition, through demonism, idolatry, occultism (inverted forms of religious interest), and mysticism all the way to religious positions that are intellectually scrutinized, articulated, and compatible with scientific thinking insofar as they involve the same epistemological processes. As here viewed, the religious urge encompasses all manifestations and questions indicative of ultimate concern, either sacred or profane, with special emphasis upon those questions that have been deemed throughout the ages as particularly worthy of reverence.

TIME OF EMERGENCE. The fact that a behavioral trait (for example, linguistic ability) is characteristic of the species does not mean, of course, that it is necessarily manifest at birth or soon thereafter. Even under privileged environmental conditions, certain dimensions of the specifically human repertory of needs—ethical, political, or esthetic—emerge only after a considerable degree of maturity and experience is gained. Therefore, a serious, autonomous, and explicit concern with metaphysical questions (as distinct from religious upbringing) is most unlikely to arise early in the developmental process. Only when the basic physical and social needs—survival, security, affiliation, and acquisition of basic skills—are to some degree assured, are the needs related to further self-differentiation and actualization apt to arise in awareness. This unreflective, quasi-organismic ordering of priorities was first noted by Maslow, who theorized that certain need categories emerge only when other, more elementary categories are satisfied (Maslow and Murphy, 1969).

Both in our culture and during our life span, metaphysical concern is most likely to come to the fore either before or after the phase of intense pursuit of education or career-building goals—that is (roughly), before the late teens and after the early fifties. Indeed, because of the powerful influence of the environment upon the nonsurvival-oriented aspects of human development, metaphysical interest may fail to manifest itself altogether—just as such natural functions as laughing, playing, and even talking may fail to emerge or, at least, develop under adverse social conditions.

The common assumption that metaphysical concern is more likely to arise in older people at the approach of death does not find support in either the literature on the subject or my experience as a clinician. True, some concern with death is unavoidably present in the aged, but it pertains to the fact of death itself rather than to the metaphysical perspectives for which death is a condition. Again, unless the individual has been sensitized to certain modes of thinking at an earlier age, he is not likely to turn in that direction later in life. On the contrary, after several decades of preoccupation with pragmatic matters, the self-structure is unable to develop tendencies that have remained latent throughout the long growing season of the human. Lack of formal or informal imprinting at a sensitive age affects the emergence of species-specific behavior in humans as well as in animals—though in far less severe and irreversible ways.

Metaphysical concern may emerge or change dramatically, however, at any age (past childhood) when traumatic events tug at the roots of a person's being. This may be the case if one suffers the loss of a significant other, serious physical or social impairment, the experience of war, or the knowledge of impending and premature death. In such cases metaphysical concern may achieve the implosive effect of a conversion or, for that matter, an apostasy; that is, it may result in either the recognition or rejection of a supernatural power. Religious concern is a natural, experiential phenomenon and is intertwined, therefore, with the affective elements and total experiential context that make up personality. Thus, the individual whose life has been marked by frustration, stress, and strain may reject the idea of a deity, while another who has experienced the goodness and blessings of life may move in the direction of discovery and acceptance of a supreme guiding power.

PHILOSOPHICAL U-TURNS. Of course, anyone, whatever his background and disposition, can make a U-turn on the religious or secular philosophical path he has walked for half a lifetime or more. Theoretically, nearly anything is *possible* in the specifically human, symbolic realm. But not everything is *probable*. Ideas never entertained and values never considered, like muscles never used, are not likely to be very serviceable.

Actually, acute scepticism about or militant opposition to metaphysical matters would seem more conducive to such turnabouts than genuine indifference. This, because scepticism and opposition are actually left-handed and often very lively forms of concern with philosophical or psychodynamic root systems so broadly ramified throughout personality that they are their own, perhaps unacknowledged, metaphysic.

Sociological Interpretations

Social scientists commonly explain religious leanings and convictions as the result of socialization exclusively. For Freud, the concept of God is a father-figure projection; for the learning theorist, religious attitudes proceed from conditioning; for the sociologist, they are a form of cultural introjection. The sociologist asks if it is possible to conceive of any behavioral manifestation that is free from either random or systematic conditioning. The basic question, however, is whether religious concern can be accounted for *solely* by sociological factors.

In attempting to evaluate the part of truth contained in these views, we must distinguish first between religious *practice* and religious *belief*. Obviously, insofar as they are ritualistic, religious practices are a function of cultural conditioning. Visiting a place of worship on a set day of the week could not possibly be explained as the coincidence of millions of individual decisions or the operation of random forces. Such practices are clearly rooted in traditional conventions and represent a part of the cumulative transmission of culture—one of man's characteristic and exclusive attributes. Even religious urges are not independent of the social environment in both their awakening and manifestations. The fact that conditioning applies to him who doesn't believe, as well as to him who does, is commonly overlooked, however.

The common failure to realize the two-sided potential of social conditioning is reflected in a student's conclusion about his fiancée who, when she was in church, acted "like a different person," becoming very solemn and hardly acknowledging his presence on the few occasions he accompanied her. He benignly submitted that "she must have been conditioned to act that way," implying that *his* attitudes toward church and behavior were *not* the result of conditioning.

Who could say which of the two is necessarily the more conditioned? To answer with any degree of validity, we would have to know a great deal more about each of them. One thing is certain: both are affected, to a variable extent, by environmental conditioning, just as both are probably acting, to some extent, autonomously. Neither's stance has its footing in a vacuum. Actually, implicit conditioning may be far more pervasive and powerful than explicit conditioning. The individual who is raised either for or against religion is aware of being told to be for or against; he is apt to question the position he is made to adopt and may turn against it as part of the self-assertion that accompanies maturation. Conversely, he who is raised without any serious mention of religion will tend to develop an attitude of indifference, more impervious than opposition.

A FUNCTION OF NEED?   Another sociological proposition holds that faith is a function of existential need: of physical, social, economic, or emotional powerlessness. According to this theory, the more the individual feels a need for succor, the more he tends to resort to supernatural agency. Here again, the question is not whether the proposition contains truth but whether the truth it contains is sufficient to explain the phenomenon. Religious belief—as distinct from its object—is a natural phenomenon. Like other natural phenomena—thirst, love, or pain—it is subject to the lawfulness that operates throughout the natural experiential order. Thus, the person who is thirsty will search for a fountain and, having found one, will drink from it. Conversely, he who is not thirsty is not likely to drink even if a fountain is available. Similarly, he who is in a desperate state of need will naturally search for help where he feels he is most likely to obtain it. If no other agency can be counted upon, he will express his need to the deity. Such behavior may appear naive to the observer. But psychodynamically, it is a natural, not a mystical or mysterious, phenomenon. Just as the fountain does not explain the drinking, however, so the petitioning does not account for the faith.

Social scientists seem to confuse the religious urge with its object. The latter, of course, is supernatural, but the former is a natural phenomenon with observable manifestations and effects. To recognize the effects of (genuine) faith, it may be necessary to participate to some degree in the attitudes that are the condition of faith—just as it may be necessary to participate in the faith which is science in order to recognize some of its significance. The difference between technological and religious effects is not that the latter are less real but that they are less recognizable by the sense organs. It takes a person to recognize that faith "works" (Polanyi).

Existential Religion: A Way of Being

Faith, then, is not a matter of knowing and understanding but of being and feeling. Is it not taking a reductionist stand, however, to say that religious urges and beliefs correspond not to a body of knowledge but to a subjective state, to a feeling? *Feeling* is something of a weasel word that may stand for phenomena extending from a passing affective ripple to an integrated state, an internal synthesis in which the individual feels himself in his most intimate and undivided wholeness. Feeling, in the sense of intuition, is a legitimate and reliable epistemological path (Royce, 1964; Merleau-Ponty, 1962; and the existentialists generally), provided the subject is congruent, that is, at one with himself. Feeling is the only way to know and test such significant experience as love, trust, hope, and similar existential states.

Like any genuine philosophy of life, faith is not, of course, something that "can be taken up anywhere at any time like baseball" (Watts, 1961,

p. 44). It requires an active and focused concern, translated into a way of life and an outlook on reality.

Religion on Trial/Religious Revival

It used to be that ups and downs were successive. Now, judging from the prevailing state of affairs in the religious sector, they can apparently be simultaneous. For there is no doubt that something of a religious renaissance is stirring among the young—not a mass movement but a part of the current scene that cannot be dismissed. At the same time, there is no doubt that religion, especially institutionalized religion, is on trial—not by any militant outside forces, as periodically used to be the case, but by the faithful themselves. Together, these antithetical currents reveal a remarkable and somewhat puzzling religious climate in contemporary society.

What strikes one first of all about this religious fermentation is its contrast with attitudes of either placid adherence, contemptuous indifference, or militant opposition that alternated throughout the history of religion in the West. Also quite novel and perhaps historically unique is the fact that the revival issues from the young, and the sophisticated young at that. Most receptive to "the call" are college students and other young people who, though not exactly intellectually oriented, are by no means holy innocents. The depth of their religious interest would be hard to assess. Judging by some of the showier aspects of the movement, it has the makings of a fad. It is certainly most unorthodox and its belief, ritual, and trappings, rather unfocused. But this is not necessarily a sign of shallowness. It may bespeak a genuine search for new forms, a keen awareness of the uniquely complex and intangible quality of its object, plus a healthy experimentation with modes of expression.

As for the trial that religion is currently undergoing, it is equally difficult to assess. In a sense, all traditional institutions currently are brought before the bench. Most characteristic of the dialectical movement surrounding these trials is the rapid succession in which prosecution and defense support and demolish their own and each other's arguments, subsequently leaving society in a state of generalized confusion or indifference.

In the case of religion, one of the predominant accusations is breach of trust by the authorities—an accusation rooted in the scepticism and resentment of the faithful for having been caught in a web of mythological doctrines, complete with do's and don't's, gradually exploded by science. However, no sooner is a plea made for factual, verifiable foundations of the kind of faith that supports science—for what May calls "the myth of no-myth"—than it is revealed that science itself relies on myth to express its usually valid but necessarily incomplete grasp of things.

Myth: The "Intercom of Culture"

A choice vantage point for understanding the contrapuntal social and intellectual processes surrounding religion is the study of the role of myth in the development and communication of thought. Until recently, Western culture regarded myths as naive symbolizations indicative of a primitive, prescientific level of thinking about the universe and the human condition—an outlook English and English (1958) confirm in their definition of myth as "1. a story that has sacred or cultlore associations, but lacks actual, historical basis. 2. a false but persistent idea or theory that is widely accepted." To this purely external description, sociology adds a psychodynamic or sociodynamic dimension, defining myth as "a collective belief, that is built up in response to the wishes of the group, rather than an analysis of the basis of those wishes."

Now, however, reputable scientists and philosophers of science regard myth as something considerably more significant than folkloric oddity. Myth is now thought to be a valid medium for the representation, communication, and unaltered transmission across the generations of certain crucial, preconceptual values and insights. "The myth at its deepest level is that collectively created thing which crystallizes the great, central values of a culture. It is, so to speak, the intercommunications system of culture" (Roszak, 1969, p. 214).

THE DEMYTHOLOGIZING OF RELIGION.   Simultaneously, however, a process has been set in motion that tends to demythologize religious belief; that is, to purge it of the mythical elements that are a part of all traditional religious systems. The process was nurtured by two independent and diametrically divergent sources: one deliberately issuing from religion itself; the other, accidental, emanating from positivistic philosophies and sciences, especially psychology and cultural anthropology.

The religious wing of the movement was represented by avant-garde theologians who endeavored to make the message of the church understandable and acceptable to secularized man. The other, far more powerful wing, offered impressive amounts of data and scholarly commentary that revealed myth as a sociologically purposeful but epistemologically dubious phenomenon. Curiously, while the findings and theories of the social scientists were entirely detached from any religious concern, they had a far more pervasive effect upon the trend away from religion than did their deliberately aggressive counterparts of the past (for example, Voltaire's scathing anticlericalism during the Enlightenment or Marx's dialectical materialism and denunciation of religion as the "opiate of the people").

Most readers will recall the existential shocker known as the "Death of God" movement, a vigorous part of the process of demythologizing religion and a favorite topic of magazine articles in the early sixties. Like many an intellectual novelty, it was born in Europe and raised (in more than one sense) in the United States. Indeed, as far back as the late twenties, certain seminal theological thinkers—Germany's Bultmann (1955) and Gogarthen (1955) at the helm—proposed a drastic reinterpretation of the ancient religious message to make it relevant to modern man. What they considered a particularly vulnerable part of religious doctrine was its use of myth, which they perceived as a barrier to faith for the educated sector. But the scholarly, near-esoteric style of these writers precluded wide dissemination of their endeavor.

To turn the original idea into an eye-catching movement, it took the dynamic and readable writings of such men as Vahanian, Altizer, and Hamilton. Their message, billed as the "Death of God," rapidly reached the marketplace, deliberately shocking both believers and unbelievers into a heightened awareness of the crude anthropomorphism and, all told, often rather unspiritual quality pervading much of traditional religion. In half-playful, half-militant language, these theologians denounced the average believer's image of God as the "Big Daddy God," the "Cosmic Bellboy," and similar epithets evocative of a solely petitionary and wish-fulfilling approach to the Deity. However, this kind of gleefully irreverent rhetoric soon declined into a bumper-sticker campaign of pro and con witnessing (for example, "Too bad about your God. Ours is still alive."). Consistent with the fate of vociferous and explosive movements generally, this, too, soon lost momentum and was replaced by a round of talks about "The God Who Wouldn't Stay Dead" (Greeley, 1968, p. 117).

Short-lived though it was, this upheaval has had a lingering effect upon the current attitude toward religion. The consequences of its overall impact appear to have been both detrimental and beneficial. They were detrimental because the vestiges of genuine religion latent under the apathy, irrelevance, and petrification that the movement sought to combat collapsed in many instances as a result of the vigor of the attempts at revival; beneficial in that the movement ushered in such significant changes as those described in a later section of this chapter.

THE MYTHOLOGIZING OF SCIENCE? Sharply contrapuntal to the demythologizing process is the recent surge of scientific and philosophical thought that tends to restore myth as a legitimate cognitive device. Surprisingly, this development did not originate in religious circles nor was it in defense of religion. Like the earlier reductionist emasculation of myth by science, its current "rehabilitation" seems entirely free of ulterior, ideological motives. Nevertheless, one cannot fail to appreciate May's comment: "Ironic as this is, it is the fate of all who engage in 'mythoclasm,' to borrow Jerome Bruner's phrase, that they find themselves in secret ways constructing new myths again" (1969, pp. 298–99).

The groundbreakers in this development are those rare personalities who combine outstanding achievement as specialists with unquestioned scholarship as generalists. Among them are Polanyi, Dubos, Julian Huxley, Boulding, and Teilhard de Chardin; the most vocal is Polanyi, the scientist-philosopher who champions the view that science at its deepest level is a faith, a subjective interpretation within a sociohistorical context (referring, no doubt, to science as theoretical explanation not as application or technology). "The premises of science on which all scientific teaching and research rest are *the beliefs held by scientists* on the general nature of things"(1946, p. 11) (italics added) and, in more personal terms: "The ultimate justification of my scientific convictions always lies in myself. At some point I can only answer, 'For I believe so.' This is why I speak of Science, Faith and Society" (p. 9). He also writes that "objective experience cannot compel a decision either between the magical and the naturalist interpretation of daily life or between the scientific and the theological interpretation of nature; it may favor one or the other, but the decision can be found only by a process of arbitration in which alternative forms of mental satisfaction will be weighed in the balance" (p. 28).*

Royce, a theoretical-experimental psychologist, echoes Polanyi's view:

> When men pool their existentially valid findings and project them out into the universe and ask the ultimate questions of life, when they, in effect, try to encompass the totality of things, they are, in my opinion, offering *a mythological statement* concerning the nature of reality. And it is my view that the best they can muster is an image of this totality— a reality image, or a myth. It happens that the view which is currently accepted as "really" real is the image we can gain from the scientific community. That is, science is what is really believed in these days. Science, therefore, is in danger of becoming ultimatized or *mythologized*. Science is in danger of religiofication, the art of turning a secular matter into a religion (1964, pp. 158–59; italics added).

Roszak is among the more activistically oriented scholars representative of this point of view. His purpose, contrary to Polanyi's or Royce's, is not to explain the nature of the epistemological process or the inescapably metaphysical bent of man's thinking but to expose the imperialistic hold that modern technocracy—the political outgrowth of applied science—exerts upon the public. His contribution, then, to the rehabilitation of the myth is only indirect and, in a sense, left-handed.

Arguing that science can be regarded as a builder of myths—sometimes with deliberately political or "imperialistic intent"—he writes:

> Objective consciousness is emphatically *not* some manner of definitive, transcultural development whose cogency derives from the fact that it is uniquely in touch with the truth. Rather, like a mythology, it is an arbitrary construct in which a given society in a given historical situation has invested its sense of meaningfulness and value. And so, like any

* Polanyi's expression "mental satisfaction" is reminiscent of Einstein's ultimate reason for preferring the theory of relativity to that of quantum physics: "I like it better."

mythology, it can be gotten round and called into question by cultural movements which find meaning and value elsewhere (1969, p. 215).

Aware of the scepticism his stand is apt to elicit, Roszak asks, "Are we using the word 'mythology' illegitimately? . . . I think not. . . . If the culture of science locates its highest values not in mystic symbol or ritual or epic tales of faraway lands and times, but in a mode of consciousness, why should we hesitate to call this a myth?" (p. 214).

These are but a few of the current testimonies of leading physical and social scientists. The thrust of their argument, of course, has nothing to do with the promotion of religion. It aims solely to correct the prevalent misunderstanding of science as a source of objective truth and omniscient guidance and to prevent the "religiofication" of science, as Royce (1964) calls it. But the rehabilitation of myth unintentionally lends support to those fields that do and must use the language of myth as an essential vehicle. The fact that myth, like any other tool, can be used for spurious as well as constructive purposes does not detract from its unique value for the symbolization and communication of complex or comprehensive matters. In light of this rediscovery of myth as a legitimate cognitive device, the demythologizing of religion—by its very representatives— appears to be a peculiarly radical and somehow defensive (if not alto- gether mistaken) effort.

From a Vertical to a Horizontal Model of Religion

The crisis revolving around religion in the context of modern thought has not been without positive effects. One of the more promising trends to emerge from it is the tendency towards substituting a "horizontal" model of religious concern for the previous "vertical" model. The earlier notion of religious involvement could appropriately be termed "vertical" because it consisted characteristically of an attempt by the individual at engaging in an intimate, one-to-one spiritual relationship between himself and his Creator, a "soul-to-soul" bond of a purely internal, contemplative nature. It was characterized by an assiduously cultivated inwardness and intense concern with personal salvation, often accompanied by ascetic tendencies leading in certain cases to complete withdrawal from the world.

This religious stance, then, assumed a socially confining rather than expanding form. Curiously, while its devotees were often extremely gen- erous in their intentions—aiming, as they did, to mediate the salvation of the world at large through the sacrifice of selfish pursuit—they carefully avoided any contact with the world they wanted to redeem. (Incidentally, such thinking does not have the irrationality in the spiritual realm that it would have in the material-social realm. It is mentioned here not by way of criticism but characterization.) In the great mystics (for example, Meister Eckhart, St. Theresa of Avila), this intensely focused state of mind culminated in renowned ecstasies. From the testimony of these mystics themselves, these ecstasies (at least in some of their sensory and emotional components) were akin to the "mind-expanding" effects of LSD and sometimes led to mystical writings that have taken their place in world literature. On the less authentically spiritual, popular level, this vertical type of religion found expression in images of an intimacy between the worshipper and his God that tended to assume a naively anthropomorphic, sometimes visibly romanticized, element—as exemplified in the lyrics of certain popular hymns ("And I walk with Him and I talk with Him/And He tells me I am His own/And the dreams we share, as we linger there/None other has ever known").

This once prevalent individualized and exclusive concept of religion —as a covenant between the "low down" to the "up high"—is apparently being replaced by a horizontal model. The earlier tendency to seek refuge at the bosom of the All-Perfect Being is shifting to something resembling an attempt at "loving thy crooked neighbor with thy crooked heart," as Dylan Thomas puts it. Medieval man accepted the churches' injunction to view the things of this world *sub specie aeternitatis*, but the new type of committed believer wants his religious convictions to be relevant to the immediate situation of which he is a part. His religion is existential, aiming to express itself in daily living with and among his fellowmen. As a result, we see the emphasis shift *from contemplation to service, from preaching to practice, from a flight toward heaven to an embracing of mankind*—an approach that prefers the din and, if must be, the vulgarity of the marketplace to the majestic solitude of the temple.

A NEW STYLE OF RELIGIOUS RESPONSE. The manifestations of this new paradigm of religious interest and concern are numerous. On the practical plane, church-affiliated people of different persuasions have substituted a mutually tolerant and appreciative attitude for the animosity and rejection that once prevailed among denominations. All sides involved seem to experience the new attitude as enhancing and enriching. Significant also is the tendency toward developing "societal" and "folk" styles of religion, as distinct from formal or ecclesiastical systems. Religious witnessing aims more and more at "encounter" with the fellow worshipper. What is sought is a genuine sharing and mutual revealing of either needful or joyful religious experience. Buber's I-Thou image of interpersonal encounter and Rogers's person-to-person concept of human relations are the new paradigms of religious communion. In line with this orientation, religious ritual assumes forms that harmonize with the contemporary mood and temper and are more expressive of the concelebrating character of communal services. There is also a shift in the locus of worship. Instead of taking place exclusively in permanently assigned, solemn, and impersonal sanctuaries, it is being brought into the home, with ordinary furniture and utensils being used and the participants wearing ordinary clothing—the whole setup aimed to heighten the life-relatedness of the event and the tacit covenant of the family of man.

On the theoretical plane there is a trend toward the psychologization of religion, in the sense that traditional theological discussion is being replaced by an analysis of the psychological processes leading to religious stances and conclusions. Other effects of this radical scrutiny brought to bear upon religious thought and behavior are the increasing attention given by serious authors to such paradoxical phenomena as "religious atheism" and the possibility that a reverently sceptical and actively questioning attitude may carry greater spiritual value and vitality than relatively mindless certainty or an all too mindful calculation.

A Spiritual and Esthetic Loss?

The disappearance, or at least the decline, of some of the time-honored religious beliefs and practices could hardly be deplored. However, certain thoughtful authors with a deep and scholarly sense of the sacred, feel that the wave of religious secularization may sweep away some of the wellsprings as well as the deadwood of the great religions. They perceive a danger of real spiritual loss in the new psychologistic-social service direction that religious interest is taking and the abandonment of the attempt to actualize a vivifying awareness of infinitude and perfection, which was part of the vertical approach at its best. They also fear that the charismatically esthetic dimension that has been associated throughout time and cultures with religious attitudes and worship is likely to disappear, thus impoverishing even the nonreligious individual.

17 The Transcending Animal

Suddenly the venerable but rather dusty word *transcendence* has sprung upon the scene as if it had been freshly minted to answer the call of some new need. Transcendence, as a human capacity, has been around as long as mankind itself; and as a concept, it is as old as philosophy and theology. But only recently has the notion been "marketed," given the sales appeal that intrigues the layman and stirs him into feeling that he may be "missing out on something"—which he quite possibly is in an age of pseudoempiricism (Bakan, 1967; May, 1958). Notwithstanding this possibility, he actually may be immersed in the process of transcendence without realizing it, for people engage in many activities whose sophisticated names they may not be acquainted with. And transcendence is not only one of man's capacities; it is also one of his tendencies. The current popularization of the notion is a good thing then, at least in principle, since it may heighten man's awareness of this capacity. In practice, however, we must wait and see, hoping that our idea of transcendence does not suffer the trivialization that is apt to be the fate of suddenly fashionable notions.

In his introduction to a brief but remarkable collection of readings on transcendence, Richardson (Richardson and Cutler, 1969) comments that "the study of transcendence is provoked by the quest for transcendence" (p. ix). Indeed, a quest of this sort has recently emerged, as anyone working among educated young adults is bound to notice. It is manifested as an urge to move from ordinary dimensions of thought and action to an awareness of extraordinary dimensions of existence and radically novel perspectives on the cosmos. Commenting on this budding ramification of contemporary thought, Richardson further states, "My own supposition is that this is one reflection of a major intellectual opening in America—an opening that may mean a more radical reorientation in outlook than the Enlightenment and the development of science, more radical because it is more discontinuous with our past intellectual and spiritual traditions" (p. xiii).

Forms of Transcendence

There is an elementary sense in which all that is alive can be said to continuously transcend itself through the processes of physical and psychological growth. This form of transcendence can be equated with the operation of what Rogers calls the "actualizing tendency" and defines as "the inherent tendency of the organism to develop all its capacities in ways which serve to maintain or enhance the organism.* It involves not only the tendency to meet what Maslow terms 'deficiency needs' for air, food, water, and the like, but also more generalized activities. It involves development toward the differentiation of organs and of functions, expansion in terms of growth, expansion of effectiveness through the use of tools, expansion and enhancement through reproduction. It is development toward autonomy and away from heteronomy, or control by external forces" (1959, p. 196).

Since transcendence literally means "over-climbing," going above and beyond one's level of being—in whatever realm it may be, social, educational, spiritual—all the preceding functions can be classified as transcendental. They all imply a movement that goes counter to inertia, deterioration, limitation, incompleteness, restriction, obstacles, and so on. Therefore, in its most general form, transcendence can be characterized as a property of life.

In this sense, however, transcendence is so ubiquitous that it cannot qualify as a specifically human capacity. Most facets mentioned in the above definition apply to animals as well as humans. Even development toward autonomy and away from heteronomy applies in variable measure to all animals in that they grow towards independence from their parents. In this sense, transcendence amounts to a nearly unavoidable movement beyond present being and capacity. To approach man's specific and unique capacity for transcendence, we must examine its symbolic aspects, for only these can modify the stream of biological and sociological determinism.

On the symbolic plane, transcendence can be represented as a three-tiered pyramid. The lowest, broadest tier is common to humanity at large; the intermediary tier requires certain attitudes, insights, or stages of consciousness that, for some cluster of as yet little-known reasons, not everybody acquires. As for the top of the pyramid, it is occupied by those who by disposition, search, or exercise find themselves developing a perspec-

* Rogers uses the term *organism* to refer to not only the physical but the total psychophysical structure that is the human being.

tive about self and reality that in some way allows their awareness to detach itself from and rise above the ordinary social-empirical world. These persons may either remain part of the everyday world for the purpose of fulfilling ordinary existential obligations or withdraw from the world and organize themselves in relative isolation.

A striking example of the latter, incipient trend is the recently "discovered" (though not so recently founded) Protestant monastery of Taize (France). In this humble place, quite devoid of the imposing architectural setting and cultural treasures of the great traditional monasteries, males of intellectually and professionally high standing and from a variety of countries pledge themselves to celibacy, community of goods and achievements, and the acceptance of authority. By choosing the rough-hewn life of service and contemplation embodied in the Taize community, these men seek to liberate themselves from the bondage of socioeconomic concerns and ascend into the spiritual realm. Curiously, it is upon the top tier of the pyramid of transcendence, exemplified by the Taize phenomenon, that the current interest is focused; for example, the crowds of young people (more than 70,000 in 1973) who choose to spend time in the tents rising on the Taize grounds and to participate in the lives of these lay monks.

SELF-ACTUALIZATION.   The act of transcending is so characteristic of man that the specifically human dimensions we have examined, taken together, are themselves The Transcending Animal. Therefore, it seems that no better characterization could be given of this first level of transcendence than a brief recapitulation of the highlights of these specific dimensions as they were discussed in the preceding chapters.

The most fundamental and ubiquitous manifestation of this phenomenon is, of course, man's symbolic ability, which frees him from stimulus-boundness by way of abstraction and generalization, allows him to identify and utilize pattern and paradigm on both the perceptual and conceptual levels, and enables him to invent and enjoy analogy, metaphor, wit, and humor. Via his reflective ability, he has the option to live in an experiential hall of mirrors. His time-binding ability allows him to capture the present moment, to enshrine it in an ever-stretching past that articulates the past of his species, and to project it in alternate perspectives of the future. He transcends every animal in the animal kingdom by his capacity to go beyond raw communication and to engage in exquisitely precise, variegated, and elegant language, expressive not merely of individual, visceral needs and pressures but of timeless concerns, insights, and discoveries. He is the animal who not only uses rudimentary tools but devises them, who makes tools that make tools: material tools and machines; intellectual tools and systems; social tools, laws, and institutions. He is the imaginative animal who can create endless forms of fun, play, and beauty and who reaches peaks of ecstasy in love. He is the animal who can choose hardship over reward, freedom over comfort; who can delay gratification; who can empathically place himself in the frame of reference of his fellow human beings and can, thereby, derive guidelines for his conduct with and toward them. Man is the animal who questions, experiences ultimate concern, penetrates beyond the world of the senses and peers into metaphysics; who knows that he will die and who can transcend this paralyzing foreknowledge to the point of utilizing it to enhance his very existence; who can conjure possibility, futurity, and alternate modes of being.

Each of these highlights represents actualization—not of an unavoidable nature such as biological growth but achievement with a variable degree of self-determined direction and purpose. As expressed by the very name of the process, it is actualization of the self by the self. Such a process does not, of course, occur in a vacuum. It involves social, biological, and physical factors but cannot be explained solely by these factors—at least it has never thus been explained.

TRANSCENDENCE OF PARTICULAR PROBLEMS. Transcendence, as we have seen, can be essentially means oriented, keyed to clearly visualized, often tangible objectives. Another form of transcendence, however, is end oriented and keyed to meaning rather than achievement. It is a more evolved form and focuses upon action, but not in the sense of doing something *in order to* obtain or achieve something beyond the action. Rather, the activity is autotelic, or self-contained; it has to do with a state of consciousness and belongs to the realm of *seeing*, hence, of *being*.

But can these two realms be equated? Seeing, in the sense of intellectual understanding of causes and effect, of antecedents and consequents, of categories and similar logical relations, clearly does not fall within the order of being. One can have a considerable amount of such knowledge and not be affected by it as a person; for example, one may be specialized in psychology, in moral philosophy, or in political science and not behave or even feel in a way that constructively articulates such knowledge. But there is another way of seeing or grasping that exerts a compelling influence upon the existential significance of experience and thereby upon one's way of being, including its expression in behavior. This is what is here meant and is explained in the following.

THE DEVELOPMENT OF ATTITUDINAL VALUES. To introduce this aspect of transcendence and to avoid falling into obscurantism—to which the topic of transcendence is subject—I will draw upon the life-related thinking of Victor Frankl. In *The Doctor and the Soul* (1955), Frankl distinguishes three value categories: creative or active values, experiential or passive values, and attitudinal values. The first two are constantly being actualized by the normally functioning person; both come naturally to man and are commonly known, though not necessarily under these names. The third, however, lies between the elementary values described in the preceding section and the relatively unfamiliar forms discussed further on under "Transcending the Human Predicament."

Attitudinal values stand out most distinctly when described against the backdrop of the other two kinds. Therefore, while the actualizations of both the active and the passive values are elementary forms of transcendence that belong in the category of self-actualization, they will nevertheless be described here for the sake of providing a contrasting backdrop for the focus of the present discussion. The actualization of the active and experiential values are special cases of the category just described under "Self-Actualization." Creative values are actualized in the active, coordinated pursuit of objectives whose complexity extends from the acquisition of such simple skills as walking and speaking to the mastery of the complex skills characteristic of membership in an evolved society (from cooking a meal, repairing a bike, tending a garden, to epochal inventions or achievements). The pursuit of these values looms large in the growth of the individual's self-concept, self-reliance, and self-esteem, and their achievement strengthens and builds the ego.

Experiential or passive values, on the other hand, are gained not through effortful pursuit but through receptive abandon of consciousness to things and events in the environment that exert an individually variable and captivating effect upon awareness. Mediated by any one of the sensory pathways with which man is equipped, and subliminally selected by the individual's unique sensitivity matrix, the stirring image of these things reverberates through the self and remains there as a fund of live, precious remembrance. Such values are garnered, for instance, through the contemplation of natural or man-made beauty; breathing the fragrance of a flower or the freshness of mountain air; savoring the taste of food or drink; enjoying the caress of warmth or coolness; listening to the voice of bird and brook, to the wind playing in pine trees, to the voice of man, and to the countless modes of his music-making talent. On a more symbolic level, experiential values can be derived from the contemplation of a kind of beauty that is independent of the senses—the beauty of loyalty, dependability, gratitude, courage, and virtue by whatever name. While active values tend to strengthen the self-structure, passive values tend to exert a purifying, uplifting, and spiritually amplifying effect upon the affective-esthetic personal economy.

Attitudinal values, in turn, are actualized whenever the individual adopts a positive stance in the face of unavoidable physical or psychological pain or loss. Frankl himself does not describe attitudinal values as transcendental. But their transcendent qualities are evident. "Unavoidable" is crucial here since positive attitudes toward avoidable pain tend to be masochistic. Attitudinal values do not come naturally to man. Though they involve both creativity and surrender, they transcend these functions in that, beyond achievement and enjoyment, they aim at meaning—overall, life-encompassing meaning that involves the total self, somehow after the model of a conversion. Characteristic of these attitudinal or transcendent values, then, is their capacity to generate meaning not out of inner strength or resources but out of extreme need, helplessness, loss, or deprivation.

It may appear at first that attitudinal values are less universal and apply only to the unfortunate, the suffering, the oppressed. They are universal, however, not necessarily in terms of particular problems but in terms of the overall predicament that Nietzsche characterizes "the disease called man."

Transcending the Human Predicament

What differentiates the transcendence achieved through the actualization of attitudinal values from what we are about to discuss is, essentially, the type and scope of the predicament upon which transcendence bears. While there is no clear-cut break between the two, they can be roughly distinguished as follows: the former is focused upon particular problems (bereavement, disease, loss of organs, function, prestige, or possession); the type of transcendence discussed in this section deals with the overall predicament inherent in human existence, quite apart from the vicissitudes of individual life.

Over the centuries, this predicament has been described in many different terms—most eloquently in recent decades by the existentialists and most concisely and starkly in Gautama Buddha's "Three Signs of Being": suffering; finiteness or transience (whose most radical expression is death); and loss of individual significance or ego power (a function of the preceding two). In what manner is the individual capable of transcending these predicaments? For a brief and lucid characterization of an often esoterically treated subject, I will draw upon Huston Smith's excellent article, "The Reach and the Grasp: Transcendence Today" (1969).

Transcendence affects man's predicaments holistically; that is, in an overall manner—not like a spotlight focused upon one problem but like a floodlight illuminating the totality of his being. "It is a gestalt phenomenon, changing nothing within the field unless it changes the field as a whole" (p. 3). Second, transcendence does not counter the problem by removing it but by transmuting it to a new level of perception and meaning. Transcendence, then, it not an anesthetic; the pain remains, but the perception of its role in the economy of one's existence is affected. Third, transcendence operates through a quality of insight so penetrating and encompassing that it accomplishes a transvaluation of the subject's world view and results in veritable self-renewal.

The effect upon the person of this transcendence is a parallel to the state of Maslow's "authentic" person who "by virtue of what he has become, assumes a new relation to his society and indeed, to society in general. He not only transcends himself in various ways; he also transcends his culture. He resists enculturation. He becomes more detached from his culture and from his society. He becomes a little more a member of his species and a little less a member of his local group" (1968, p. 11).

As for the particular paths along which transcendence proceeds in dealing with the human predicament, that most frequently recognized by authorities on the subject is the path of love. Only when the self focuses upon and fuses with another self (or selves) does it achieve unity (Kierkegaard, 1946). Next to love, the most promising, most commonly chosen path is hope (Bloch, 1959; Ellul, 1973; Marcel, 1962). And for those to whom these paths offer no appropriate solution, there is the path of commitment (Bühler, 1959; Frankl, 1962). Together these paths lead to the core of existential thinking, especially in its therapeutic applications.

ONTOLOGICAL TRANSCENDENCE.   Ontological transcendence is the ultimate or cosmic form. Both in process and outcome, it consists of seeing *through* and *beyond* what is called, in Eastern philosophy, the *maya,* that is, the illusion that is the familiar, empirical, "real" world of everyday things and events.

The values just mentioned—love, hope, commitment—can prove effective, for a time, to anyone seeking to transcend the predicament of human existence. Many find lasting sustenance in one or more of them. But there are others, apparently not just a few, to whom these sources do not afford lasting fulfillment. While not abjuring the meaning and joy that these sources have lent to his life, the person thus affected cannot deny to himself the insufficiency of the perspective afforded by them. Discovering the limits, touching the bottom of these sources of fulfillment, represents to this person the ultimate crisis, skirting the void of meaninglessness. At this stage, *new objects* of hope, of love, or of commitment are powerless to fill "the abyss of longing" as the existentialists call the sense of infinity by which certain individuals are possessed (Levinas, 1969).

For those inveterate searchers, there remains one further plateau. Transcendence in this key begins with a dawning awareness of living on the verge, on the threshold of "something more" than is currently apprehended or assumed. This "more" is not a matter of either increased quantity or even of increased quality. For the subject does not seek more of the things that make up his familiar, empirical existence nor a better version of the existence he knows. This ultimate form of transcendence is beyond concern with the solution of predicaments. Instead, it focuses upon an understanding of being itself (hence it is called ontological transcendence), a stance derived from the notion that there is more to "reality" than we normally perceive or assume—more not only in an intellectual sense but also in a value sense (Teilhard de Chardin, 1965) that allows the individual to see himself as part of a world that contains new, unsuspected dimensions and allows him to see his existence from a different, richer, infinitely meaningful, more personalized yet cosmic perspective.

The notion of ontological transcendence—especially its personal value-dimension—may be uncongenial, actually distasteful and even threatening to the "encapsulated man" (Royce, 1964), the individual accustomed to thinking within a narrow, exclusively empiricist frame of reference. Such a notion also tends to have psychotic overtones to a culture highly sensitized to psychopathology and rather intolerant of departures from tangible and/or socially validated reality. Notions of this kind appear to have a mystical flavor. Yet this flavor is precisely what scientists are uncovering as they probe deeper and deeper into nature. "From the radiant energy of the total electromagnetic spectrum, human eyes register only a slender band. Similarly, we hear only a fraction of sound waves. Radio, X-, and gamma rays don't register with our senses at all. . . . Given different sense receptors, we would perceive an unimaginably different world" (Smith, 1969, p. 11).

At first sight, the notion of "an unimaginably different world" may sound fantastic. Yet mankind has been faced twice before by the discovery of such worlds, and has long since integrated these worlds into ordinary thinking. Indeed, before the invention of the telescope, the microscope, and the theories and applications connected with their use, the world of sense perception was the only world we knew. Now we know that it is only an intermediary realm, a macro-world situated between the mega-world of astronomy and the micro-world of quantum physics. Hence Smith's conclusion that "there is no reason to presume that these three worlds are exhaustive" (1969, p. 11). In fact, scientists are currently searching for the reality that may lie beyond the mega- and micro-worlds. The "different world" referred to in ontological transcendence is, however, not a world of waves and particles but a world whose essential dimension is axiological, that is, related to value.

Ontological transcendence, then, represents a state of being that is intuited by certain individuals and attracts them. At the currently prevailing level of human awareness, these individuals are few and rather reticent. The great mystics of all ages are among those who have achieved insight and participation in this realm of being. And in an entirely secular vein, increasing numbers from among the most highly trained of our contemporaries are also attaining this expanded insight. As may be inferred from his posthumously published diary, *Markings* (1964), Dag Hammarskjöld, the Swedish economist and former Secretary General of the United Nations, can be regarded as one of these.

In summary, ontological transcendence corresponds to a vision of reality capable of affecting even rational adults with a sense of wonderment and stimulation to action. What it involves is not solely a matter of insight or vision but a process of becoming: "The More we seek . . . is a More we can become" (Richardson, in Richardson and Cutler, 1969, p. x). This form of transcendence, then, seems to represent the ultimate in human growth, personally and socially.

The Good
Life

My purpose has been to offer a sampling of what is human about human beings. I have emphasized throughout that man can be understood and can reveal himself only in his wholeness: conscious, active, reflective, creative, value questing, playing, loving, transcending. This last section offers a brief glance at *the most holistic of man's attributes*—his search for something he perceives only dimly but pursues relentlessly and that may be called the "good life."

The good life! What on earth is it? A mirage in the eye of the desert traveler? Born of his longing and the numbing bleakness around him? The magical carrot that keeps the rabbit running, doggedly? One more notion to be demythologized by a generation grown familiar with the null hypothesis? Or is there really something that, mysteriously but urgently, prompts people to muddle through, to overcome, to meander onward like roots relentlessly searching the dark earth? This side of eternity, it seems that is the question.

The desire for something indefinite but deeply and lastingly satisfying seems operative throughout the life of any healthy individual, whatever the conditions in which he happens to exist—primitive or evolved, stimulating or depressing, wealthy or poor. Though people are usually rather inarticulate about the nature of the thing, they are readily able to name it. From the man in the street to the writers of constitutions, all seem to concur that the name is *happiness*. The term has indeed a long and venerable tradition, having had currency even in antiquity, when philosophers used it interchangeably with the notion of the good life.

The popular image of happiness is extraordinarily versatile; hence Charles Schulz's apt series *Happiness Is. . . .* To the child, with his undeveloped sense of time and wholeness, happiness is related to particular experiences, to fun times. So also to the immature adult who vaguely conceives of it as some endless chain of exciting events. Even otherwise realistic people often continue to visualize happiness as something of a protracted "peak experience" (clearly a contradiction in the terms since peaks, by definition, have little extension). As a result of such unrealistic expectations, many conclude, with a mixture of resignation and nostalgia, that while they "can't complain," neither can they call themselves "happy."

In reaction to such romantic views there are others who dismiss the notion of happiness altogether as a naive projection. As for the mature person, while he may admit to the possibility and reality of something like the good life, he is often reluctant to define it as "happiness." To him the term evokes something either too effervescent or too idyllic to be realistic. And when asked what, then, the good life is, even thoughtful people tend to conclude, after some groping, that it cannot be defined, that it is too utterly subjective, too much a matter of taste and preference.

Unfortunately, such vague or false notions of happiness tend to interfere with its achievement. While it is true that precise knowledge about a thing carries no guarantee of its acquisition, ignorance about what may legitimately be termed the good life reduces one's chances of achieving it. He who roams the oceans without map or compass has less chance of successfully completing his course than one equipped for the journey.

A Good Life or a Good Time?

The vagueness or naiveté of the common image of the good life may be explained once we realize the confusion between "a good time" and "a good life." Good times are highly subjective. What some may consider a good time, others may not. As for a lifelong good time, it is, of course, inconceivable in either principle or fact. If all is good, nothing is good, since no quality can be experienced in its specificity unless there is some other quality within the same class that differs from it. Identification presupposes differentiation. As for the practical impossibility of a continued good time, it is only too well known by all who have even a minimum of life experience.

One major difference between a good life and a good time is the primary and most obvious characteristic of good times: they are enjoyable. The good life, on the other hand, is not primarily characterized by fun. There is no doubt that the good life is supremely gratifying, but, to the extent that it can be achieved at the present juncture of human evolution, the fun and pleasure content of a good life may vary and fluctuate considerably. Many a life may be regarded—and experienced by the subject— as good yet may comprise a relatively scant measure of what is commonly called fun and enjoyment. Among those who hold an examined view of the subject, few would deny that a fair share of the goodness of life fell to such persons as Abraham Lincoln, Gandhi, Louis Pasteur, Albert

Schweitzer, Dorothea Dix, Dietrich Bonhoeffer, Pope John XXIII, Martin Buber, and Martin Luther King. Hardly anyone, however, would say that these persons' lives were marked by lots of fun. Such contamination of the notion of the good life with that of a good time obscures and distorts the issue.

Life as a Whole

Whether or not a particular life qualifies as good cannot be decided on the basis of some selected segments but on the basis of the whole of that life. I do not necessarily mean the absolute whole, realized only at death, but the whole of life at any given time the (adult) subject examines it. The configurational, or gestalt, quality of our lives is susceptible to modification by the addition of new elements, and because life is composed of numerous interacting factors—physical, social, personal, some dependent, others independent of the subject—the vicissitudes of each may easily affect the whole for good or ill.

Take, for example, the person whose need spectrum is so abundantly satisfied that his life could be termed very good were it not for his poor health, an element without which no life can be considered good. (And, for the sake of simplicity, let us assume that the individual does not transcend his predicament.) In spite of much good fortune, then, the life of this person cannot be regarded as good. Suppose, now, that some medical breakthrough proved capable of curing his illness; he would then not only be restored to full health but would almost certainly enjoy an exceptional awareness and appreciation of his newly gained normal condition— an asset the average person usually overlooks, hence fails to value. In addition, former learnings may have equipped him with a high tolerance for frustration and hardship, attributes that also enhance the goodness of life. Since we have posited that this individual has as much of the personal, social, and economic goods as is realistically possible, we may conclude that while his earlier existence could not be termed good, its goodness can now be scored very high indeed.

In the above example, goodness is gained essentially through a fortuitous circumstance. (See below, "The Goods of Chance and the Goods of Choice.") Even the person's keen awareness and enjoyment of blessings arose primarily as a consequence of previous conditions. Therefore, his life as a whole is good despite (not, of course, because of) earlier deprivation. One could, of course, continue the discussion and argue that after the first wave of appreciation, this person reflects bitterly on all that he perceives he has missed during the many years of his illness. But this outcome would only support the point that a life must always be judged in its totality in light of its latest episode. If bitterness and envy are the eventual outcome of the cure, this person's life is hardly better than before—it is, perhaps, worse.

Now for an example of the hitherto good life that subsequently loses this quality through personal agency: the individual who "has everything" but ruins this fortunate state by a criminal action that earns him a long-term prison sentence. Despite all earlier assets, his life can no longer be regarded as good. He has lost not only his freedom, with all that this implies, but also the esteem of the community and, quite likely, his self-esteem, all of which are essential elements of the good life. The previous goodness of his life must now be reassessed and deemed cancelled by his regrettable action and its consequences.

In other instances, a combination of fortuitous and self-determined factors might also terminate the goodness of a life. Imagine an instance of perfectly happy parents of an only child whom they have the misfortune to lose. If they fail to recover after a reasonable period of mourning, their lives can no longer be considered good, not only because of the bereavement but because these parents have apparently vested the meaning of their lives exclusively and irreversibly in their child. In summary, each example shows that life can be evaluated only in terms of its latest antecedents.

Can the Good Life Be Defined?

Many, as I have pointed out, believe that the good life is too personal, too completely subjective to be defined, implying therefore that it is purely a matter of taste. Anything that has reality, however qualitative its nature, can be judged for goodness or lack of it. Granted, *good* detached from anything substantive cannot be specified, since it cuts across the categories. But the goodness of a thing, event, or process can most certainly be consistently (if schematically) defined. Since life is real, its goodness can be assessed as well as that of anything else, be it a mate, a job, a house, or anything not purely fanciful.

Definitions, by nature, do not specify particulars; they describe the substructure rather than the surface. Because a person's ignorance or biases may cause him to focus upon characteristics incidental or even foreign to the subject, he may fail at first to recognize the validity of a given definition. But definitions are essential, especially to evaluations. One determines the goodness of human life, then, by defining *goodness*, whatever its object.

WHAT IS GOODNESS? In the proceedings of a symposium published under the title *New Knowledge in Human Values*, Hartman proposes that *good* can legitimately be applied to "any object that fulfills its concept" (1959, p. 20). This may at first seem a hopelessly abstract statement. Applying it to specific instances, however, one discovers that it is as apt as it is concise. Take the elementary case of a simple tool—a knife, a spade, a yardstick.

We call it good when it cuts well, digs well, measures accurately; that is, when it does well what it is designed to do. A slightly more complex example would be a car: it may be called good if it is reliable, economical, durable, easily maneuvered, and the like. It may not be a sporty or conspicuous status symbol, but it does what a car is supposed to do and does it well; it thoroughly "fulfills the concept" of a car.

The good, then, contrary to the attractive or the enjoyable, is not a matter of taste and preference, but is inherent in the object and independent of the subject. Valid criteria for its evaluation are based, therefore, not upon particular value angles but upon an analysis of the concept of the object. Particular instances, then, of the object, state, or process are good to the extent that they incorporate the attributes corresponding to these inherent criteria.

But is such a simple, operational definition applicable to a process as complex and dynamic as the life of a human being? The answer is unhesitatingly affirmative, since the evaluation focuses not upon individual cases and their differences but on their common humanity; the complexity, variety, and variability of human beings poses no difficulty.

KEYED TO A CONCEPT OF MAN. Does it follow from Hartman's paradigm of the "good" and the rational analysis that hinges upon it that there is an objective and universal notion of the good life? Because these terms are often used in an unwarranted absolutistic sense, the answer must be qualified. The notion of the good life here offered, keyed as it is to a certain concept of man and a certain epistemology, is objective in the sense that it will be agreed upon by all who share the same concept of human nature. However, since there is no universal agreement about the concept of man, there can be no universal agreement about the good life. It should be emphasized, however, that there is now and has been throughout history a very large measure of agreement among philosophers and otherwise educated persons about that which constitutes the essentials of human nature. Only in modern times, especially since the rise of the social sciences, has controversy about human nature been brought into focus. (In this connection see the section on the development of a naturalistic concept of man in chapter 12.)

Notions of the good life will vary according to the particular world view—materialistic, idealistic, fascistic, democratic, or humanistic-personalistic. An example is the well-known difference between Rogers's and Skinner's concept of human nature: Rogers affirms the reality of human freedom while Skinner denies it. Consequently, their concept of the good life must necessarily differ, freedom being a prime requisite in Rogers's concept, a dangerous illusion in Skinner's.*

* Actually, if both Rogers and Skinner were to formulate their respective concept of the good life, formally and exhaustively, the outcome probably would not differ significantly because of the existential inconsistency of Skinner's concept of man.

One way, then, to avoid arbitrary or doctrinaire approaches in determining the goodness of a thing lies in an analysis of its concept, essentially of its purpose. What, then, is the concept of the nature of man—more bluntly, what is man for? In a personalistic-humanistic framework, the answer is unambiguous: for the satisfaction of his needs and the actualization of his potential. But is this not an essentially egotistic view of human life and purpose? It would be indeed if we forget that man has social, ethical, and spiritual needs that will, ideally, prevent him from lapsing into crude egotism. In addition, the satisfaction of many of his needs does not arise automatically from favorable conditions but presupposes the exercise of the characteristically human functions of choice and effort, as we will soon see.

On the biological-physical level man's needs are easily discernible, and most of psychology has focused upon the investigation and description of this level. Man needs the goods of the body—adequate food, clothing, shelter, rest, exercise, recreation, and cleanliness.* Social needs are somewhat more difficult to specify. All higher and some lower animals have social needs; in the case of man, however, they are intimately intertwined with specifically human needs. It is precisely the level of the characteristically human needs and capacities that calls for articulation, clarification, and dissemination, and this work has attempted to bring them into sharper focus and to provide heightened awareness of this neglected area of the human picture.

A Paradigm of the Good Life

Weaving together the strands of the preceding chapters, a tapestry of the good life begins to emerge. Most prominent among its features is the realm of the symbolic, not the sensory. Thus, for instance, love will emerge as more important than sex; knowledge more precious than possessions; being more fundamental than having; transcendence of problems superior to passive acceptance—always assuming, of course, the satisfaction of survival needs or, better, a balanced satisfaction of needs. Ideally, the good life would further allow man's urge for autonomy to express itself under optimal conditions, permitting him the latitude to shape his life in a unique and satisfying way while providing him with the knowledge and skills necessary to avoid jeopardizing his precious assets in the pursuit of his autonomy. Such a life would have adequate room for fun and recreation as well as the enjoyment and creation of beauty. It would prepare man to give and receive love in its many forms by making him loveable, appreciative, joyfully sensitive to others, and

* Cleanliness is seldom mentioned in psychological works, perhaps because of its obviousness; yet even animals manifest a certain need for bodily cleanliness in their elaborate self- or mutual grooming rituals.

responsibly concerned about all—those different, far away, or yet to come, as well as those to whom he is related by the bonds of intimacy, inter-dependency, or proximity.

In such a life, the individual would be capable, stimulated, and free to be esthetically, socially, and technologically creative—beautifying his world, improving the human condition, facilitating the production and dissemination of goods, augmenting the amenities, and reducing the menial burdens of existence to the extent that personal endowment and existing conditions permit. Such a life would be characterized by a high level of reflective awareness, the unique apanage of man; it would be enriched by formal and informal education, aimed at not only a well-informed but a well-formed mind, capable of further enriching and en-joying itself in the process. It would equip man to understand as much about human nature as is known at any particular juncture of history and leave him the mental freedom to dream intelligently about the unknown.

In matters of religion, it would be a life as free from indoctrination as from deliberate, planned ignorance. In the ethical sphere, one would be capable of seeing the beauty, wholeness, and harmony of ethical con-duct and, correspondingly, aversive to moral disorder. It would be a life free from cheap or hazardous illusion, realistically aware of its finiteness and capable of transforming this awareness into keen appreciation of the fleeting moment—a life, finally, capable of facing its unavoidable con-clusion manfully and generously, if regretfully.

A tall order, then, the good life. So tall that one can safely assume it has never been fully achieved in historical reality. Many individuals have, or have had, a highly privileged life, but it is improbable that anyone, however favored by fortune, ever had the opportunity to develop all his potentialities. Nor is anyone ever likely to have experienced satisfaction of the full gamut of his needs. For example, a person's social-ethical needs could not have received full satisfaction in the past if only because he lacked information about the conditions of his fellow men and hence was not fully aware of his obligations. This picture of the good life, therefore, is decidedly paradigmatic or theoretical.

Balanced Satisfaction: The Reality

If the good life is one in which the full spectrum of needs of the whole man are satisfied and his potentialities actualized, then, practically, a life qualifies as good when and to the extent that it approaches this ideal. More precisely, a life is good when the vital needs without which no life could be called good are provided for, when at least the most outstanding elements from among an individual's manifest potential have an opportunity for actualization, and when that opportunity is effectively utilized.

In reality, then, rather than representing the *summum bonum,* one's life may be called good when it represents the balanced satisfaction of one's needs. That is, certain needs may be fully satisfied, certain others satisfied only adequately or occasionally, and a few may not be met for a long time, even a lifetime. As for the actualization of potentialities, one widespread misapprehension calls for correction. Few would deny that the kind and number of man's potentialities are almost infinite. However, actualization is a process that occurs in time and usually involves the expenditure of a fair amount of effort. Consequently, only a limited number of these possibilities can be developed in real life; the development of one potential necessarily cancels another. Only a limited range of the spectrum of possibilities can simultaneously—or, for that matter, successively—be realized. Unactualized potentialities do not necessarily detract from the goodness of a life but may reflect upon the richness of the person's endowment.

"THE GOODS OF CHANCE AND THE GOODS OF CHOICE." At this stage in human evolution—and in some measure, probably at all times in the future—the goodness of the actually lived life is something short of perfection. In Adler's crisp characterization, actual empirical existence is constituted by "the goods of chance and the goods of choice," the former fortuitously, the latter fallibly, determined (1970, p. 165).

The goods of chance include the conditions of birth and early development, whose staggeringly important role in the individual's destiny—including such powerful forces as his attitudes toward the world, life, and self—are well known. But intertwined with these external factors are the determinants issuing from the individual himself. Probably most humanistically oriented authors will agree that, except in extremely unfortunate cases, the factors of choice are, at least potentially, the more powerful in any attempt to achieve the good life.

Among the determinants issuing from within, the most powerful—capable of overarching the errors of choice as well as the blows of chance—is man's potential for transcendence. This uniquely human characteristic allows man to overcome symbolically many—in principle, all—of the deprivations and predicaments that fall to him as an individual and, unavoidably, as a member of the human species. This view clearly implies a concept of man as agent, not product, of social and other contingencies. (See Chapter 11.)

EXPERIENCE IS ESSENTIAL. So far, the discussion may seem to have omitted the experiencing subject who has, however, been silently present throughout. His absence would have been inconsistent with an existential approach, and now is the time to make his part explicit. What is the relation between a life that may be called good according to legitimate, objective criteria and the individual's experience of that life? Can it be good if the subject does not experience it as such? From a particular or partial point of view—social, moral, civic—perhaps it can, but from a wholly human and existential, indeed, an ontological, point of view, very definitely not.

The proposition that the subject who has the good life must be aware of it probably calls for some clarification. Having defined the good life as that which fulfills the concept of human life, let us first look at the theoretical case of the individual whose needs (again, not his wants) are all fulfilled—including the actualization of his preferred potentialities. Would it automatically follow that he would be happy, in the sense of being aware of and valuing the goodness of his life? It may not seem that this would necessarily be the case, but upon analysis, it does follow. Indeed, if, as we have posited, all of an individual's needs are satisfied, this implies that along with all the organismic and specifically human needs, the need for meaning, perhaps the cornerstone of any life, would also be satisfied.

Although moderate, the notion of a balanced satisfaction of needs nevertheless refers to a level of need satisfaction that the vast majority of existent human beings—and an even larger majority of those in the past—never attain. Few serious authors have claimed the contrary. However, because this conclusion is derived from the point of view of the experiencing subject, it must nevertheless be regarded as an interpretation and one that might well be mistaken in quite a few cases.

What is there, however, that warrants the assumption that people who suffer from ill-health, poverty, tyranny, or any other gross impediments to the good life might nevertheless experience it as good, if demanding? The answer lies in the peculiarly human capacity I have repeatedly mentioned—the capacity for transcendence; that is, for symbolic reassessment of one's lot in function of one leading value or another.

Proceeding to the actual, in which only a balanced satisfaction of needs is achieved, does it still follow that the individual would recognize his life as happy? The answer is apparently affirmative and for very much the same reason as in the preceding cases: There could be no question of balanced satisfaction unless the need for meaning were included in the balance.

Regarding the question of meaning, however, an important clarification must be made. Meaning does not arise spontaneously, the way a gestalt quality emerges from a particular configuration of elements. Rather, it exists as a result of the individual's creative trust and capacities operating within and upon the totality of his existence. Meaning is not a given but a function of symbolic creativity, of commitment, effort, care, and concern—in sum, a function of personal investment.

Finally, that the good life is necessarily experienced as good is not a reversible proposition; in other words, the individual who experiences his life as good does not necessarily have the good life in the ontological sense. Because of his particular make-up or values or because of his ignorance about what a humanly good life is, he may enjoy the life he has, be contented and indeed exhilarated by it. But all these are only emotionally positive states; they do not necessarily imply an ontological basis. Conversely, the ontologically good life necessarily implies the subject's awareness of its goodness, though that awareness may fall far short of exhilaration.

Characteristics of the Good Life

By now, it is evident that the good life comes closer to fulfillment than to excitement. There seems to be a tendency in common usage to either sell fulfillment short—as if it were a consolation prize for something short of happiness—or to oversell it as a state in which one's fondest wishes come true. Fulfillment, however, must be understood with reference not to one's dreams but to one's potential and efforts. That the fulfillment of one's fondest wishes is an inadequate yardstick with which to measure the good life is immediately apparent when we reverse the proposition: The individual whose fondest wishes haven't come true is not necessarily unfulfilled or unhappy. Because of the dissatisfaction, the sense of defeat that often accompanies this faulty conception of fulfillment, many throw themselves into activities that fill their every hour. Instead of achieving a full life, they end up with a cluttered one.

Another notion popularly associated with the good life is peace of mind. In the sense of a clear conscience, peace of mind is doubtless an essential ingredient of the good life. However, the demands of conscience are often incompatible with peace of mind. More serious is the fact that peace of mind is a state into which one can be coaxed, preached, or conditioned. Winston Smith, Rutherford, and other figures in Orwell's *1984* ended up with peace of mind: an at-oneness with their world, however sinister; an absence of conflict; the wet-eyed docility of the cud-chewing oxen.

Peace of mind, then, is a somewhat ambiguous attribute not only because it evokes a placidity that is the rightful apanage of the tired and the innocent, but also because it can be the cop-out of those who are unaware and uninformed due to indifference or false piety. Rather than relinquish one's life to such a complacent state, it seems that anyone with enough vigor, insight, and courage would opt for "a lover's quarrel with the world," as Robert Frost (1967, p. 237) described his dialogue with existence.

The kind of life an individual fashions for himself is (to the extent that personal agency permits) largely a matter of the attitudes with which he approaches his life. Thus, an appreciation of and gratitude for past and present assets and a realistic trust in the promise of the future exerts a kind of magnetic effect, attracting more assets and justifying more trust. Of course, such welcoming attitudes per se will not secure the good life. Conversely, scepticism, cynicism, indifferentism, or otherwise untoward attitudes can (almost by definition) interfere so powerfully with the conditions of the good life as to preclude every chance for achieving it. Persons affected by such attitudes fail to register the good that resides in all but the most unfortunate of lives. They are also directly opposed to any normal effort toward transcending the equally unavoidable deficiencies of any real-life situation. Few processes appear to be as sensitive to the effects of the self-fulfilling prophecy as those that shape a life.

Prospects for the Good Life

The terminology and climate of growth psychology are so exhilarating that one often forgets that growing, becoming, actualizing one's potential, and so forth, involve danger and pain as well as excitement. Reading and talking about growing are certainly stimulating; *doing* the growing can be a very different thing. Rogers, who has authored some of the best work on growth psychology, describes the process of becoming that he sees as the good life:

> For me, adjectives such as happy, contented, blissful, enjoyable, do not seem quite appropriate to any general description of this process I have called the good life, even though the person in this process would experience each one of these feelings at appropriate times. But the adjectives which seem more generally fitting are adjectives such as enriching, exciting, rewarding, challenging, meaningful. This process of the good life is not, I am convinced, a life for the faint-hearted. . . . It *involves the courage to be* (1961, pp. 195–96; italics added).

The good life is not a fixed state; it is, in Rogers's words, "a journey, not a destination." Whether or not this journey is embarked upon and whether it spirals upwards or downwards would seem to depend upon whether the individual is sensitized to the broader, more encompassing—if less tangible—possibilities of human existence.

How likely, then, is the average individual to achieve the object of his deepest urge, the good life? A single chapter in an introductory text cannot cover the question exhaustively, and there is good reason to assume that, in any case, no final answer can be provided. Sketched here in rough outline, however, are the cornerstones of my position: the principle of finality and the plasticity of human need fulfillment.

THE PRINCIPLE OF FINALITY. According to this philosophical proposition, every species-wide urge is geared toward a commensurate object or end—whether or not the subject knows that end in its concrete reality. A commensurate end is a valid end that satisfies the urge or tendency when reached. Thus, the urge for food leads to behavior aimed at satisfying (reducing) the hunger drive by prompting a search for objects suitable for consumption. In the case of hunger, the relation between tendency and object and the vital importance of the relation are obvious. Indeed, the craving that sets off the search for food is, in principle, as vital as the food itself: no hunger, no food intake.

On the surface, the principle of finality parallels the psychological proposition that all behavior is goal directed. It differs from that general tenet in that it applies only to behaviors prompted by species-specific urges whose built-in end or goal is of vital importance for the individual, for example, sexual longings, the quest for knowledge, metaphysical aspirations, dreams of happiness.

The principle of finality, however, specifies nothing about the length of time that may elapse between the call of the urge and its satisfaction. On the physical level, the time between these two poles of the process is usually brief. On the specifically human level, the time unfortunately increases. As for a worldwide fulfillment of so encompassing a human aspiration as the good life, the prospects seem remote but real—remote because the achievement of such a state involves not merely positive altruistic feelings but deep ethical concern and a readiness to face sacrifices. Still the prospects are real because the enlightened person's enjoyment of the good life implies a concern about the conditions for extending this blessing to the less fortunate.

THE PLASTICITY OF SYMBOLIC NEED FULFILLMENT. In the questing dialectic of life—that is, the back and forth process of the search for need fulfillment—the urge is the call, its object the response. This correspondence between urge and object is clearly visible on the biological level where *function* is substantiated by *organ* or organ system; thus, the wings of birds are geared to flying, the gills of fish to breathing under water, the genitals of the higher animals to copulation.

By contrast, the quest for human fulfillment is elicited not by the call of organ-determined ends or objects but by symbolic values that by their nature are multivalent. (See Chapter 1.) A particular value, then, may be recognized and pursued in a variety of objects: love may find expression in erotic relations, parenthood, friendship, worship, civic responsibilities, service to the community, and so forth. Similarly, a particular object may represent a number of values: money may denote purchasing power, independence, fun, security, luxury, philanthropy, or self-affirmation, depending upon the individual.

In the human sphere both the need and the object have a versatility and multivalence that is nonexistent in the nonhuman sphere. In other words, on the human level, the correspondence between need and object (or category of objects) is not limited in a one-to-one manner, as is the case on the biological level. The Symbolic Animal, contrary to other animals, is not stimulus bound; his need objects are multivalent, their satisfaction found in a multitude of situations, goals, and actions. By the same token, however, he is liable to project value into objects unsuited to meet his needs. For, unlike his lesser brothers, he is subject to error in regard to both the identification and satisfaction of his basic needs.

In conclusion, the plasticity of symbolic need fulfillment and the principle of finality are mutually reinforcing in that the versatility of the symbolic needs facilitates the resolution of the need-object polarity involved in the pursuit of the good life.

EVERY MAN'S CHANCES: BETTER THAN EVER? *In principle*, every man's chances to obtain a fair share of the good life are better than ever in history. Never before have the conditions permitting the greatest good for the greatest number been present to the degree they now are. Due to prodigious technological advances, toward which man has exerted his creative capacities most persistently and successfully, the world now has the potential to provide its population with the external ingredients of the good life: food, clothing, shelter, health needs, education, recreation, esthetic enjoyment, communication, transportation, and an extended life span.

This vast capacity for production has been realized at so high a cost that it threatens one of man's most precious assets: a habitable, enjoyable, and beautiful planet. But this situation can largely be remedied. Our dawning ecological awareness presages a promising new course of action in man's dealings with his planet. It is also true that the resources that allow fulfillment of mankind's material needs are not infinite, while humanity itself—although perhaps not infinite—is free from definite ceiling that exists, for instance, in the mineral reserves. The frightening prospects of radical shortages of raw materials can be mitigated, however, by the knowledge of man's seemingly endless capacity for creating substitute goods and commodities. Moreover, and again, the growing awareness of and concern for the limits of raw materials spur social responsibility and policy. This leads us to the social angle of the human picture.

Man's prodigious technological capacity for production, though fundamental, must now be supplemented and humanized by another achievement, namely, effective and responsible management and distribution. A distribution understood not solely in the economic sense of creating markets but in the *social*-economic sense of meeting existing needs—without the prospect of full and tangible compensation. Not a perennial dole, with its pernicious side effects for all concerned, but a responsible arrangement that aims to maintain the incentive to work in the ones while stimulating it in the others. This requires a mode of thought and conduct that does not come easily, a serious care and concern for others, even those who are personally unknown and potentially ungrateful. To be effective this concern must reach deeper than the sharing of surpluses, personal or national. It must reach our actual lives—what we call a lowering of our standards of living—but would better designate as a raising of our awareness in the use of goods and opportunities.

Can it realistically be expected that man will move fast enough and far enough on the social-moral plane to reach this insight and implement it? On the basis of past evidence, it seems doubtful. But is the past a fully adequate basis for answering this question? On the face of it, history may appear to follow a circular pattern. There is ample evidence, however, that the circles are open-ended and form a slowly widening spiral. On the intellectual-technological plane, that spiraling movement is conspicuous. On what principle could it be claimed that man's evolution stops short of his social-ethical and affective potential?

In trying to reach a conclusion on issues of this kind, we must not overlook that past conditions have never been like their present counterparts. In the past, sharing was optional—somewhat like a gallant gesture. In the present, it is becoming necessary, hence compelling. The interdependence now arising between the "haves" and the "have-nots" is potentially so perilous that it is likely to spur the former to social efforts such as were never before envisaged. What centuries of moral and religious exhortation could not achieve may come to pass under the pressure of imminent threat to safety and survival. Such progress may not be glorious in its initial impetus, since it would stem in the last analysis from self-serving considerations. My point is not that man is glorious but that he can be trusted in his matchless capacity for adaptation and problem solving. In due time, what started out as self-protective strategy may acquire genuinely moral status once it becomes voluntarily sanctioned as part of a new way of life.

TOO OPTIMISTIC A STANCE? At the present particularly somber nexus of time and events, the position here expressed, though duly qualified, may appear to some as lacking factual support. Indeed, despite our enormous potential for production, reports keep coming in about sporadic shortages in basic necessities and even about a decline in literacy in various quarters of the globe—other than those temporarily suffering from the effects of drought, floods, or other natural disasters. Though sadly accurate, such reports do not invalidate the proposition that the necessary external conditions for the achievement of the good life are better now than they ever were and can be so maintained—barring unforeseen developments—provided mankind adopts sound and far-reaching policies fast enough to save its ecological niche. Progress, especially in its human dimensions, is not linear, nor does it move in one united front; rather, it develops sporadically and unevenly, moving in and out of the human scene, perplexing the observer, challenging his faith in and commitment to his kind.

It seems that our generation is inclined to equate a positive outlook with naiveté and a negative one with realism. Actually, conclusions about vast issues such as the reality or fallaciousness of human progress are interpretations, not inventories. The evidence supporting such interpretations is not only in constant flux, it is necessarily incomplete. Furthermore, even the most careful conclusions pertinent to questions this large and complex involve a selection of evidence. The evaluator's attitudes, beliefs, and values, his concept of the world, combine to play an elusive but probably important part in the selection and weighing of the evidence. Finally, and perhaps most significantly, his position and its effect upon others tend to affect the course of events in the direction of that position.

In Conclusion

Upon reflection and analysis, the good life appears as a real, definable, essentially achievable state, but one so diverse in its outward manifestations that it may go unrecognized by all but its beneficiaries. Even they may not be able at all times to maintain a clear vision of this most precious of assets—obscured as that vision is apt to be by the physical-social vicissitudes of existence. Once glimpsed, however, the good life keeps beckoning around the successive bends of man's typically winding path.

Largely responsible for man's unsure grasp of this essential good is his tendency to confuse the good life with good times. These two sources of satisfaction, though not mutually exclusive, are surprisingly independent of one another when viewed in the perspective of individual existence as a whole—the only vantage point from which a verdict on the matter can be reached. For the goodness of a life (or its opposite) is retroactive, just as the value of a journey is retroactive—determined, as it is, by the outcome.

The good life is neither a given nor a possession. Karl Barth's metaphor of truth as "a bird in flight" applies here. Just as a bird in flight cannot be captured without ceasing to be a bird in flight, so the good life cannot be secured, once and for all, either for self or others. Nor can it be directly pursued, for it is a gestalt that emerges from a mode of living, a mode that is in accord with one's specific nature.

Because man's specific nature lies in his symbolic ability and because the good life is ultimately a matter of meaning and insight rather than of facts and events, achievement of a fair measure of this supreme value lies in man's own hands. As the meaning-giving animal, he is capable of fashioning a good life out of the most unlikely or unyielding materials—barring severe and lasting impairment or deprivation. Some exceptional individuals may be able to achieve it almost regardless of conditions. The bulk of humanity, however, requires at least minimally propitious conditions of livelihood, education, and leisure in order to pursue satisfactions that go beyond survival-related needs. Liberated, as most of humanity now is, from the burden of lifelong subsistence work and severe ignorance, the full range of human needs and capacities can now come to the surface and strive for actualization.

Formulated with special reference to the task of psychology, the following conditionally phrased proposition expresses the major tenets of humanistic thinking on the issue:

If, as is widely accepted, individual behavior is essentially a function of the self-concept, that is, if man actually tends to enact the image he has of himself;

if the diminished and fragmented image that has prevailed in recent decades can be restored to wholeness by inclusion of man's specific needs and capacities and if psychology's emphasis can be shifted from the characteristics that man shares with more elementary forms of life to those that are distinctively his own;

if as a result of this corrected image man can come to think differently about himself and the nature of his fulfillment;

if it is true that, on the phylogenetic plane, mankind is still evolving —not in his physical structure but in his powers of awareness and insight —and if, under the pressure of necessity, he learns to move forward on the social and moral planes as he has on the intellectual and technological;

if, therefore, his past may be considered a prologue to his future rather than a blueprint of it;

then, we may conclude, with Jacob Bronowski that mankind is indeed ascending, moving toward the good life.

BIBLIOGRAPHY

Adams, Joe K. "The Hidden Taboo on Love." In *Love Today*, edited by Herbert A. Otto. New York: Association Press, 1972.

Adler, Mortimer J. *The Difference of Man and the Difference It Makes*. New York: Holt, Rinehart and Winston, 1967.

————. *The Time of Our Lives: The Ethics of Commonsense*. New York: Holt, Rinehart and Winston, 1970.

Alland, Alexander. *The Human Imperative*. New York: Columbia University Press, 1972.

Allport, Gordon W. *Becoming*. New Haven, Conn.: Yale University Press, 1955.

Altizer, Thomas J. *The Gospel of Christian Atheism*. Philadelphia: Westminster Press, 1966.

Altizer, Thomas J., and Hamilton, William. *Radical Theology and the Death of God*. Indianapolis: Bobbs-Merrill, 1966.

Altizer, Thomas J., ed. *Toward a New Christianity: Readings in the Death of God Theology*. New York: Harcourt Brace Jovanovich, 1967.

Anand, Mulk. *The Third Eye: A Lecture on the Appreciation of Art*. Chandigarh (India): Punjab University, 1963.

Anderson, Alan R., ed. *Minds and Machines*. Englewood Cliffs, N.J.: Prentice-Hall, 1964.

Andreski, Stanislav. *Social Sciences as Sorcery*. London: Andre Deutsch, 1972.

Archives of the Foundation of Thanatology. See, *Journal of Thanatology*.

Ardrey, Robert. *The Territorial Imperative*. New York: Atheneum, 1966.

Arendt, Hannah. *Eichmann in Jerusalem: A Report on the Banality of Evil*. New York: Viking Press, 1963.

————. *The Human Condition*. Garden City, N.Y.: Doubleday, Anchor, 1959.

Arieti, Silvano. "Volition and Value: A Study Based on Catatonic Schizophrenia." *Comprehensive Psychiatry* 2, No. 2 (April 1961): 74–82.

————. *The Will to Be Human*. New York: Quadrangle Books, 1972.

Avorn, Jerry. "Beyond Dying: Experiments Using Psychedelic Drugs to Ease the Transition from Life." *Esquire*, March 1973, pp. 56–60.

Ayers, A. J. *Language, Truth and Logic*. London: Gallancz, 1936.

Bakan, David. "Psychology's Research Crisis." *The Michigan Psychologist* 26 (October 1967): 20–33.

————. *Slaughter of the Innocents*. San Francisco: Jossey-Bass, 1971.

Baldwin, James, and Avedon, Richard. *Nothing Personal*. New York: Dell, 1964.

Bantam, Katherine M. "The Development of Affectionate Behavior in Infancy." *Journal of Genetic Psychology* 76 (1950): 283–89.

Beauvoir, Simone de. *Encounters with Death*. New Brunswick, N.J.: Rutgers University Press, 1973.

Becker, Ernest. *The Denial of Death*. New York: The Free Press, 1973.

Benedict, Ruth. *Patterns of Culture*. New York: New American Library, 1951.

Bennett, Jonathan. *Rationality: An Essay Towards an Analysis*. London: Routledge & Kegan Paul, 1964.

Bergson, Henri. *Essai sur les données immediates de la conscience*. Geneva: Editions Albert Skira. (No date of publication is given in this book; however, the preface is dated 1888.)

————. *Time and Free Will: An Essay on the Immediate Data of Consciousness*. Translated by F. L. Pogson. London: George Allen & Unwin; New York: Macmillan, 1959.

————. *The Two Sources of Morality and Religion*. Garden City, N.Y.: Doubleday, 1935.

Berne, Eric. *Games People Play*. New York: Grove Press, 1964.

Berscheid, Ellen, and Walster, Elaine. "Beauty and the Best." *Psychology Today*, March 1972, pp. 42–46, 74.

Bettelheim, Bruno. *The Empty Fortress*. New York: The Free Press, 1967.

Bhave, Vinoba. In cover story, *Time*, 11 May 1953, pp.

Biegel, Hugo G. "Romantic Love." *American Sociological Review* 16 (June 1951): 326–35.

Blau, Theodore. "The Love Effect." In *Love Today*, edited by Herbert A. Otto. New York: Association Press, 1972.

Blauner, Robert. "Death and Social Structure." *Psychiatry* 29 (1966): 378–94.

Bloch, Ernst. *Das Prinzip Hoffnung*. 2 vols. Frankfurt am Main: Suhrkamp Verlag, 1959.

Bloom, Martin. "Toward a Developmental Concept of Love." *Journal of Human Relations* 15, No. 2 (1967): 246–63.

Bonhoeffer, Dietrich. *Letters and Papers from Prison*. New York: Macmillan, 1967.

Bonner, Hubert. *On Being Mindful of Man*. Boston: Houghton Mifflin, 1965.

Bossart, William H. "Heidegger's Theory of Art." *Journal of Aesthetics and Art Criticism* 27, No. 1 (Fall 1968): 57–66.

Bridgman, P. W. *The Way Things Are*. Cambridge, Mass.: Harvard University Press, 1959.

Bronowski, Jacob. "On the Limits of Scientific Knowledge." In *Man and the Science of Man*, edited by William R. Coulson and Carl R. Rogers. Columbus, Ohio: Charles E. Merrill, 1968.

————. *Science and Human Values*. New York: Harper & Row, 1965.

————. "The Values of Science." In *New Knowledge in Human Values*, edited by Abraham H. Maslow. New York: Harper & Row, 1959.

Bronowski, Jacob, and Bellugi, Ursula. "Language, Name, and Concept." *Science* 168 (1970): 669–73.

Brown, Norman O. *Life Against Death*. Middletown, Conn.: Wesleyan University Press, 1959.

————. *Love's Body*. New York: Random House, 1966.

Bruner, Jerome. "Myth and Identity." In *The Making of Myth*, edited by R. M. Ohmann. New York: G. P. Putnam's Sons, 1962.

Buber, Martin. *I and Thou*. New York: Charles Scribner's Sons, 1958.

Bugental, James F. T. *Challenges of Humanistic Psychology*. New York: McGraw-Hill, 1967.

Bühler, Charlotte. "Theoretical Observations About Life's Basic Tendencies." *American Journal of Psychotherapy* 13 (1959): 561–81.

Bühler, Charlotte, and Allen, Melanie. *Introduction to Humanistic Psychology*. Belmont, Calif.: Wadsworth, 1972.

Bultman, Rudolf and Jaspers, Karl. *Myth and Christianity*. New York: Noonday Press, 1958.

Burke, Kenneth. Cited in Warren Shibles, *Metaphor*. Whitewater, Wisc.: The Language Press, 1971.

Bynner, Witter. *The Way of Life According to Laotzu*. New York: John Day, 1944.

Campbell, Elizabeth W. "First Things Looked Upon." *Childhood Education* 25 (1949): 295–98.

Campbell, Joseph. *Myths, Dreams, and Religion*. New York: E. P. Dutton, 1970.

Camus, Albert. *The Myths of Sisyphus and Other Essays*. New York: Alfred A. Knopf, 1955.

Cantril, Hadley. *The "Why" of Man's Experience*. New York: Macmillan, 1950.

Carpenter, Edmund, and Heyman, Ken. *They Became What They Beheld*. New York: Outerbridge & Dienstfrey, 1970.

Carrell, Alexis. *Man the Unknown*. New York: Harper & Bros., 1935.

Casler, Lawrence. "This Thing Called Love Is Pathological." *Psychology Today*, December 1969, pp. 18–20.

Cassirer, Ernst. *An Essay on Man*. New Haven, Conn.: Yale University Press, 1944.

Child, Irvin L. *Humanistic Psychology and the Research Tradition*. New York: John Wiley & Sons, 1973.

Ciardi, John. "The Gift." *The Saturday Review of Literature*, 7 September 1963, p. 51.

Clarke, Arthur. *2001*. New York: New American Library, 1968.

Clay, Felix. *The Origin of the Sense of Beauty*. London: John Murray, 1917.

Coleman, James C. *Abnormal Psychology and Modern Life*. 3rd ed. Chicago: Scott, Foresman, 1964.

Collier's Encyclopedia, 1965, s. v. "Lemming."

Coulson, William R., and Rogers, Carl R., eds. *Man and the Science of Man*. Columbus, Ohio: Charles E. Merrill, 1968.

Culican, William C. "Wheel." *Encyclopaedia Britannica*. Chicago: University of Chicago, 1972.

D'Arcy, Martin. *The Mind and Heart of Love*. New York: Holt, 1947.

DeRopp, Robert S. *The Master Game*. New York: Delacorte Press, 1968.

Diggory, James C., and Rothman, Doreen Z. "Values Destroyed by Death." *Journal of Abnormal and Social Psychology* 63 (1961): 205–10.

Diringer, David D. *The Alphabet: A Key to the History of Mankind*. New York: Philosophical Library, 1948.

Dollard, John; Auld, Frank, Jr.; and White, Alice Marsden. *Steps in Psychotherapy*. New York: Macmillan, 1953.

Donnelly, Margaret E. "Toward a Theory of Courtship." *Marriage and Family Living* 25 (August 1963): 290–93.

Doss, S. R. "Copernicus Revisited: Time Versus 'Time' Versus *Time*." *Philosophy and Phenomenological Research* 31 (December 1970): 193–211.

Drews, Elizabeth Monroe. "Fernwood, A Free School." *Journal of Humanistic Psychology* 8 (Fall 1968): 113–22.

Dreyfuss, Henry. *Symbol Sourcebook*. New York: McGraw-Hill, 1972.

Driver, G. R. *Semitic Writing*. London: Oxford University Press, 1954.

Dubos, René. *A God Within*. New York: Charles Scribner's Sons, 1972.

———. *The Torch of Life*. New York: Simon and Schuster, 1962.

Dumazedier, Joffre. "Leisure." *International Encyclopedia of the Social Sciences*, vol. 9. New York: Macmillan, The Free Press, 1968.

Edel, Abraham. *Ethical Judgment.* Glencoe, Ill.: The Free Press, 1955.

Eiseley, Loren. *The Invisible Pyramid.* New York: Charles Scribner's Sons, 1970.

Ellul, Jacques. *Hope in Time of Abandonment.* Translated by C. Edward Hopkin. New York: The Seabury Press, 1973.

Emmet, Dorothy. *Rules, Roles, and Relations.* New York: St. Martin's Press, 1966.

English, H. B., and English, A. C. *A Comprehensive Dictionary of Psychological and Psychoanalytical Terms.* New York: David McKay, 1964.

Farber, Leslie H. *The Ways of the Will.* New York: Basic Books, 1966.

Farber, Seymour M., and Wilson, Roger H. L. *Control of the Mind.* New York: McGraw-Hill, 1961.

Farber, Seymour, ed. *Conflict and Creativity.* New York: McGraw-Hill, 1963.

Feifel, Herman. *The Meaning of Death.* New York: McGraw-Hill, 1959.

Feigenbaum, Edward, and Felman, Julian. *Computers and Thought.* New York: McGraw-Hill, 1963.

Feibleman, James K. "Man as the Key to His Meaning." *The Saturday Review of Literature,* 24 November 1962, p. 29.

Fraisse, Paul. "Time: Time and Duration," *International Encyclopedia of the Social Sciences,* vol. 16. New York: Macmillan, The Free Press, 1968.

Fraisse, Paul, ed. "Perception et estimation du temps." *Traité de psychologie experimentale,* vol. 6. Paris: Presses Universitaires de France, 1963.

Frankl, Viktor E. From Address Before the Third Annual Meeting of the Academy of Religion and Mental Health, 1962. *Universitas, Zeitschrift für Wissenschaft, Kunst und Literatur* (Quarterly English Language Edition) 5 (1962): 273–86.

———. *The Doctor and the Soul.* Translated by Richard and Clara Winston. New York: Alfred A. Knopf, 1955.

———. *Man's Search for Meaning.* Rev. and enl. Translated by Ilse Lasch. Boston: Beacon Press, 1962.

Freud, Sigmund. "Mourning and Melancholia." In *The Complete Psychological Works of Sigmund Freud,* vol. 14. Translated by Mrs. Alix Strachey. London: The Hogarth Press and The Institute of Psychoanalysis, 1968.

Frick, Willard B. *Humanistic Psychology: Interviews with Maslow, Murphy, and Rogers.* Columbus, Ohio: Charles E. Merrill, 1971.

Fromm, Erich. *The Art of Loving.* New York: Harper & Row, 1956.

———. *Escape from Freedom.* New York: Holt, Rinehart and Winston, 1941.

———. *The Sane Society.* New York: Holt, Rinehart and Winston, 1955.

Frost, Robert. "The Lesson for Today." *Selected Poems of Robert Frost.* New York: Holt, Rinehart and Winston, 1967.

Fuller, Lon L. *Anatomy of the Law.* New York: New American Library, 1968.

———. "Jurisprudence." *Encyclopaedia Britannica.* Chicago: University of Chicago, 1972.

Fulton, Robert. *Death and Identity.* New York: John Wiley & Sons, 1965.

Gadd, Cyril John. "Hammurabi." *Encyclopaedia Britannica.* Chicago: University of Chicago, 1972.

Gallico, Paul. *The Snow Goose.* New York: Alfred A. Knopf, 1972.

Gardner, Allen R., and Gardner, Beatrice T. "Teaching Sign Language to a Chimpanzee." *Science* 165 (1969): 664–72.

Gibran, Kahlil. *The Prophet.* New York: Alfred A. Knopf, 1964.

Gilbert, G. M. "Sex on the Campus." In *About the Kinsey Report,* edited by Donald Porter Geddes and Enid Curie. New York: New American Library, 1948.

Giorgi, Amadeo. *Psychology as a Human Science.* New York: Harper & Row, 1970.

Giorgi, Amadeo; Fisher, William F.; and von Eckartsberg, Rolf, eds. *Duquesne Studies in Phenomenological Psychology*, vol. 1. Pittsburgh: Duquesne University Press, 1971.

Giraudoux, Jean. *Amphitryon 38*. New York: Random House, 1938.

Goble, Frank G. *The Third Force*. New York: Grossman Publishers, 1970.

Gogarthen, Friedrich. *Demythologizing and History*. New York: Charles Scribner's Sons, 1955.

Goldschmidt, Walter. *Exploring the Ways of Mankind*. New York: Holt, Rinehart and Winston, 1960.

Goldschmidt, Walter, ed. *Ways of Mankind*. Boston: Beacon Press, 1954.

Goodman, Paul. *Growing Up Absurd*. New York: Random House, 1956.

———. *Making Do*. New York: Macmillan, 1963.

Gordon, David Cole. *Overcoming the Fear of Death*. New York: Macmillan, 1970.

Gordon, Ernest. *Through the Valley of the Kwai*. New York: Harper and Bros., 1962.

Gorer, Geoffrey. *Death, Grief, and Mourning in Contemporary Britain*. London: The Cresset Press, 1965.

Greeley, Andrew M. "The God Who Wouldn't Stay Dead." In *What Do We Believe?* edited by Martin E. Marty, Stuart E. Rosenberg, and Andrew M. Greeley. New York: Meredith Press, 1968.

Greenberg, Joseph H. "Language and Linguistics." *The Voice of America Forum Lectures*. Behavioral Science Series, No. 11. New York: 1961.

Greening, Thomas C. "Commentary." *Journal of Humanistic Psychology* 11, No. 2 (Fall 1971): 107–08.

Harlow, Harry F. *Learning to Love*. San Francisco: Albion Publishing, 1971.

Harlow, Harry F.; Harlow, Margaret Kuenne; and Meyer, Donald R. "Learning Motivated by a Manipulation Drive." *Journal of Experimental Psychology* 40 (1950): 228–34.

Harper, Robert. "Honesty in Courtship." *The Humanist* 18, No. 2 (March 1958): pp. 103–07.

Hartman, Robert S. "The Science of Value." In *New Knowledge in Human Values*, edited by Abraham H. Maslow. New York: Harper & Row, 1959.

Hattwick, La Berta. "More Than Skin Deep." *Childhood Education* 25 (1949): 292–94.

Haythorn, W. W., and Altman, I. "Together in Isolation." *Trans-action* 4, No. 3 (1967): 18–22.

Hebb, Donald. *A Textbook of Psychology*. Philadelphia: W. B. Saunders, 1958.

Heidegger, Martin. *Being and Time*. Translated by John Macquarrie and Edward Robinson. London: SCM Press, 1962.

———. *On "Time and Being."* Translated by Joan Stambaugh. New York: Harper & Row, 1972.

Heimann, Eduard. *Freedom and Order*. New York: Charles Scribner's Sons, 1947.

Hein, Hilde. "Play as an Aesthetic Concept." *Journal of Aesthetics and Art Criticism* 27 (Fall 1968): 67–71.

Heine, Ralph W. In Salvatore R. Maddi and Paul T. Costa, *Humanism in Personology*. Chicago: Aldine-Atherton, 1972.

Hesse, Hermann. *Magister Ludi*. Translated by Mervyn Savill. New York: Henry Holt, 1959.

Hoagland, Edward. " 'No Groveling, Death!' " *Newsweek*, 30 July 1973, pp. 8–9.

Hobbes, Thomas. *Leviathan*. Oxford: Clarendon Press, 1909.

Hoebel, E. A. "Law, Primitive." *Encyclopaedia Britannica*. Chicago: University of Chicago, 1972.

Hook, Sidney. *Dimensions of Mind*. New York: New York University Press, 1960.

Huizinga, Jacob. *Homo Ludens: A Study of the Play-Element in Culture*. London: Routledge & Kegan Paul, 1949.

Hunt, Morton M. *The Natural History of Love*. New York: Alfred A. Knopf, 1959.

Huxley, Aldous. *Brave New World*. New York: Bantam, 1968.

———. *Le Plus sot animal*. Paris: La Jeune Parque, 1946.

Huxley, Julian. "Transhumanism." *Journal of Humanistic Psychology* (Spring 1968): 73–76.

———. *The Uniqueness of Man*. London: Chatto and Windus, 1943.

James, William, *Principles of Psychology*, vol. 2. New York: Dover, 1950.

Janet, Pierre. *L'Evolution de la memoire et la notion du temps*. Paris: Chahine, 1928.

Johnson, Pamela Hansford. *On Iniquity: Some Personal Reflections Arising out of the Moors Murder Trial*. London: Macmillan and Co., 1967.

Jourard, Sidney M. *Healthy Personality*. New York: MacMillan, 1974.

———. *Self-Disclosure*. New York: John Wiley, 1971.

Journal of Humanistic Psychology, The Association for Humanistic Psychology, 325 Ninth Avenue, San Francisco, Calif. 94103.

Journal of Thanatology, Foundation of Thanatology, 630 W. 168th Street, New York, N.Y. 10032. (Originally published as *Archives of the Foundation of Thanatology*)

Journal of Transpersonal Psychology, Anthony J. Sutich, Transpersonal Association, Stanford, California, 94305.

Jung, C. G. *The Archetypes and the Collective Unconscious*. Translated by R. F. C. Hull. New York: Princeton University Press, Bollingen Foundation, 1969.

———. *Flying Saucers: A Modern Myth of Things Seen in the Skies*. Translated by R. F. C. Hull. New York: Harcourt Brace Jovanovich, 1959.

Kagan, Jerome. "Kagan Counters Freud, Piaget Theories on Early Childhood Deprivation Effects." *A.P.A. Monitor* 4, No. 2 (February 1973): 1, 7.

Kagawa, Toyohiko. *Love and the Law of Life*. Chicago: John C. Winston, 1951.

Kalish, Richard A. "Death and Bereavement: A Bibliography." *Journal of Human Relations* 13 (1965): 118–41.

Kastenbaum, Robert. "The Dimensions of Future Time Perspective: An Experimental Analysis." *Journal of General Psychology* 65 (1961): 203–18.

Kellogg, Winthrop Niles, and Kellogg, L. A. *The Apes and the Child*. New York: Hafner, 1933.

Keen, Sam. "Transpersonal Psychology. The Cosmic Versus the Rational." *Psychology Today*, July 1974, pp. 56–59.

Kerr, Walter. *The Decline of Pleasure*. New York: Simon and Schuster, 1962.

Kesey, Ken. *One Flew over the Cuckoo's Nest*. New York: New American Library, 1962.

Kierkegaard, Soren. *Works of Love*. Princeton, N.J.: Princeton University Press, 1946. Translated by David F. Swenson and Lillian Marvin Swenson.

King, Richard. "The Eros Ethos Cult in the Counterculture." *Psychology Today*, August 1972, pp. 35–39.

Klaw, Spencer. "Harvard's Skinner: The Last of the Utopians." *Harper's Magazine*, April 1963, pp. 45–51.

Koch, Sigmund. "The Image of Man Implicit in Encounter Group Theory." *Journal of Humanistic Psychology* 11 (Fall 1971): 109–33.

———. "Psychology Cannot Be a Coherent Science." *Psychology Today*, September 1969, p. 14.

Koch, Sigmund, ed. *Psychology: A Study of a Science,* vol. 3. New York: Mc-
Graw-Hill, 1959.

Köhler, Wolfgang. *Gestalt Psychology.* New York: Liveright, 1947.

———. *The Mentality of Apes.* Translated by Ella Winter. New York: Harcourt Brace Jovanovich, 1925.

Korzybski, Alfred. *Manhood of Humanity.* 2nd ed., enl. Lakeville, Conn.: The
International Non-Aristotelian Library, 1950.

———. *Science and Sanity: An Introduction to Non-Aristotelian Systems and
General Semantics.* 3rd ed. Lakeville, Conn.: The International Non-
Aristotelian Library, 1950.

———. *Time-Binding: The General Theory.* Lakeville, Conn.: The International Non-Aristotelian Library, 1924.

Krauss, Reinhard. "Uber Graphischen Ausdruck." *Zeitschrift für Angewandte
Psychologie,* Beiheft 48 (1930): 1–141.

Krutch, Joseph Wood. *The Measure of Man.* New York: Grosset & Dunlap,
1954.

Kubie, L. S., and Ribble, Margaret A. "The Rights of Infants: Comments." In
The Psychoanalytic Study of the Child, vol. 1, edited by O. Fenichel et. al.
New York: International Universities Press, 1945.

Kübler-Ross, Elisabeth. *On Death and Dying.* New York: Macmillan, 1969.

LaBarre, Weston. *The Human Animal.* Chicago: University of Chicago Press,
1961.

Langer, Susanne K. *An Introduction to Symbolic Logic.* 3rd ed. New York:
Dover, 1967.

———. *Philosophy in a New Key.* 3rd ed. Cambridge, Mass.: Harvard University Press, 1963.

van Lawick-Goodall, Jane. *In the Shadow of Man.* Boston: Houghton Mifflin,
1971.

———. *My Friends: The Wild Chimpanzees.* New York: The National Geographic Society, 1967.

Lepp, Ignace. *The Psychology of Loving.* Baltimore: Helicon Press, 1963.

Levin, Meyer. *Compulsion.* New York: New American Library, 1968.

Levinas, Emmanuel. *Totality and Infinity.* Translated by Alphonso Lingis.
Pittsburgh: Duquesne University Press, 1969.

Lewis, C. S. *The Discarded Image.* London: Cambridge University Press, 1970.

———. *The Four Loves.* New York: Harcourt Brace Jovanovich, 1960.

Lorenz, Konrad Z. *King Solomon's Ring.* Translated by Marjorie Kerr Wilson.
New York: Thomas Y. Crowell, 1952.

———. *On Aggression.* Translated by Marjorie Kerr Wilson. New York: Harcourt Brace Jovanovich, 1966.

Lowen, Alexander. "The Spiral of Growth: Love, Sex and Pleasure." In *Love
Today,* edited by Herbert A. Otto. New York: Association Press, 1972.

MacCorquodale, Kenneth. "Behaviorism Is a Humanism." *The Humanist,*
March-April 1971, p. 12.

MacIver, Robert. "The Essentials of Law and Order." In *Exploring the Ways of
Mankind,* edited by Walter Goldschmidt. New York: Holt, Rinehart and
Winston, 1960.

MacLeish, Archibald. "Why Do We Teach Poetry?" *Atlantic Monthly,* March
1956, pp. 48–53.

Maddi, Salvatore R., and Costa, Paul T. *Humanism in Personology.* Chicago:
Aldine-Atherton, 1972.

Malinowski, Bronislaw. *Magic, Science and Religion.* Garden City, N.Y.:
Doubleday, Anchor, 1954.

Malson, Lucien. *Wolf Children and the Problem of Human Nature.* Translated by Edmund Fawcett, Peter Ayrton, and Joan White. New York: Monthly Review Press, 1972.

Marcel, Gabriel. *Du refus à l'invocation*. Paris: Librairie Gallimard, 1950.

——. *Homo Viator: Introduction to a Metaphysic of Hope*. Translated by Emma Craufurd. New York: Harper & Row, 1962.

Marcuse, Herbert. *Eros and Civilization*. Boston: Beacon, Vintage, 1955.

——. *Negations: A Critique of Norman O. Brown*. Translated by Jeremy J. Shapiro. Boston: Beacon, 1968.

——. *One-Dimensional Man*. Boston: Beacon, 1964.

Marler, Peter. "Learning, Genetics, and Communication." *Social Research* 40, No. 2 (Summer 1973): 293–310.

Marty, Martin E.; Rosenberg, Stuart E.; and Greeley, Andrew M. *What Do We Believe?* New York: Meredith Press, 1968.

Maslow, Abraham. *Eupsychian Management*. Homewood, Ill.: Richard D. Irwin and The Dorsey Press, 1965.

——. *The Farther Reaches of Human Nature*. New York: Viking Press, 1971.

——. *Toward a Psychology of Being*. 2nd ed. Princeton, N.J.: D. Van Nostrand, 1968.

Maslow, Abraham H., ed. *New Knowledge in Human Values*. New York: Harper & Row, 1959.

Maslow, Abraham H., and Murphy, Gardner, eds. *Motivation and Personality*. New York: Harper & Row, 1969.

Massarik, Fred. "La Force Est Morte—Vive Les Forces." *Journal of Humanistic Psychology* 8, No. 3 (December 1971): 1–5.

Matson, Floyd W. *The Broken Image*. New York: George Braziller, 1964.

——. "Humanistic Theory: The Third Revolution in Psychology." *The Humanist*, March-April 1971, pp. 7–11.

——. *Without/Within*. Belmont, California: Wadsworth, 1973.

May, Rollo. *Love and Will*. New York: W. W. Norton, 1969.

——. *Psychology and the Human Dilemma*. Princeton, N.J.: D. Van Nostrand, 1967.

May, Rollo; Angel, Ernest; and Ellenberger, Henri F., eds. *Existence*. New York: Basic Books, 1958.

Mead, George Herbert. *Mind, Self and Society*. Chicago: University of Chicago Press, 1955.

Mendelsohn, Everett. *Time*, 23 April 1974, p. 84.

Menninger, Karl. *Time*, 16 April 1951, pp. 63–65.

Mercer, Samuel A. B. *The Origin of Writing and Our Alphabet*. London: Luzac & Co., 1959.

Merleau-Ponty, M. *Phenomenology of Perception*. Translated by Colin Smith. New York: Humanities Press, 1962.

Michotte, Albert. *The Perception of Causality*. Translated by R. C. Oldfield. New York: Basic Books, 1963.

Miller, Henry. *Time*, 1 April 1966, p. 40.

Miller, James G. "The Individual Response to Drugs." In *Control of the Mind*, edited by Seymour M. Farber and Roger H. L. Wilson. New York: McGraw-Hill, 1961.

Mitchell, Gary; Redican, William K.; and Gomber, Jody. "Males Can Raise Babies." *Psychology Today*, April 1974, pp. 63–68.

Mitford, Jessica. *The American Way of Death*. New York: Simon and Schuster, 1963.

Montagu, Ashley, ed. *The Meaning of Love*. New York: Julian Press, 1953.

Morris, Desmond. *The Naked Ape*. London: Jonathan Cape, 1968.

Moutakas, Clark. *Loneliness*. Englewood Cliffs, N.J.: Prentice-Hall, 1961.

Mullin, C. S., Jr. "Some Psychological Aspects of Isolated Antarctic Living." *American Journal of Psychiatry* 117 (1960): 323–25.

Mumford, Lewis. *The Myth of the Machine.* New York: Harcourt Brace Jovanovich, 1967.

Murphy, Gardner. "Determinants of Personality." In *Conflict and Creativity,* edited by Seymour Farber. New York: McGraw-Hill, 1963.

———. *Human Potentialities.* New York: Basic Books, 1958.

Murray, Henry. "Toward a Classification of Interaction." In *Toward a General Theory of Action,* edited by T. Parsons and E. A. Shils. Cambridge, Mass.: Harvard University, 1954.

Nardini, J. E. "Navy Psychiatric Assessment Program in the Antarctic." *American Journal of Psychiatry* 119 (1962): 97–105.

Nicholl, Donald. *Recent Thoughts in Focus.* New York: Sheed and Ward, 1953.

"Norman O. Brown's Body: A Conversation Between Brown and Warren G. Bennis." *Psychology Today,* August 1970, pp. 43–47.

Nygren, Anders. *Agape and Eros.* New York: Harper & Row, 1969.

Omega. Greenwood Periodicals, Inc., 51 Riverside Avenue, Westport, Conn. 06880.

Orlinsky, David E. "Love Relationships in the Life Cycle: A Developmental Interpersonal Perspective." In *Love Today,* edited by Herbert A. Otto. New York: Association Press, 1972.

Orwell, George. *1984.* New York: New American Library, 1961.

Otto, Herbert A. *Love Today.* New York: Association Press, 1972.

Parsons, Talcott. "Death in American Society—A Brief Working Paper." *American Behavioral Scientist* 6 (May 1963): 61–65.

Paton, Alan. *Cry, the Beloved Country.* New York: Charles Scribner's Sons, 1948.

Penfield, Wilder. "The Physiological Basis of the Mind." In *Control of the Mind,* edited by Seymour M. Farber and Roger H. L. Wilson. New York: McGraw-Hill, 1961.

Peter, Lawrence J. "Peter Principle Game." *Psychology Today,* October 1973, p. 94.

Peters, R. S. *The Concept of Motivation.* London: Routledge & Kegan Paul, 1958.

Piaget, Jean. *Le Development de la notion de temps chez l'enfant.* Paris: Presses Universitaires de France, 1946.

———. *The Moral Judgment of the Child.* Translated by Marjorie Gabin. Glencoe, Ill.: The Free Press, 1955.

Pieron, Henri. "Les Problèmes psychophysiologiques de la perception du temps." *Année Psychologique* 24 (1923): 1–25.

Pinneau, S. R. "A Critique on the Articles by Margaret Ribble." *Child Development* 21 (1951): 203–28.

Polanyi, Michael. *Personal Knowledge.* New York: Harper & Row, 1964.

———. *Science, Faith and Society.* Chicago: University of Chicago Press, 1966.

Potter, Stephen. *The Theory and Practice of Gamesmanship.* New York: Henry Holt, 1947.

Powell, John. *Why Am I Afraid to Love?* Chicago: Argus Communications, 1967.

Putney, Snell, and Putney, Gail J. *The Adjusted American.* New York: Harper & Row, 1964.

Ravetz, Jerome R. "Science, History of." *Encyclopaedia Britannica. Macropaedia,* vol. 16. Chicago: University of Chicago Press, 1974.

Read, Herbert. *To Hell With Culture.* London: Routledge & Kegan Paul, 1963.

Reichenbach, Hans. *Elements of Symbolic Logic*. New York: The Free Press, 1947.

Reik, Theodor. *A Psychologist Looks at Love*. New York: Farrar & Rinehart, 1944.

Review of Existential Psychology and Psychiatry. 140 Glenwood Road, Englewood, New Jersey, 07631.

Rheingold, Harriet L. "The Modification of Social Responsiveness in Institutional Babies." Society for Research in Child Development, Monograph 21, No. 2 (1956).

Ribble, Margaret. *The Rights of Infants*. New York: Columbia University Press, 1943.

Richardson, Herbert W., and Cutler, Donald R. *Transcendence*. Boston: Beacon Press, 1969.

Riesman, David. *The Lonely Crowd*. New Haven, Conn.: Yale University Press, 1958.

Riley, John W., Jr. "Death and Bereavement." *International Encyclopedia of the Social Sciences*, vol. 4. New York: Macmillan, The Free Press, 1968.

Rogers, Carl R. *Becoming Partners*. New York: Delacorte, 1972.

Rogers, Carl R. *Carl Rogers on Encounter Groups*. New York: Harper & Row, 1970.

————. *On Becoming a Person*. Boston: Houghton Mifflin, 1961.

————. "A Theory of Therapy, Personality, and Interpersonal Relationships, as Described in the Client-Centered Framework." In *Psychology: A Study of a Science*, vol. 3, edited by Sigmund Koch. New York: McGraw-Hill, 1959.

Rogers, Carl R., and Stevens, Barry. *Person to Person*. Palo Alto, Calif.: Science and Behavior Books, 1970.

Rohrer, J. H. "Interpersonal Relations in Isolated Small Groups." In *Psychophysiological Aspects of Space Flight*, edited by B. E. Flaherty. New York: Columbia University Press, 1961.

Roszak, Theodore. *The Making of a Counterculture*. Garden City, N.Y.: Doubleday, 1969.

Royce, Joseph R. *The Encapsulated Man*. Princeton: D. Van Nostrand, 1964.

Runes, Dagobert. *Despotism: A Pictorial History of Despotism*. Philosophical Library, 1963.

Russell, Bertrand. *The Autobiography of Bertrand Russell*. London: Allen & Unwin, 1967.

Sartre, Jean Paul. *Being and Nothingness*. Translated by Hazel Barnes. New York: Philosophical Library, 1956.

Sayre, Kenneth M., and Crosson, Frederick J. *The Modelling of Mind*. Notre Dame, Ind.: University of Notre Dame Press, 1963.

Schaller, George B. *The Year of the Gorilla*. Chicago: University of Chicago Press, 1964.

Schutz, William C. *Joy*. New York: Grove Press, 1967.

Scriven, Michael. "The Compleat Robot: A Prologomena to Androidology." In *Dimensions of Mind*, edited by Sidney Hook. New York: New York University Press, 1960.

————. "The Mechanical Concept of Mind." In *Minds and Machines*, edited by Alan Ross Anderson. Englewood Cliffs, N.J.: Prentice-Hall, 1964.

Severin, Frank T. *Discovering Man in Psychology*. New York: McGraw-Hill, 1973.

————. *Humanistic Viewpoints in Psychology*. New York: McGraw-Hill, 1965.

Shibles, Warren. *Metaphor*. Whitewater, Wisc.: The Language Press, 1971.

Shneidman, Edwin S. "Death Questionnaire." *Psychology Today*, August 1970, pp. 66–72.

————. "You and Death." *Psychology Today,* June 1971, pp. 43–45 (results of "Death Questionnaire").

Shostrum, Everett L. *Man, the Manipulator.* New York: Abingdon Press, 1967.

Simons, Joseph B., and Reidy, Jeanne. *The Risk of Loving.* New York: Herder and Herder, 1968.

Skinner, B. F. *About Behaviorism.* New York: Alfred A. Knopf, 1974.

————. *Beyond Freedom and Dignity.* New York: Alfred A. Knopf, 1972.

————. "Humanistic Behaviorism." *The Humanist,* May-June 1971, p. 35.

————. *Walden Two.* New York: Macmillan, 1948.

Smith, Huston. "The Reach and the Grasp: Transcendence Today." In *Transcendence,* edited by Herbert W. Richardson and Donald R. Cutler. Boston: Beacon Press, 1969.

Snow, C. P. *The Two Cultures: And a Second Look.* New York: Cambridge University Press, 1963.

Snygg, Donald, and Combs, Arthur W. *Individual Behavior.* New York: Harper & Brothers, 1949.

Sorokin, Pitirim A. "The Powers of Creative Unselfish Love." In *New Knowledge in Human Values,* New York: Harper & Row, 1959.

————. *The Ways and Power of Love.* Boston: Beacon Press, 1954.

Sorokin, Pitirim A., ed. *Explorations in Altruistic Love and Behavior.* Boston: Beacon Press, 1950.

Steiner, Jerome. "Group Function Within the Mourning Process." *Archives of the Foundation of Thanatology* 2 (Summer 1970): 80–82.

Stevens, John O. "Determinism: Prerequisite for a Meaningful Freedom." *Review of Existential Psychology and Psychiatry* 7 (Fall 1967): 201–23.

Stevenson, Charles L. *Ethics and Language.* New Haven, Conn.: Yale University Press, 1944.

Stewart, Omer C. "Fire." *Encyclopaedia Britannica.* Chicago: University of Chicago Press, 1972.

Strupp, H. H., and Bergin, A. E. "Some Empirical and Conceptual Bases for Coordinated Research in Psychotherapy: A Critical Review of Issues, Trends, and Evidence." *International Journal of Psychiatry* 7, No. 2 (1969).

Sumner, William G. *Folkways.* New York: Ginn and Co., 1940.

Szasz, Thomas S. *The Myth of Mental Illness.* New York: Dell Publishing, 1961.

Teilhard de Chardin, Pierre. *The Phenomenon of Man.* Translated by René Hague. New York: Harper & Row, 1965.

Thorpe, W. H. *Science, Man and Morals.* London: Methuen, 1965.

Tillich, Paul. *The Courage to Be.* New Haven, Conn.: Yale University Press, 1952.

Toffler, Alvin. *Future Shock.* New York: Bantam Books, 1970.

Tonnies, Ferdinand. *Gemeinschaft und Gesellschaft.* Berlin: Curtius, 1912.

Tubbs, Walter. "Beyond Perls." *Journal of Humanistic Psychology* 12 (Fall 1972): 5.

Turing, A. M. "Computing Machinery and Intelligence." In *Computers and Thought,* edited by Edward Feigenbaum and Julian Feldman. New York: McGraw-Hill, 1963. Also in *Minds and Machines,* edited by Alan Ross Anderson. Englewood Cliffs, N.J.: Prentice-Hall, 1964.

Vahanian, Gabriel. *The Death of God.* New York: George Braziller, 1961.

————. *No Other God.* New York: George Braziller, 1966.

————. *Wait Without Idols.* New York: George Braziller, 1964.

Vercors (Jean Bruller). *Plus ou moins homme.* Paris: Edition Albin Michel, 1950.

von Bertalanffy, Ludwig. *Robots, Men and Minds.* New York: George Braziller, 1967.

Waddington, C. H. *The Ethical Animal*. London: Allen & Unwin, 1960.
Wainwright, Loudon. "A Lesson For Living." *Life,* 21 November 1969, pp. 36–42.
Watson, Robert I. *Psychology of the Child*. New York: John Wiley & Sons, 1958.
Watts, Alan W. *Psychotherapy East and West*. New York: New American Library, 1961.
Weber, Max. *The Methodology of the Social Sciences*. Glencoe, Ill.: The Free Press, 1949.
Wertenbaker, Lael Tucker. *Death of a Man*. New York: Random House, 1957.
Whyte, William H., Jr. *The Organization Man*. Garden City, N.Y.: Doubleday, Anchor, 1956.
Wood, Ernest. *Zen Dictionary*. New York: Philosophical Library, 1962.
World Book Encyclopedia, 1971 ed., s. v. "Lemming."
Wright, Iovanna Lloyd, with Nicholson, Patricia Coyle, ed. *Architecture: Man in Possession of His Earth*. Garden City, N.Y.: Doubleday, 1962.
Yerkes, Robert M. *Almost Human*. New York: Century, 1925.
———. *The Mind of a Gorilla*. Worcester, Mass: Clark University, 1926–28.
Yerkes, Robert M., and Yerkes, Ada W. *The Great Apes*. New Haven, Conn.: Yale University Press, 1929.

ACKNOWLEDGMENTS AND COPYRIGHTS

(Continued from p. iv)

Harcourt Brace Jovanovich, Inc. For "The Hollow Men" from *Collected Poems 1909–1962* by T. S. Eliot. Reprinted by permission of the publisher.

Harper & Row, Publishers, Inc. For excerpts from *The Phenomenon of Man* by Pierre Teilhard de Chardin. Copyright © 1959 by Pierre Teilhard de Chardin. Reprinted by permission of Harper & Row, Publishers, Inc.

Houghton Mifflin Company. For an excerpt from "Why Do We Teach Poetry" by Archibald MacLeish from *Atlantic Monthly* (March 1956). Reprinted by permission of Houghton Mifflin Company.

Journal of Humanistic Psychology. For "Beyond Perls" by Walter Tubbs from *Journal of Humanistic Psychology* 12 (Fall 1972).

Journal of Human Relations. For Table I on pages 249–50 from "Toward a Developmental Concept of Love" by Martin Bloom from *Journal of Human Relations* 15, No. 2 (1967). Reprinted by permission of Central State University, Wilberforce, Ohio.

Alfred A. Knopf, Inc. For "Li Fu-jen" from *Translations from the Chinese* by Arthur Waley. Copyright 1919 and renewed 1947 by Arthur Waley. Copyright 1941 and renewed 1969 by Alfred A. Knopf, Inc. Reprinted by permission of the publisher.

David McKay Company, Inc. For two excerpts from *A Comprehensive Dictionary of Psychological and Psychoanalytical Terms* by Horace B. English and Ava Champney. Used with permission of the publishers.

Macmillan Publishing Co., Inc. For excerpts from "Death: Death and Bereavement" by John W. Riley, Jr.; "Leisure" by Joffre Dumazedier; and "Time: Psychological Aspects" by Paul Fraisse from *International Encyclopedia of the Social Sciences,* D. L. Sills, ed. Copyright © 1968 by Crowell Collier and Macmillan, Inc. Reprinted by permission of Macmillan Publishing Co., Inc.

Walter Tubbs. For "Beyond Perls" by Walter Tubbs from *Journal of Humanistic Psychology* 12 (Fall 1972).

D. Van Nostrand Company. For excerpts from *Psychology and the Human Dilemma* by Rollo May. © 1967 by Litton Educational Publishing, Inc. Reprinted by permission of D. Van Nostrand Company.

INDEX

Building, as a specifically human function, 137
Bultmann, Rudolf, 213

C

Cage, John, 135
Campbell, Elizabeth W., 134
Campbell, Joseph, 114, 118
Camus, Albert, 202
Carpenter, Edmund, 28, 134–35, 142
Carrell, Alexis, 1
Casler, Lawrence, 122, 128
Cassirer, Ernst, 14–15
Ciardi, John, 203
Clay, Felix, 135
Cognition, 37, 189–90, 193; and comprehension, 192; and understanding, 191–92. *See also* Thinking
Coleman, James C., 185
Combs, Arthur W., 156
Communication. *See* Language
Community versus society, 162
Comparative psychologists, 4, 12, 16, 72, 99. *See also* Mechanism; Methodology
Computer, 28, 55, 62–65, 157, 171
Comte, August, 168
Concept of man. *See* Man
Conscience, 162, 184
Conscious experience. *See* Consciousness
Consciousness, 24, 27–29, 32, 37, 222; and ability to discriminate, 28–29; human type of, 28; and transcendence, 221. *See also* Reflection consciousness; Thinking
Creativity, interpersonal, 78, 92–112. *See also* Love
Cruelty, 146, 184–85
Culican, William, 61
Culture, 48; versus biological determinants, 3, 178; versus genetic determinants, 53; versus heredity, 70–71; and sociological determinants, 153
Culture making, 3
Cybernetics. *See* Computer

D

Dancing honey bee, 12, 52–53, 68–69, 141
Darwin, Charles, 168
Death, 45, 61, 103, 188, 195–205; and academic psychology, 196, 204; and afterlife, 197–98; attitudes toward, 197–99; and Christianity, 198; cosmeticized, 200; existentialist view of, 201, 203–04; and love, 200–01; and mourning, 199–200; and psychoanalysis, 196, 204
Deception, 179–82
de Ropp, Robert S., 82–85
Determinism, methodological: versus ontological, 13
Diringer, David D., 17
Dix, Dorothea, 108
Dollard, John, 92
Donne, John, 93
Dooley, Thomas, 108
Doss, S. R., 35
Drews, Elizabeth Monroe, 134
Dreyfuss, Henry, 14
Drugs, 148, 204; abuse of, 162
Dubos, Rene, 98, 214
Dumazedier, Joffre, 89
Duration, 34–35, 37, 41; estimates of, 35. *See also* Time

E

Ecological awareness, 238, 239
Ecology, 16
Education, 176, 204, 232
Einstein, Albert, 214
Eiseley, Loren, 27, 98, 127
Eliot, T. S., 9
Empiricism: Locke's, 167; pseudo, 218. *See also* Science
Encounter, 105, 113; authentic, versus role, 105
Energy binding, 41
English, A. C., and English, H. B., 136, 212
Epistemology, 167, 212, 230; empirical, 153; mechanistic, 153, 155; phenomenological, 153, 155–56
Eskimo customs, 73
Esthetic urges, 4. *See also* Beauty
Ethics, 3, 16, 72–73, 146, 161–77, 179, 232; and analytical philosophy, 170; and behaviorism, 169; and biological and social forces, 168; common, 171–73; and environmental conditions, 163, 168; and hedonism, 170; and law, 71; and logical positivism, 170; naturalization of, 165–71; and psychoanalysis, 169–70; reductionism in, 164, 168–70; and religion, 166; and science, 166; and social sciences, 166–69; and utilitarianism, 170, 239

Ethical absolutism, 164
Ethical behavior, 39
Ethical progress, 174
Ethical relativism, 164
Ethologists, 12, 69, 99
Eupsychian psychology, 178
Existentialism, 37, 40, 97, 205, 223–24, 233. *See also* Phenomenology
Experimental method, 13, 18. *See also* Science
Eysenck, H. J., 98

F

Farber, Leslie, 149
Feifel, Herman, 202–04
Fiedler, F. E., 98
Finiteness. *See* Death
Fire, 60–61
Fraisse, Paul, 34, 35, 37
Frankl, Viktor E., 98, 202, 224. *See also* Values
Freedom, 48, 146–60, 176; as autonomy, 147, 158; and biological and social variables, 152; and choice, 153, 205; conditions for, 149–52; and determinism, 158–59; and genetic determinants, 153; and the good, 150; and human fulfillment, 87, 224; as independence, 147; and indeterminism, 158; and lawfulness of existence, 148; as liberty, 158; and responsibility, 155; and self-determination, 157; and sociological determinants, 152; and unfreedom, 158
Free will, 148–49, 152, 158
Freud, Sigmund, 115–16, 196, 199, 209
Friendship, 93, 100, 104–08, 129, 200. *See also* Love
Fromm, Erich, 87, 97, 127
Frost, Robert, 20–21
Fulfillment, 188, 224, 237. *See also* Good life; Happiness
Fuller, Buckminster, 137
Fuller, Lon L., 67, 71
Future. *See* Time

G

Gallico, Paul, 108
Games, 79–91; colloquial corruption of, 81; and competition, 80–82; definition of, 79–80; fun, 82, 84–85; game playing, 85–86; life, 82–83, 88; neu-

rotic, 84; new meaning of, 80–81; nogame, 85; object, 83; as play, 80; psychiatric usage of, 81; and sport, 84–85; and stakes, 80; theory of, 81; types of, 81–84. *See also* Metagames
Gardner, Allen R., and Gardner, Beatrice T., 25
Gibran, Kahlil, 113
Giraudoux, Jean, 203
Goble, Frank G., 189
Gödel, Kurt, 32
Gogarthen, Friedrich, 213
Goldschmidt, Walter, 173
Gomber, Jody, 72
Good life, 86, 89, 177, 203, 205, 226–41; versus good time, 227–28. *See also* Fulfillment; Happiness
Goodman, Paul, 116
Goodness, 171, 228, 230; definition of, 229
Gordon, Ernest, 109
Gorer, Geoffrey, 200–01
Greenberg, Joseph H., 50

H

Hamilton, William, 213
Hamlet, 9
Hammarskjöld, Dag, 225
Hammurabi, Code of, 74–75
Happiness, 127, 226–27. *See also* Fulfillment; Good life
Harlow, Harry F., 42, 99, 189
Hartman, Robert S., 229–30
Hattwick, LaBerta, 134
Hebb, Donald, 141
Heidegger, Martin, 37–38, 89, 97, 152, 202
Hein, Hilde, 80, 85
Hesse, Herman, 84
Hobbes, Thomas, 168
Homicide, 184–86. *See also* Infanticide; Senilicide
Huizinga, Jacob, 79–80, 172
Human nature. *See* Man
Human predicament, 222–24
Humor, 149, 220
Husserl, Edmund, 40
Huxley, Aldous, 65, 95, 205
Huxley. Julian, 29, 54, 186, 214

I

Ideals, versus goals, 84
Identity of man. *See* Man

Ideology, 5, 12
Imprinting, 208
Independence, 66–67. *See also* Autonomy; Freedom
Infanticide, 73
Interanimation, 93
Interpersonal creativity. *See* Love
Intuition. *See* Epistemology

J

James, William, 26, 201
Janet, Pierre, 35
Jefferson, Thomas, 174
Johnson, Pamela, 186
Journal of Human Relations, 101
Jung, Carl G., 109, 121

K

Kafka, Franz, 35
Kagan, Jerome S., 96
Kant, Immanuel, 35
Kellogg, W. N., and Kellogg, L. A., 57
Kerr, Walter, 82
Kesey, Ken, 108
Kierkegaard, Sören, 87, 97, 202, 224
King, Martin Luther, Jr., 111
Kinget, G. Marian, 21
Köhler, Wolfgang, 20, 54, 57
Korzybski, Alfred, 41, 172, 175
Krauss, Reinhard, 21
Krutch, Joseph Wood, 16
Kubie, L. S., 96
Kübler-Ross, Elisabeth, 196

L

Langer, Susanne, 18, 24, 51, 142
Language, 3, 44, 48–55; as communication, 49, 52; computer, 55; and consciousness, 24; conversational, 55; culturally determined, 53; and dancing honey bee, 52–53; genetically determined, 53; human and animal, 49–50, 52, 54; and human linguistic behavior, 52–54; interspecies ubiquitousness of, 53; machine, 55; and need reduction, 54; potentiality versus actuality, 53; propositional, 52–53; and self-expression, 54; sentence making in, 53; as speech, 49, 51; syntactical, 50–52
Lao-Tsu, 107
Law, 48, 66–76, 86, 179; and cultural factors, 70–71; definition of, 66; and ethnics, 71, 173; and hereditary factors, 70; and political activity, 68, 70; and regulated behavior, 71; of retribution, *lex talionis,* 74; in time, 73
van Lawick-Goodall, Jane, 56–58, 67, 69, 99, 184
Leakey, Louis B., 58, 192
Leisure, 85, 92; and life, 89; work and, 89
Lemmings. *See* Suicide
Levin, Meyer, 185
Lewis, C. S., 97, 107, 117, 119, 126, 143, 175
Locke, John, 167
Loneliness, 27
Lorenz, Konrad, 54, 141, 184, 189
Love, 92–131, 141, 162, 186, 220, 231, 237; and archetypes, 22, 120–21; and biological determinants, 104, 118; and child development, 95–96; companionship as a type of, 93, 100, 103–05, 108; concept of, 94; and counterculture, 116; cosmetic image of, 120, 128; desire as part of, 119; developmental stages of, 101–02; emotion versus sentiment in, 124–25; filial, 100, 200; forms of, 99–112; fulfillment in, 125, 127; function of, in the human economy, 96; generic, 92–94; as a lifelong phenomenon, 99; and marriage, 127–29; parental, 100, 200; relation of, to death, 200; as self-rehabilitation, 99; status of, within American psychology, 94–95; transference, 95; and transcendence, 224. *See also* Agape; Friendship; Romantic love; Sex
Lowen, Alexander, 114
LSD, 139, 216

M

Machine. *See* Technology
MacLeish, Archibald, 142–43
Malinowski, Bronislaw, 183
Man: concept or nature of, 48, 64, 230–31, 233, 240; Dionysian, 116; evolutionary character of, 171–72, 176; qualitative difference of, 12; quantitative difference of, 12, 196; radical difference of, 29; as rational animal, 9–11, 191
Marasmus, 96
Marcel, Gabriel, 97, 224

Marcuse, Herbert, 116
Maslow, Abraham, 96, 111, 149, 178, 207
Matson, Floyd, 64
Maturity, 128, 147, 148
May, Rollo, 38, 43, 87, 93, 97, 148, 157, 213
Maya, 90, 224. *See also* Zen Buddhism
Mead, George Herbert, 88
Meaning, need for, 192, 234
Mechanistic psychology, 169
Meister Eckhart, 216
Memory, 42
Mendelsohn, Everett, 12
Menninger, Karl, 97, 206
Mercer, Samuel, 17
Merleau-Ponty, M., 40, 210
Metagames, 83
Metaphysical concern, 4, 61, 136, 208. *See also* Religion; Ultimate concern
Methodology, 2, 12; and principle of parsimony, 26, 31; and research, 16. *See also* Science
Michotte, A., 21, 156
Miller, Henry, 201
Miller, James G., 150
Minkowski, Eugene, 38
Mitchell, Gary, 72
Mitford, Jessica, 197–98, 200
Morality. *See* Ethics
Morris, Desmond, 67, 69
Mourning. *See* Death
Mumford, Lewis, 64
Murphy, Gardner, 192, 207
Myth, 20, 22, 211–15; definition of, 212. *See also* Religion; Science

N

NASA (National Aeronautics and Space Administration), 104
Neurosis: and alienation, 182; collective, 204–05; experimental, 181
Nietzsche, Friedrich, 223
Nightingale, Florence, 109
Nygren, Anders, 109

O

Omega, 196
Operational criterion, 11
Operationism, 11
Orlinsky, David E., 99
Orwell, George, 235

P

Pansexualism, 115. *See also* Sex
Paton, Alan, 108
Peking Man, 61
Perception, 156–57; versus stimuli, 156; symbolic tendency of, 21
Perceptual thinking, 13
Perls, Fritz, 130
Peter, Lawrence J., 84
Peter Principle Game, 84
Peters, R. S., 69
Phenomenology, 16, 27, 33, 37, 90–91, 133, 153, 155–57; and epiphenomenalism, 4. *See also* Existentialism
Philosophy of life, 124, 193–94; and world view, 230
Phylogenetic, 2
Piaget, Jean, 35, 172
Pieron, Henri, 35
Pinneau, S. R., 96
Plato, 88–89, 198
Play, 78–91; and the child, 88; as a model for life, 88–91; and need for freedom, 86; and reality-unreality, 90; and recreation, 231. *See also* Games
Polanyi, Michael, 29, 210, 214
Political activity. *See* Law
Polymorphous sexual perversion, 116
Potter, Stephen, 82
Principal of finality, 236–37
Progress, 172–73; ethical, 174, 239; human, 174, 177, 239
Psychotherapy. *See* Therapy
Putney, Snell, and Putney, Gail J., 126, 128
Pyramids. *See* Death

R

Rational, the, 9–11, 191; versus the reasonable, 10; and the transrational, 192
Read, Herbert, 132
Recreation. *See* Play
Redican, William K., 72
Reductionism, 28, 94, 111, 176, 183, 210
Reflection, 3, 23–24, 26, 40, 195, 225, 232; significance of, 23. *See also* Consciousness; Thinking
Reflective awareness. *See* Reflection
Regulated behavior: versus rule following, 68
Reichenbach, Hans, 13, 15
Reik, Theodore, 114

Relativism, ethical. *See* Ethics

Religion, 206–17, 232; and conditioning, 209; and the "Death of God" movement, 212–13, 215; demythologizing of, 212, 215, and ethics, 165–66; existential view of, 110, 210; and Gallup polls, 206; as natural phenomenon, 210; psychologization of, 217; revival of, 211; and social scientists, 210; and sociological interpretations and influences, 209–10, and the supernatural, 210; time of emergence of, 207; universality of, 207; from a vertical to a horizontal model, 215–16. *See also* Metaphysical concern; Ultimate concern

Ribble, Margaret, 95–96, 99

Richardson, Herbert W., 218, 225

Riesman, David, 86

Riley, John W., Jr., 195, 197, 199–200

Rogers, Carl R., 95, 98, 106, 127, 151, 176, 216, 219, 230, 236

Romantic love, 83, 99–100, 109, 113, 116–22, 125, 128, 200. *See also* Love

Roszak, Theodore, 64, 212, 214–15

Royce, Joseph, 14, 27, 28, 210, 214, 225

Runes, Dagobert, 184

Russell, Bertrand, 98, 170

S

Sadism, 185–86

Sartre, Jean Paul, 40, 152, 180, 205

Schaller, George, 67, 184

Science, 10, 18, 20, 210–12, 215, 218; and methodology, 214; mythologizing of, 213; premises of, 214. *See also* Experimental method; Methodology

Scientific humanism, 4; interdisciplinary character of, 5

Scriven, Michael, 32

Self, 24–25, 179, 182. *See also* Reflection

Self-actualization, 220–21

Self-awareness, 27

Self-concept, 240

Self-consciousness, 29

Self-fulfilling prophecy, 174, 236

Self-knowledge, 32

Self-reference, 23

Self-transcendence, 55, 111. *See also* Transcendence

Senilicide, 73

Sensory deprivation, 104

Sex, 94, 113–15, 231; and death, 201; determinants of, 115; and love, 115; neurological bases of, 115; and sexuality, 115–16. *See also* Love; Pansexualism

Shakespeare, 9

Shostrom, Everett, 161

Signals, 14–16. *See also* Signifier; Signs; Symbols

Signifier, 13–15. *See also* Signals; Signs; Symbols

Signs, 12–13; as operators, 15–16; conventional, 14; iconic, 14, 18; indexical, 13; noniconic, 17. *See also* Signals; Signifiers; Symbols

Skinner, B. F., 4, 16, 72, 153–57, 159, 177, 230

Smith, Huston, 223, 225

Snygg, Donald, 156

Social animal, 92. *See also* Law

Socrates, 190, 198

Space binding, 41

Species predictability, 141

Species specificity, 42, 78

Speech. *See* Language

Steiner, Jerome, 200

Stevens, John O., 159

Stevenson, Charles L., 170, 177

Straus, E., 98

Suicide, 40, 182–84; and lemmings, 183; sociological and biological determinants of, 183; Trobriand Islanders and, 183

Sumner, William G., 169

Symbolic animal, 40, 165, 180, 184, 186, 191

Symbolic capacity, 8, 11–12, 89, 176, 181, 195, 220

Symbolic need fulfillment, 237–38

Symbolism, 21; and metasymbolism, 22

Symbols, 12–19, 34, 41, 49, 202; and alphabet, 17; as designator, 14–16; nonconventional types of, 20–21. *See also* Sign; Signal; Signifier

Szasz, Thomas, 82, 85, 182

T

Technological advances: and the good life, 238

Technology, 34, 48, 61–62, 65; benefits of, 65; effects of, upon man, 63–64; and machine, 32; and man as attend-

Technology *(cont.)*
ant, 62; and robot proletariat, 32. *See also* Tools
Teilhard de Chardin, Pierre, 23, 98, 112, 176, 186, 214, 224
Temporal horizon, 36
Territoriality, 68
Test: Rorschach Inkblot, 21; Thematic Apperception, 21; Wartegg Drawing Completion, 21
Therapy: client-centered, 43; insight-centered, 98; relationship-centered, 98; Rogerian, 43
Thinking: and animals, 30–31; characteristics of, 29; conceptual, 13, 23, 26–27, 29–30; definition of, 30; perceptual, 27, 30. *See also* Reflection
Thinking machines, 31. *See also* Computer
Thomas, Dylan, 216
Thorpe, W. H., 52
Tillich, Paul, 206
Time, 33–45, 188; and age gap, 43; and being, 37–38; and the child, 36; and clocks, 34, 64; duration of, 34–35, 37; and freedom, 40; future, 38–39, 42; and healing, 44; historical awareness as, 4; Kant on, 34; and the meaning of life, 39; measurable, 34; and motion, 34; Newton on, 34; past, chronological, 43; past, existential, 43; psychophysics of, 35; representations of, 36; and space, 33, 41, 44; technological, 44
Time binding, 41, 220
Tools, 3, 56–65; effects of, upon man, 63–64; evolution of, 62; history of, 60; and Man the Artisan, 62; and non-human primates, 57–58. *See also* Technology
Traherne, Thomas, 127
Trained incapacity, 193
Transcendence, 143, 188, 218–25, 233–34; and attitudinal values, 221–23; as commitment, 224; and consciousness, 221; forms of, 219–23; as hope, 224; of the human predicament, 222–24; as love, 224; ontological, 224–25; of particular problems, 221; as self-actualization, 220

Trobriand Islanders. *See* Suicide
Tubbs, Walter, 130
Turing, A. M., 31
Turing's game, 31, 55

U

Ultimate concern, 20, 206–07. *See also* Metaphysical concern; Religion
Unfinished animal (or species), 112, 146, 186

V

Vahanian, Gabriel, 213
Values, 188; attitudinal, 221–23; creative or active, 222; experiential or passive, 222; and freedom, 150
Vercors (Jean Bruller), 52

W

Wagner, Richard, 142
Waley, Arthur, 142
Walster, Elaine, 139
Watts, Alan, 90, 210
Weber, Max, 10
Wertenbaker, Lael, 203
Wheel, 17, 61–62
White, Alice Marsden, 92
Whyte, William H., Jr., 106
Wild Boy of Aveyron, 50
Wood, Ernest, 90

Y

Yerkes, Robert M., and Yerkes, Ada W., 57
Yin/Yang, 19, 121

Z

Zen Buddhism, 121. *See also* Maya
Zuni Indians, 82

A 5
B 6
C 7
D 8
E 9
F 0
G 1
H 2
I 3
J 4